for Pension Costs

by

David Campbell
of Bacon & Woodrow

and

Teresa Sienkiewicz
of Touche Ross & Co.

Tolley Publishing Company Limited
A UNITED NEWSPAPERS PUBLICATION

While all reasonable care has been taken in the preparation of this book no responsibility is accepted by the authors, nor by Bacon & Woodrow and Touche Ross & Co. for any errors it may contain, whether caused by negligence or otherwise; or for any loss, howsoever caused, occasioned by any person by reliance on it.

Published by
Tolley Publishing Company Limited
Tolley House
2 Addiscombe Road
Croydon, Surrey CR9 5AF England
081-686 9141

Typeset in Great Britain by
Touche Ross & Co
Hill House
1 Little New Street, London EC4A 3TR

Printed and bound in Great Britain by
Biddles Ltd, Guildford and King's Lynn

ISBN 08559 513-9

Preface

Our aim in writing this book is to provide an essentially practical rather than theoretical guide to Statement of Accounting Practice number 24, 'Accounting for pension costs'. SSAP 24 has radically changed UK accounting practice in this area and, to assist in the understanding of the context in which the new standard operates, the book examines the background to pensions in the UK, before describing the content of the Statement and analysing the issues which need to be dealt with in its application. Each chapter is designed to be self-contained as far as possible. The text also reviews in each chapter the major practical problems which have arisen or are likely to be encountered under the particular subject heading and suggests solutions. We have included useful reference material in the appendices.

The authors would like to thank their colleagues and clients for their contributions in highlighting the issues raised in the SSAP and those who commented and made suggestions on the text, especially Peter Morgan and Peter Randall of Bacon & Woodrow, Martyn Jones and Craig Foreman of Touche Ross & Co and Bryn Davies. Our grateful thanks are due to Ken Wild of Touche Ross for his contributions throughout.

We must make special mention of Rex de Saram of Tolley Publishing Company Limited for his invaluable editorial assistance and of Margaret Wilson and Sheila Gillis for undertaking the typing of the manuscript.

We also wish to acknowledge our gratitude to the Pensions Management Institute for consent to include as an appendix a large part of the booklet 'Pensions terminology', and also the Accounting Standards Committee and the Auditing Practices Committee which kindly gave permission to reproduce SSAP 24 and the Practice note respectively. These appendices help to make this book a comprehensive guide to the subject.

Finally, lest anyone be in doubt, references to 'he' in the text apply equally to 'she'.

David Campbell
Bacon & Woodrow
B & W House
55 East Street
Surrey KT17 1BP

Teresa Sienkiewicz
Touche Ross & Co
Hill House
1 Little New Street
London EC4A 3TR

Abbreviations

APB	Accounting Principles Board
APC	Auditing Practices Committee
ASB	Accounting Standards Board
ASC	Accounting Standards Committee
AVC	Additional voluntary contributions
CA	Companies Act
DSS	Department of Social Security
EEC	European Economic Community
ED	Exposure draft
FA	Finance Act
FAS	Statement of Financial Accounting Standards
FSA	Financial Services Act
FSAVC	Free standing additional voluntary contributions
GAAP	Generally accepted accounting principles
GMP	Guaranteed minimum pension
IAS	International Accounting Standard
IASC	International Accounting Standards Committee
ICAEW	Institute of Chartered Accountants in England and Wales
ICTA	Income and Corporation Taxes Act 1988
IR	Inland Revenue
NI	National Insurance
OPB	Occupational Pensions Board
para	paragraph
PHI	Permanent health insurance
PRAG	Pensions Research Accountants Group
RPI	Retail price index
s	section
sch	schedule
SERPS	State Earnings Related Pension Scheme
SFO	Superannuation Funds Office of the Inland Revenue
SI	Statutory Instrument
SORP	Statement of Recommended Practice
SSA	Social Security Act
SSAP	Statement of Standard Accounting Practice
SSPA	Social Security Pensions Act
TR	Technical release of the ICAEW
UK	United Kingdom
US	United States of America
4 Sch.4	Schedule 4, Para 4

Contents

Chapter 1

Introduction

The background

1.1 Over the last two decades, occupational pension schemes to provide benefits for employees on their retirement have become almost universal for employers in the UK. This trend has been actively encouraged by a favourable tax régime. The usual pattern is for both employee and employer to pay regular amounts, based on a percentage of the employee's salary, into a pension scheme over the working lifetime of the employee, the amounts being subject to actuarial review, usually every three years.

Prior to the introduction of Statement of Accounting Practice No. 24 [SSAP 24], pension cost in the accounts of employing companies was almost universally determined on the basis of funding, i.e. the amount of contributions payable into the scheme each year by the employer. However, such amounts depend on, *inter alia*, investment returns, salary levels, staff turnover and ages, and consequently funding requirements may vary considerably from valuation to valuation. The result was that cost could fluctuate from year to year and not match the provision of benefits with the service of the employee.

Such distortions became increasingly evident as many occupational pension schemes moved into substantial surplus in the early eighties. As a result, the subject came under increasing scrutiny by the accounting profession. SSAP 24 was, however, to have a lengthy gestation period. The Accounting Standards Committee (ASC) published its first exposure draft (ED) on pension costs, ED 32 'Disclosure of pension information in company accounts', in 1983 but the proposed issue of a standard which dealt only with disclosure was rejected by the accounting profession. A Statement of Intent was issued instead which was subsequently reproduced substantially in ED 39, which was released in May 1986. Although there were some changes, this was eventually accepted by the ASC and released in May 1988 as SSAP 24. This standard was to apply as soon as possible and for UK companies and Irish companies quoted on The International Stock Exchange of the United Kingdom and Ireland was to apply to accounting periods beginning on or after 1 July 1988 [*SSAP 24 para 93*]. For other Irish companies, the accounting requirements for defined benefit schemes and the associated actuarial disclosures are not mandatory until accounting periods beginning on or after 1 January 1993.

The new approach

1.2 The new standard, unlike most other accounting standards which codify existing best practice, is for many employers a radical departure from previous practices of accounting for pension costs. SSAP 24, para 16, states that from the point of view of the employer, a pension is part of the cost incurred in obtaining the employee's services. The accounting objective therefore requires the employer to recognise the cost of providing pensions on a systematic and rational basis over the period during which the employer derives benefit from the employees' services. How this is achieved depends on the nature of the pension scheme commitment.

There are two main types of occupational pension schemes in the UK:

(a) defined benefit schemes, in which the rules specify the benefits to be paid (usually based on the employee's average or final pay and the number of years of membership of the scheme), the scheme being financed accordingly, and

(b) defined contribution (commonly called money purchase) schemes, where the rate of contribution is normally specified in the rules. The individual member's benefits are determined by reference to contributions paid into the scheme in respect of that member, usually increased by an amount based on the investment return on those contributions.

In a defined contribution scheme, the employer's cost comprises the contributions payable, so employers who operate such schemes for their employees will not find their costs affected by the standard, though certain additional disclosures are now required. For those employers with defined benefit schemes the situation is rather more complex; the benefits to be paid are dependent on the average or final pay of each employee, whether he leaves service or whether he dies in service or retirement, and the number and relationship of his dependants. The impossibility of precisely determining the pensions, benefits and investment returns on contributions in advance means that the pension cost for each financial year can only be assessed by actuarial estimation. Actuarial advice has always been essential in the administration of pre-funded schemes i.e. money is paid to a fund based on actuarial advice, to assist the employer to determine how and when the scheme should be funded. SSAP 24 has extended the rôle of the actuary by requiring actuarial involvement in the accounting for pension costs.

SSAP 24 in practice

1.3 All pension arrangements, prefunded or unfunded, contractual or *ex gratia*, are caught by SSAP 24. Defined contribution, defined benefit and hybrid schemes, both UK and overseas all fall within its scope. This book aims to be an essentially practical guide on SSAP 24. It examines the background to pensions in the UK, the content of the SSAP and the issues which need to be dealt with in its implementation. It suggests practical solutions to the major problem areas which are likely to be encountered including the application of SSAP 24 to post-retirement benefits other than pensions (see 3.15, 11.10), groups and deferred tax. The appendices have been chosen with a view to their relevance to the subject and include the full text of SSAP 24 and the Auditing Practices Committee's practice note on liaison between the auditor and the actuary. Whilst SSAP 24 includes a list of definitions to be applied, we have also included extensive extracts of terms from the Pensions Management Institute/PRAG publication 'Pensions Terminology' which readers may come across in the context of pension cost.

The International and US standards

1.4 As there are many UK companies with undertakings or parent companies overseas, there is a discussion of International Accounting Standard 19, and the US Statements of Financial Accounting Standards numbers 87 and 88. A comparison of these with SSAP 24 is included.

Chapter 2

Pensions in the UK

Methods of funding

2.1 An employer can arrange to pay for employees' pensions in four main ways:

(a) from current revenue (pay-as-you-go);

(b) by paying a capital sum, usually to an insurance company, for an annuity when the employee retires (terminal funding);

(c) by charging an actuarially calculated amount for pension cost for the year in the profit and loss account and crediting a pension reserve, the 'book reserve' method; and

(d) by prefunding, paying regular contributions into a pension scheme during the employees' working lives.

Methods (a)-(c) of financing pensions do not by themselves provide security of pension payments to employees. This security is achieved by method (d), i.e. prefunding.

Pay-as-you-go

Pay-as-you-go is an arrangement under which benefits are paid out of revenue and no provision is made for future liabilities. In the UK, the vast majority of pensions being paid on this basis are state pensions. The basic old age pension and the State Earnings Related Pension Scheme (SERPS) are the most obvious examples, but state employees' pensions are also paid on this basis, for example, those of civil servants and teachers. These schemes are not prefunded because the government levies sufficient taxes to ensure that the pensions can be paid in full as they fall due. Such schemes have rarely been operated in the private sector except on a discretionary, *ex gratia* basis. Cash flow problems resulting from poor trading results or from expansion could jeopardise the payment of pensions, and the employer's liquidation would of course mean that the pension would cease.

Terminal Funding

Similar problems can exist when pensions are funded only when retirement occurs. The cash needed to purchase an annuity for each retiring employee may be beyond the resources of the company at the time this is required.

Book reserve

As with pay-as-you-go and terminal funding, this method does not ensure that cash will be available to pay benefits when they fall due. There is no prefunding and in the UK this method of charging does not attract tax relief except to the extent that allocations to the reserve are matched by actual benefit payments or annuity purchases. It is, therefore, most unusual in this country, although it may become more common with the imposition by the *Finance Act 1989* of cash limits upon benefits from tax-approved pension funds. However, as the accounts of multinational corporations demonstrate, it is used in Europe, particularly in Germany, (see 13.4), where there are certain safeguards for employees in the event of the company having financial problems.

Prefunding of pensions

In the UK, most private sector and many public sector employers, such as local authorities and the state monopolies (including British Rail and the Post Office) fund their pension liabilities in advance. Payments are made on a regular actuarially-calculated basis to either an insurance company or to a separate trust, so that on retirement there are sufficient assets either to purchase an annuity or to ensure the payment of the pension.

Inter-relationship with the SERPS

2.2 Everyone who has met the minimum contribution requirements by working and paying national insurance contributions is entitled to the basic component of the state pension scheme, i.e. the 'state flat rate pension'. Pension provision over and above this basic can be achieved in a number of ways, but for employees there are three main methods:

(i) To contract in, i.e. to participate in the State Earnings Related Pension Scheme (SERPS) which provides an earnings-related element or 'additional component' to the state pension, based on pay between 'band' earnings for National Insurance purposes. The maximum level of earnings upon which the SERPS pension is paid is relatively modest. Some occupational pension schemes are contracted into SERPS. In such cases, the employer and employee pay full rate National Insurance contributions, but the employee will receive both a SERPS pension and a pension from the occupational scheme. It should be noted that SERPS benefits are based on average (but revalued) pay and not on final earnings. A contracted-in scheme can provide benefits based on final pay rather than a career average.

(ii) To contract out of SERPS, by being a member of a contracted-out pension scheme run by employers. Nearly all large occupational schemes are contracted-out. The practical implications are that the employer pays national insurance at a lower rate but contributes a percentage of the employees' earnings to the scheme which undertakes to provide a benefit broadly equivalent to SERPS, the 'Guaranteed Minimum Pension', or, in money purchase schemes 'Protected Rights' (see (iii) below), as part of the benefit from the occupational scheme.

(iii) To join a personal pension plan. Such a plan could be contracted-in to SERPS, or contracted-out of SERPS. In the latter case, full National Insurance contributions continue to be paid, but the Department of Social Security pays part of these, together with tax relief at the basic rate on the employee's share of the rebate, directly to the pension plan. Benefits secured by the investment of these contributions are known as 'protected rights'. These will provide a pension in place of SERPS but because investment conditions cannot be foreseen it could be higher or lower than a SERPS pension.

All employees must either participate in SERPS (i.e. contracted-in) or be contracted-out through an occupational scheme or personal pension. There is no compulsion, either by the government or employers, to do more than participate in SERPS.

Types of scheme

2.3 There are basically two main types of scheme with respect to benefits, defined contribution and defined benefits. A defined contribution scheme (more familiarly known as a money purchase scheme) is one where the rules specify the rate of contribution. The individual's benefits on retirement are generally determined by the contributions paid into the scheme on the member's behalf and by the investment returns on those contributions. In contrast, a defined benefit scheme is one where the rules specify the benefits to be paid, the scheme being financed accordingly. Benefits are usually calculated at a fixed fraction, e.g. a sixtieth or eightieth, of pensionable pay prior to retirement for each year of pensionable service, irrespective of the scheme's investment performance. Defined benefit schemes, often known as final salary schemes, presently comprise the large majority of UK schemes, including the public sector. For employees, this type of scheme offers certainty of benefit and protection from adverse fluctuations in the value of investments, particularly at retirement date.

Some schemes provide a mix of money purchase and final salary benefits. For example, a final salary scheme may have provision for money purchase additional voluntary contributions, and some are hybrids, i.e., the benefit is calculated as the better of two alternatives such as final salary or money purchase.

Maxima and minima

2.4 An essential feature of occupational pension schemes in the UK is the favourable tax treatment of contributions to and benefits from such schemes and the income and gains from funds held by the schemes themselves. Provided that the funding is within the prescribed statutory guidelines, income and capital gains arising from the scheme's assets are free of taxation. Lump sums available to the members on retirement (see 2.5 below for further details) are tax-free and the pension is treated as earned income for tax purposes. It is not surprising therefore that the main legislation controlling occupational and other pension schemes is contained in the *Income and Corporation Taxes Act 1988* (a consolidation of earlier legislation) and the *Finance Act 1989*. The essential features of this legislation are set out in the Inland Revenue Superannuation Funds Office 'Practice Notes'. To qualify for tax relief on personal contributions, the employee must belong to an approved scheme and the aggregate of his annual contributions must not normally exceed 15% of remuneration. Employers must contribute at least part of the cost and the general rule is that the employer's contribution must be at least 10% of the total cost – token contributions are not acceptable if a scheme is to receive 'exempt approved' status which makes it eligible for the exemptions from income and capital gains tax. Ordinary annual contributions by employers to such a scheme are deductible as an expense for tax purposes. In exceptional cases (e.g. a lump sum contribution to meet the capital cost of improving benefits) the Inland Revenue may require the tax allowance to be spread forward for up to five years.

2.5 In the great majority of schemes, benefits are subject to certain maximum limits. The maximum pension is normally two-thirds of final remuneration, but may be lower in certain cases. It is common for an employee to be able to commute part of his pension for a lump sum at retirement. The Inland Revenue allows an amount of at least 3/80ths of final pay for each year of service. This amount may be greater where maximum pension benefits accrue over periods of less than forty years. In all cases there is a maximum of one-and-a-half times final salary for members of defined benefit schemes. These maxima and minima are presented in tabular form in Appendix C. There are also certain minima for contracted out scheme benefits. There must be a spouse's provision and each member must be provided with at least a Guaranteed Minimum Pension, broadly a SERPS equivalent.

It should be noted that the *Finance Act 1989* introduced a cap on pensionable earnings of £60,000 per annum for those joining an occupational scheme established on or after 14th March 1989 or joining a scheme existing before that date on or after 1st June 1989. This earnings cap increases in line with the retail price index, rounded up to the nearest £600 (*ICTA 1988 s590C(5)(b)*). Thus the maximum pension in 1989-90 in these circumstances was £40,000. The earnings limit for 1990-91 has been set at £64,800.

The Inland Revenue limits which apply to most money purchase occupational schemes are identical to those to which final salary schemes are subject.

However, rules governing maxima and minima set by the Inland Revenue are also affected by social security legislation, trust law and employment law, which also impact on the level of pension benefits. Social security legislation includes preservation, anti-franking and revaluation and transfer requirements. Trust law concerns the investment of funds, refunds, appointment of trustees and powers to amend the rules, and it is the scheme rules which include benefit details. Employment law also impacts on this area as contracts of employment often contain clauses relating to pensions. There has been much concern over the position of early leavers, an issue considered by the Occupational Pensions Board (OPB) in its 1989 report 'Protecting Pensions'. The OPB examined ways in which the minima might be improved and the government is poised to introduce new legislation concerning the revaluation of all early leavers' pension rights. The rules on minimum pension for early leavers will change in the near future when the *Social Security Act 1990* is implemented.

Inland Revenue rules on scheme surpluses

2.6 The *Finance Act 1986* introduced new rules for schemes in surplus. Surpluses above 105%, determined within guidelines prescribed by the government actuary, must be removed within 5 years if the scheme is to continue to enjoy in full the privileges of exemption from capital gains and income tax (*ICTA 1988 ss 603, 603* and *Sch 22*). Scheme surpluses may be reduced by taking contribution holidays (by both employer and employees but in practice usually only the former), improving benefits or sometimes refunding a surplus to the employer. If this last course is taken, the assets may not be reduced to less than 105% of the liabilities as calculated on the prescribed basis. The option of a refund may also be restricted by the Social Security Act 1990.

Chapter 3

Overview of SSAP 24

Scope

3.1 The purpose of this chapter is to give a brief overview of the key points of SSAP 24. Detailed considerations of the implications of the different points are set out in subsequent chapters and a cross reference is provided. The full text of the SSAP is reproduced as Appendix A.

SSAP 24 should be applied by all employers who have explicit or implicit commitments to provide, or contribute to, pensions for their employees, unless the amounts involved are immaterial. The Statement is not limited to companies, but is intended to apply to all employers whose accounts are intended to give a true and fair view. It applies to all types of pension scheme, including:

(a) defined contribution and defined benefit schemes;

(b) prefunded and unfunded schemes;

(c) insured and self administered schemes.

SSAP 24 also addresses *ex gratia* pensions, i.e. those which the employer has no commitment to provide, discretionary or *ex gratia* increases in pensions, foreign schemes and group schemes. The principles set out in the SSAP may also be applied to the cost of providing other post-retirement benefits (see 3.15) but do not apply to either state social security contributions or redundancy payments.

Accounting objective

3.2 The accounting objective of the Statement is that 'the employer should recognise the expected cost of providing pensions on a systematic and rational basis over the period during which he derives benefit from the employees' services'. This acknowleges the fact that the cost to an employer of providing a pension is a part of the cost incurred in obtaining the employee's services. Consequently, the cost should be matched to the period when the benefit of the employee's service is received.

SSAP 24 is designed to smooth pension costs and takes a profit and loss account approach. Actuarial surpluses or deficits are not consolidated in the balance sheet (although curiously the transitional provisions of SSAP 24 do permit this treatment), because of the volatility which might arise from such a policy. In addition, the timescale involved in assessing pension cost is so long and the estimates are subject to such inherent uncertainty that the figures can only be an approximation.

Defined contribution schemes

3.3 For defined contribution schemes the charge against profits should be the amount of contributions payable to the pension scheme in respect of the accounting period (see also 10.1).

Defined benefit schemes

3.4 For defined benefit schemes the charge against profits should be calculated using actuarial methods aimed at achieving the accounting objective of the Statement. SSAP 24 recognises two elements of pension cost: the regular cost, which mainly depends on the actuarial method and assumptions used for the population of employees involved, and variations from regular cost, to adjust for the particular experience of the scheme over time (see 6.2, 6.3).

Regular cost

3.5 The regular cost is the actuary's best estimate of the consistent ongoing cost of providing for the pensions and should be a substantially level percentage of the annual pensionable payroll (see 6.1, 6.2).

Variations from regular cost

3.6 Since the pensions will not, on average, be paid for many years, the actuary is required to make assumptions of future events, and estimates of financial effects, over a long period. It is inevitable that the estimated cost will have to be revised from time to time to take account of differences between actual events experienced compared to those previously predicted, and for changed future expectations. The revised estimates will result in variations from the regular cost. Variations from the regular cost arise for a number of reasons including:

(a) experience surpluses or deficiencies, e.g. better or poorer than expected returns on investments;

(b) changes in actuarial method or assumptions, e.g. an increase in the salary inflation applied;

(c) retrospective changes in benefits or in conditions for membership, such as inclusion of part-time employees; or

(d) increases to pensions in payment or to deferred pensions which had not been previously provided for in the actuarial assumptions.

(See 6.2, 6.3).

Accounting for variations

3.7 The basic requirement of the SSAP is that variations from the regular cost should be spread over the expected remaining service lives of the current employees in the scheme. A period representing the average remaining service lives may be used if desired. SSAP 24 does not prescribe the method of amortisation to be applied (see 6.23-6.25)

There are a limited number of circumstances in which there may be a departure from the spreading requirement. These circumstances arise

(i) when there is a significant reduction in the number of employees covered by the pension scheme;

(ii) where an unexpected major event or transaction has occurred;

(iii) where prudence may require a material deficit to be recognised over a shorter period, or

(iv) where the employer has received a refund of a surplus that is subject to deduction of tax in accordance with the provisions of what is referred to in the SSAP as the UK *Finance Act 1986* or equivalent legislation, now the *ICTA 1988 ss 601, 602, 603* and *22 Sch* (see 6.11-6.22).

Ex gratia pensions

3.8 The capital cost of an *ex gratia* pension should, to the extent that it is not covered by a surplus, be charged to the profit and loss account in the period in which it is granted (see 6.13). If it is implicit in the employer's actions that there is a commitment to provide such a pension, (i.e. such pensions are normally granted to employees who are not in a scheme), then the Statement requires that these be accounted for in the same way as pensions provided from a formal scheme [*SSAP 24, para 2*].

Discretionary and *ex gratia* increases in pensions

3.9 The preferred treatment of discretionary increases in pensions which are likely to be granted on a regular basis, is that they be allowed for in the actuarial assumptions made to estimate the normal ongoing cost [*SSAP 24, para 35*]. Where allowance has not been made, the capital cost of any such increases should, to the extent they are not covered by a surplus, be charged to the profit and loss account in the period in which they are initially granted (see 6.12, 6.13).

Foreign schemes

3.10 An employer who has an obligation to provide pensions under foreign schemes should, in principle, account for those obligations in the same way as the SSAP requires UK obligations to be accounted for, or he should make an adjustment on consolidation. The SSAP recognises that in some cases it may be impractical to meet this requirement because of the difficulties and cost of obtaining the necessary actuarial information, or because the nature of the commitment is very different from that which is customary in the UK. In such cases the amount charged and the basis of its calculation should, as a minimum, be disclosed in the consolidated financial statements (see 11.4).

Balance sheet presentation

3.11 SSAP 24 is, as stated in 3.2, a profit and loss account based statement. Differences arising between the amounts charged as pension cost and amounts paid to a scheme as contributions are shown in the balance sheet effectively as a balancing figure. If the cumulative amount charged to the profit and loss account exceeds the amount paid in contributions, the excess should be shown as a net pension provision. Conversely, an excess of contributions paid over the cumulative cost charged to the profit and loss account should be shown as a prepayment (see 9.5). These balances effectively represent the cumulative timing difference for the purposes of deferred tax (see chapter 8), and for the computation of interest (6.26). It may seem a contradiction in terms that where a scheme is overfunded and contributions are reduced a provision is created and where scheme is underfunded, special contributions or higher contribution rates can lead to a prepayment. These balances are effectively cumulative amounts waiting to be amortised through the profit and loss account in future periods and arise because of the smoothing of costs in the profit and loss account.

Deferred taxation

3.12 Tax relief for pension costs is normally granted in respect of the amounts actually paid. Timing differences between the amount paid and the pension cost charged to the profit and loss account, following the application of SSAP 24, may have deferred tax implications. This is explored in depth in chapter 8.

Disclosures

3.13 SSAP 24 requires companies to make considerable disclosures of information about their pension arrangements. For defined benefit schemes this includes details about the scheme's financial position and most recent actuarial valuation. The specific disclosure requirements, together with those required by the Companies Act 1985, are explained in detail in chapter 9 for defined benefit schemes and in chapter 10 for defined contribution schemes.

Group schemes

3.14 Where an employer participates in a group scheme to which a common group rate of contribution is paid, the SSAP allows a common group rate to be determined for pension cost purposes and used by members of a group, even though the true costs may vary between the employers if calculated on an individual company basis (11.2, 11.8). The SSAP also grants certain relaxations in the disclosure requirements for a subsidiary company with UK or Irish parents (see 11.2).

Application of SSAP 24 to other post-retirement benefits

3.15 In July 1989, the Accounting Standards Committee issued a statement on the application of the principles of SSAP 24 to other post-retirement benefits. It refers to paragraph 75 of SSAP 24 which states:

> 'Although this Statement primarily addresses pensions, its principles may be equally applicable to the cost of providing other post-retirement benefits.'

The rest of the ASC's statement is as follows.

> 'It has been questioned whether this information is intended to be a binding requirement. For the removal of doubt, the Accounting

Standards Committee states that paragraph 75 is indicative only. It is intended to suggest to companies how they might account for other post-retirement benefits in the absence of a Statement of Standard Accounting Practice. The ASC at present has no plans to develop a Statement on accounting for other post-retirement benefits. Until such time as it does, there is no obligation for companies to apply the principles of SSAP 24 to such benefits, although they may consider it appropriate to do so.'

(See 11.10)

Chapter 4

Defined benefit or defined contribution scheme?

Introduction

4.1 SSAP 24 draws a distinction between defined benefit schemes and defined contribution schemes because of the different nature of the employer's commitment (see 2.3). In the latter case, there is unlikely to be any change of accounting policy on implementing SSAP 24 because the cost of pensions will continue to be measured by the contributions due for the accounting period. In contrast, the prescribed treatment of defined benefit schemes will sometimes require a change of policy. This change may have a significant effect on corporate earnings and on the balance sheet.

Before SSAP 24 can be applied, it is necessary to determine whether the pension scheme in question should be treated according to the requirements for a defined benefit scheme or those for a defined contribution scheme. This is not always straightforward and if there is any doubt as to how a scheme should be treated the question should be discussed by the sponsoring company, the auditor and the actuary at an early stage. The decision may have significant financial consequences.

Many schemes will be easy to categorise even if they do not wholly fit the definition given in SSAP 24. The different categories are stated below.

Defined benefit schemes

4.2 A defined benefit scheme is a pension scheme in which the rules specify the benefits to be paid and the scheme is financed accordingly. These schemes usually pay the member a pension related to pay at or near the date of retirement. A typical pension formula is

$$\frac{\text{years of pensionable service x final salary}}{60}$$

Because of the timescale and the variables involved (including length of service and the salary on which the pension will be based), funding and pension cost can only be based on estimates.

There are other formulae, where the defined benefit treatment is less obvious. For example, the following types of scheme fall into the definition of defined benefit for the purposes of SSAP 24.

(a) A final salary scheme which includes refunds of employees' contributions on death in service and money purchase AVCs. The employer's contributions are determined by the actuarial valuation.

(b) On retirement from a pension scheme, the annual pension equals 50% of the total contributions paid by the member to the scheme during his membership. Members pay 5% of earnings to the scheme. The employer's contributions are determined by the actuarial valuation.

This example is an average pay scheme. There is no attempt to bring the employer's contributions into the calculation of the retirement pension.

(c) As (b) above, except that the pension is 25% of total member's contributions accumulated with interest at 7.5% per annum.

Defined contribution schemes

4.3 A defined contribution scheme, often referred to as a money purchase scheme, is one where an individual member's benefits are determined by reference to contributions paid into the scheme in respect of that member, usually increased by an amount based on the investment return on those contributions. The rate of contribution is normally specified in the rules of the scheme and the employer has no additional funding obligation. Thus the cost to the employer of providing the pension can be measured with reasonable certainty.

As with defined benefit schemes, there are many defined contribution schemes which have some minor benefits which do not fit the definition. For example, a money purchase scheme with a salary-related ill health retirement pension underpinning the money purchase benefit would be treated as a defined contribution scheme.

'Hybrid' schemes

4.4 Some schemes will be far less easy to categorise. SSAP 24 para 39 states:

> 'A few schemes are hybrid in nature combining features of defined contribution and defined benefit schemes. In such instances the rules or trust deed should be carefully studied and the operation of the scheme in practice, or its proposed method of operation, taken into

account when determining the appropriate accounting treatment. The accounting treatment adopted should be in accordance with the underlying substance of the scheme.'

The determination of a scheme as defined benefit or defined contribution is an essential prerequisite in arriving at the decision on accounting treatment.

Deciding the underlying substance of a 'hybrid' scheme

4.5 In the case of a 'hybrid' scheme, the sponsoring company will probably need to discuss the question with its auditors and actuary.

The simplest case is that of a scheme with different types of benefits for different categories of member. Different benefit scales may be provided from within the same scheme for a variety of reasons. A senior executive scale may apply only to selected members of a scheme which provides a routine scale of benefits for all other employees. In another scheme, employees may be offered a choice of scales of benefits and contributions. If the benefit scales are all of the same type, then the scheme will be treated as defined benefit or defined contribution as appropriate. If there are benefit scales of different types, each should be considered as a separate scheme and a decision about the appropriate treatment made in each case. The accounting calculations will then normally be carried out separately for each section of the scheme. The figures may need to be disclosed separately for each scale, if the accounts are to give a sensible picture of the nature of the scheme. This will only be necessary, however, if each scale is financially significant in its own right.

In more difficult cases, the trust deed may not be entirely consistent, or may fail to address some relevant issues such as the permitted courses of action to eliminate a surplus or deficit. A decision on the accounting treatment of such a hybrid scheme still needs to be taken. As a side issue, a review of the trust deed may be indicated.

4.6 The appropriate accounting treatment should normally be decided on the following key points taken together. If a decision cannot be reached on this basis, it will be necessary to consider secondary factors to see whether they tip the balance one way or the other.

(a) Retirement benefits

It is suggested that the nature of the retirement benefits should usually be considered in isolation from the other benefits. This would only be inappropriate if the cost of retirement benefits is very much less than the cost of the other benefits.

Example

A final salary scheme into which a money purchase underpin has been introduced at a level designed to compete with personal pensions for young early leavers would probably be treated as a defined benefit scheme.

(b) How are company contributions set?

If contributions are dependent on the results of the actuarial valuation, then this would indicate a defined benefit scheme.

If contributions are specified in the trust deed or are held fixed in any way, the trust deed must be examined to see what action is taken if a surplus or deficit arises. If the employer has an obligation under the deed to adjust his contributions in these circumstances (or if he would assume such an obligation in practice or take a refund of surplus) then a defined benefit treatment would be appropriate.

If the trust deed is silent, it may be helpful to consider the options available to the scheme under the Inland Revenue rules if a statutory surplus were to arise.

(c) Are the company contributions allocated to particular employees?

SSAP 24, para 62, which contains a definition of a defined contribution scheme, implies that company contributions are allocated to particular employees.

Examples

(i) A money purchase scheme is contracted-out by means of GMPs (Guaranteed Minimum Pensions required to replace State Earnings Related Pensions). Combined contributions of 10% of PAYE earnings are paid to each employee's account. The following criteria indicate the type of the scheme:

Retirement benefits	Most frequently money purchase
Company contributions	Defined, but minor supplements will be needed
Allocated contributions	Yes

The scheme is, in spirit, a defined contribution scheme. Two out of three major points also indicate this. The scheme is probably best treated as a defined contribution scheme for accounting purposes.

(ii) As (i) above, except that combined contributions of 5% of PAYE earnings are paid to each employee's account.

Retirement benefits	Most frequently GMP in early years of scheme operation
Company contributions	Substantial supplements to defined contributions likely to be needed for some years
Allocated contributions	Yes

The scheme is, in spirit, defined contribution but is likely to be defined benefit in practice for several years. It is probably most appropriate to treat it as a defined benefit scheme with a review after 5 years. The disclosure of the nature of the scheme may need to be carefully worded to prepare readers of the accounts for a possible change of treatment.

(iii) Fixed employer and employee contributions are paid to a final salary scheme. The trust deed is silent on what happens if the scheme has a deficit or surplus. In practice, any surplus is used to pay pension increases, which are not explicitly funded.

Retirement benefits	Defined benefit
Company contributions	Defined
Allocated contributions	No

Two of the major points suggest a defined benefit treatment. Unless the directors are able to indicate that contributions would not under any circumstances vary (or a refund of surplus be paid), the suggested treatment is that of a defined benefit scheme. A review of the trust deed may be appropriate to incorporate clauses detailing what would happen in the event of a deficit or if action were required under the surplus regulations.

(iv) In a money purchase scheme, the rate of interest on members' accounts is declared from time to time by trustees. They are not permitted to declare a negative rate. The fund is self-administered and the employer is obliged to top up the fund if there is a deficit.

Retirement benefits	Defined contribution

Company contributions	Defined, but subject to upward or downward movement
Allocated contributions	Yes

The spirit of the scheme is defined contribution and this would be the appropriate accounting treatment provided that the trustees maintain reasonable levels of reserves so that adjustments to contributions because of deficits or because there was a statutory surplus are likely to be small or infrequent.

Secondary factors

4.7 The following secondary factors may be relevant in deciding on the treatment of a particular scheme, if a decision cannot be reached on the basis of key points (a), (b) and (c) stated in 4.6 above.

(i) Is the decision sustainable from one year to another?

If a particular treatment is likely to be sustainable in normal circumstances for a period of 4 or 5 years then the likelihood of change after that time need not influence the immediate decision.

If a change within this timescale is possible in the normal course of events, treatment as a defined benefit scheme would be consistent with the spirit of SSAP 24. If such a change would only occur in very exceptional economic conditions, treatment as a defined contribution scheme would be acceptable.

(ii) How do employees, the employer and shareholders perceive the scheme? Will expectations be affected by describing the scheme in a particular way?

(iii) Will the disclosures resulting from the type of scheme chosen be acceptable to the directors? In particular, what impression will be given by disclosure of the funding level if the defined benefit treatment is adopted?

Treating a 'hybrid' scheme as defined contribution

4.8 If the scheme is treated as defined contribution, prepayments or provisions may arise if contributions are adjusted to levels other than those defined. This may happen as a result of a surplus, for example, or because a with-profits style self-administered arrangement gets into deficit. In such a situation the contributions actually paid to the scheme may be adjusted in practice, but if the trust deed does not provide for this, the contributions payable in accordance with the rules (and hence the pension cost) will not change.

Treating a 'hybrid' scheme as defined benefit

4.9 If a 'hybrid' scheme is funded by a fixed contribution rate, pension cost under SSAP 24 is very likely to differ from the contributions being paid. This may result in a prepayment or provision which while not material initially may continue to increase. If it does so, it may be necessary to explain in the notes to the accounts the way in which the balance has arisen.

Chapter 5

Defined benefit scheme – assumptions and methods for calculating pension cost

Introduction

5.1 In a defined benefit scheme the choice of the actuarial method and assumptions determines the allocation of pension cost between years. This chapter sets out the criteria which must be applied in determining pension cost and the limits which these criteria place on the choice of the valuation method and actuarial assumptions.

Actuarial methods and funding

5.2 Where pensions are paid for in advance, this is usually achieved by paying money into a segregated fund with the intention that it will be sufficient to pay future benefits. There is a whole range of methods which can be used to estimate the amount and timing of the contributions which are required to meet that objective. The timing of contributions does not affect the ultimate cost of the scheme (subject to the impact of investment returns) in terms of benefits paid in accordance with the rules, but simply determines when that cost is met. The contributions also determine the size of the fund at any time and hence the degree of security afforded to members.

The level of funding of any scheme is usually a matter to be determined by the employer and scheme trustees subject only to the relatively wide limits set by the requirements of the Inland Revenue and, where appropriate, the contracting-out provisions. This gives wide flexibility to the employer, particularly in the treatment of surpluses and deficits.

Employers, therefore, can choose in consultation with their actuary whatever funding method and assumptions that best meets their objectives within very broad constraints. This is not to say, however, that all approaches are equally prudent and the scheme's trustees will want to ensure that the funding method chosen provides adequate security for the members and beneficiaries.

5.3 *Defined benefit scheme – assumptions and methods for calculating pension cost*

The choice of assumptions and method for accounting purposes

5.3 SSAP 24, para 18 deals with the selection of the actuarial method and the assumptions to be used in the case of a defined benefit scheme.

> 'The selection of the actuarial method and assumptions to be used in assessing the pension cost of a defined benefit scheme is a matter of judgement for the actuary in consultation with his client, taking account of the circumstances of the specific company and its workforce.'

The statement also lays down the following criteria to be applied in exercising the choice. The assumptions and method must:

(a) take account of the circumstances of the specific company and its work force;

(b) satisfy the accounting objective i.e. lead the employer to recognise the expected cost of providing pensions on a systematic and rational basis over the period during which he derives benefit from the employees' services;

(c) when taken as a whole, be compatible and lead to the actuary's best estimate of the cost of providing the pension benefits promised;

(d) be used consistently and should be disclosed;

(e) recognise the effect of expected future increases in earnings, including merit increases, up to the assumed retirement date or earlier date of withdrawal or death in service;

(f) take account of expected future increases in deferred pensions and pensions in payment where the employer has an express or implied commitment to grant such increases;

(g) make full provision for the expected benefits over the anticipated service lives of employees; and

(h) be based on the situation most likely to be experienced and not on a contingent event unlikely to occur.

SSAP 24 para 18 also states that if there is a change of method, this fact should be disclosed and the effect quantified.

The Statement does not refer explicitly to methods for valuing assets for the purpose of calculating pension cost although it refers in paras 63 and 66 and Appendix 1 to the 'actuarial value of assets'. The criteria which apply to the method and assumptions as a whole do call for the calculation of pension cost to be carried out on a systematic and rational basis and lead to a best estimate. Clearly, therefore, the assets should be valued by a method and on assumptions which are compatible with those used for the valuation of liabilities. Market value related methods of valuation can be acceptable under SSAP 24.

Some employers will want to use the method and assumptions already in use for funding purposes. Others will select the method and assumptions for accounting purposes independently, and then perhaps review their approach to funding.

Use of the funding method and assumptions

5.4 There are a number of circumstances in which it will not be possible to use calculations undertaken for funding purposes to estimate pension cost. Situations where this arises include the following cases.

(a) Where there are any unfunded elements of retirement benefit liabilities, as no funding calculations will be available.

(b) If an unacceptable actuarial method is employed for funding purposes.

(c) For a scheme funded with no allowance for pension increases, where it has been decided to allow for discretionary pension increases in regular cost.

(d) Where the funding assumptions and method cannot reasonably be regarded as giving the best estimate of the cost.

There may be circumstances in which the funding method and assumptions used for funding purposes would be acceptable for calculating pension cost, but a different method and assumptions may be adopted for accounting purposes. This might be the case, for example, in the following circumstances.

(i) Where the holding company directors decide that pension cost is to be calculated on a uniform basis across all group schemes, even though the funding bases differ.

(ii) Where it is decided that best estimates of the pension costs require differing funding methods and assumptions, even though a uniform funding basis is used across all group schemes.

(iii) To permit different allowances for discretionary pension increases in accounting from those used in funding.

There is no requirement to use a common basis for all schemes within a group of companies. Differing membership or experience may be used to justify different bases.

The acceptability of particular methods

5.5 There is a large number of actuarial methods in use for funding purposes. They can be classified into groups of methods with common characteristics. The disclosures required under SSAP 24 may lead to the adoption of generic titles for methods.

The Institute and Faculty of Actuaries have codified actuarial valuation methods in their booklet 'Pension Fund Terminology'. This is primarily intended to be a reference document to provide common understanding (both within and outside the actuarial profession) where pension funding methods are described only by their title.

The codification does not include all methods in common use for funding, nor all of those that may be acceptable for SSAP 24 purposes. The methods which are described in that publication and indications of those which are likely to be acceptable for calculating pension cost are set out in 5.6 below.

It is vital to appreciate that a judgement on the acceptability of a particular method may only be made in the knowledge of the actuarial assumptions to be used in conjunction with it.

Definitions of funding methods in the Institute and Faculty of Actuaries' 'Pension Fund Terminology'

5.6 In 'Pension Fund Terminology' the funding methods are defined in terms of a standard contribution rate and the level of assets which, when taken with the standard contribution rate, would meet the scheme's liabilities. That level of assets may be regarded as the target fund inherent in the method. If all went according to plan, the employer would pay the standard contributions and the fund would stabilise at the target level.

In practice it is likely that, at any given time, the assets will not equal the target fund, thereby giving rise to an adjustment to the standard contribution rate to reflect the difference. This adjustment may be upwards or downwards, depending on whether the assets are less or greater than the target fund. For funding purposes, there is usually some flexibility in deciding the period over which the adjustment to the additional contribution is to be applied in order to bring actual assets into line with the target fund. SSAP 24, on the other hand, imposes more constraints by specifying the treatment of such adjustments or 'variations' for the calculation of pension cost (see 6.6-6.22).

5.7 The main methods set out in 'Pension Fund Terminology' are as follows:

(a) projected unit method;

(b) current unit method;

(c) entry age method;

(d) attained age method; and

(e) aggregate method.

A full description of each method is given in Appendix E.

Expressed simply, the standard contribution rate payable under each method can be summarised as follows:

(a)	Projected unit method:	–	The cost of providing this year's benefits based on earnings expected at retirement
(b)	Current unit method:	–	The cost of providing this year's benefits based on current earnings plus the cost of uprating past benefits in line with earnings
(c)	Entry age method:	–	The average annual cost of providing all future benefits for an entrant at normal entry age
(d)	Attained age method:	–	The average annual cost of providing all future benefits for existing members
(e)	Aggregate method:	–	This is not applicable as the standard contribution rate is not separately identified

Analysis of the main actuarial valuation methods set against SSAP 24 criteria

5.8 An analysis of the five main actuarial valuation methods defined in 'Pension Fund Terminology' set against the criteria of SSAP 24 is summarised below:

Method	**Acceptability**
Projected unit	Yes
Current unit	No
Entry age	Yes
Attained age	Yes
Aggregate	No

The current unit method does not meet the criteria because:

(a) it is not based on the situation most likely to occur. It is a discontinuance method and discontinuance is an unlikely event for the great majority of schemes;

(b) it does not recognise the effect of expected future increases in earnings; and

(c) it does not make full provision for the expected benefits over the service lives of employees.

The aggregate method as strictly defined does not deal properly with those items of surplus or deficit which do not fall to be spread. Therefore, it cannot in general be used to calculate pension cost. If the method is being used loosely enough to comply with the SSAP 24, it should probably be described as the attained age method.

Frequency of valuations

5.9 Valuations are required at regular intervals to compare the assets with the accrued pension liabilities so that the employer can make decisions on funding and benefits to ensure that the scheme can meet its obligations. 'The Occupational Pension Scheme (Disclosure of Information) Regulations 1986' [SI 1986 No 1046] require an actuarial valuation at least once in every period of three and a half years. This rule does not apply to unfunded and money purchase schemes.

One of the consequences of SSAP 24 is that the usual triennial valuation may not be adequate for computation of pension cost without some updating if a material event, such as the closure of a significant part of the business or a substantial rise in pensions in payment, takes place in a financial year between valuations (see 6.5).

Chapter 6

Defined benefit scheme – calculation of pension cost

Introduction

6.1 SSAP 24 requires an employer to recognise the expected cost of providing pensions on a systematic and rational basis over the period during which he derives benefit from the employees' services.

SSAP 24, para 20, identifies two components of pension cost for a defined benefit scheme which are:

(a) *regular cost* which is intended to be the underlying, ongoing cost of pensions based on the current 'best-estimate' actuarial assumptions and method; and

(b) *variations* which reflect the cost of actual past conditions where these differed from earlier estimates, and changed expectations about the future.

A third element, interest on any provision or prepayment, may be added to these costs.

Calculating regular cost

6.2 Where a stable contribution rate for regular contributions, expressed as a percentage of pensionable earnings, has been determined, that rate will provide an acceptable basis for calculating the regular cost under the stated accounting objective so long as it makes full provision for expected benefits over the anticipated service lives of employees. [*SSAP 24, para 20*]. SSAP 24 states that 'the method of providing for expected pension costs over the service lives of employees in the scheme should be such that the regular pension cost is a substantially level percentage of the current and expected future pensionable payroll in the light of the current actuarial assumptions' [*SSAP 24, para 79*].

Regular pension cost may be taken as the standard contribution rate calculated on an acceptable actuarial method before allowing for any adjustment for a surplus or deficit and may be seen as the projected cost of pensions accruing in the year in question. If benefits or assumptions about the future are changed, regular cost will change. Thus there will be a new regular cost.

It should be noted that some actuarial methods (e.g. the attained age method) by their nature lead to at least some surplus or deficit and, in such cases, regular cost will include an allowance for this. Pension cost as calculated under SSAP 24 must take into account whether the actuarial method used will produce such a surplus or deficit and be adjusted to eliminate it.

Variations

6.3 Variations are adjustments to regular cost. They result from experience surpluses or deficits such as differences in investment performance from that anticipated by the actuarial valuation, changes in benefits and changed assumptions about the future (see 3.6). The period over which a variation applies to regular cost depends on the reason for the corresponding surplus or deficit, or in actuarial terms, 'source'. The accounting surplus or deficit arising at a valuation will have come from a number of different sources. The spreading period for a variation is usually determined by its source, although in certain circumstances the Statement allows a choice. Most surpluses or deficits are written off over the expected remaining service life with the company of the present members of the scheme. SSAP 24, para 80 permits a period representing the average remaining services lives, if this is desired. Surpluses from some sources, however, have to be written off over a period shorter than this and in certain cases must be written off in a single accounting period. It is therefore necessary to identify the 'special sources' of surpluses and deficits. Generally, only major sources need to be identified and quantified, as the amount relating to other sources will not be material.

When should pension cost be calculated?

Straightforward cases

6.4 In circumstances where all the employer's schemes are funded and no special calculations are needed, SSAP 24 implies that the calculation of the pension cost for each accounting period should be based on the most recent formal actuarial valuation of the scheme in question.

Valuations are required at regular intervals to compare the assets of the scheme with the accrued pension liabilities, so that the employer can make decisions on funding and benefits to ensure that the scheme can meet its obligations (see 5.9).

Normally, the percentage contribution rate representing regular cost and the percentage contribution rates or monetary amounts representing variations will be calculated at the time of the funding valuation of each pension scheme. Changes in variations between valuations will occur only in special circumstances.

At the time of the regular funding valuation, there may be several variations in operation, resulting from earlier calculations of pension cost. The valuation will be an opportunity to review these in the context of any new variations arising. In particular, it may be acceptable to combine all variations into one figure which operates with effect from the current date (see 6.33).

Each year, when the company accounts are prepared, the total net percentage rate for each of the employer's schemes will be applied to the appropriate pensionable payroll for the accounting period. Any additional amounts (such as the capital cost of a one-off pension increase) will be added. The interest on the balance sheet items will be calculated and added or subtracted. Finally, the results for all the employer's schemes will then be summed. The resulting total for pension cost is used in the accounts unless the figure is negative when further considerations may apply (see 6.27 below).

A valuation date will probably be established for unfunded schemes and calculations carried out at convenient three yearly intervals in the same way as for funded schemes (see 12.3).

Interim valuations and reviews of pension cost

6.5 Interim valuations or reviews may be carried out for a variety of reasons, for example, proposals to improve benefits or to merge schemes. Pension cost should be revised as part of such a review if the change is likely to be material.

Experience surpluses or deficits will usually be taken formally into account in the calculation of pension cost only when a routine valuation is carried out. However, it may be necessary to calculate and apply a variation in respect of a significant deviation from the assumptions earlier than this if the accounts are to show a true and fair view. For example, an approximate valuation might be carried out if there has been a very substantial influx of new entrants which requires a change to pension cost.

The accounting treatment of variations

6.6 The accounting treatment of variations from regular cost can be divided into three main categories:

(i) spread forward over the expected (or average) remaining service lives of employees;

(ii) recognised immediately; or

(iii) recognised as the associated reduction in contributions occurs.

The source of the variation usually determines which alternative applies, but they are not invariably mutually exclusive, as demonstrated by the treatment of refunds (see 6.19-6.22) and may be overridden by prudence (see 6.18).

Appendix G gives a table summarising the treatment of variations according to their source.

Variations which must operate over the expected remaining service life

6.7 Most variations must be spread forward over the expected remaining service lives of employees in the scheme. These comprise experience surpluses and deficits, changes of actuarial assumptions or method and benefit improvements (excluding pension increases).

Experience surplus or deficit

6.8 Variations due to the experience of the fund being different from that previously assumed for accounting purposes are to be spread over the expected remaining service life of current members. This would include, for example, variations arising from investment returns and salary increases different from the rates assumed.

Change of actuarial assumptions or method

6.9 The surplus or deficit resulting from a change in the actuarial assumptions or method used to calculate pension cost must be spread over the expected remaining service life of current members.

The surplus or deficit arising from a change of method must be separately identified for disclosure purposes.

Benefit improvements

6.10 Retroactive benefit changes (including granting benefits in respect of pre-scheme service) are not dealt with by means of a prior year adjustment, even where they relate to past service costs, i.e. the change in liabilities in respect of completed service. Instead, they should be spread over the expected remaining service life of current members. This rule may not apply in certain circumstances where *ex gratia* pensions and discretionary and *ex gratia* pensions increases are granted (see 6.12 and 6.13 below).

Major improvements made between valuations should be taken into account from the date the improvement becomes effective, by calculating a new variation in respect of any past service costs. Modest improvements which are not material need not be accounted for until the following routine valuation. Regular cost may also need to be revised if the change in benefits affects those to be earned for future service by the employees.

Variations which are to be accounted for in a particular accounting period

6.11 Some variations should be dealt with in a particular accounting period. These are essentially restricted to two main areas. The first is where pensions increases and *ex gratia* pensions have not been allowed for in the computation of pension cost and where there is insufficient surplus to meet the increased liability. In such circumstances the capital cost is to be charged to the profit and loss account at the time when the benefits are promised. The second relates to extraordinary events.

Pension increases and ex gratia pensions

6.12 SSAP 24 requires that where an employer has a legal, contractual or implied commitment to provide pensions to employees then the cost should be recognised in the employer's accounts during the period of their employment. Thus guaranteed increases will be allowed for in regular cost.

Where discretionary increases 'are likely to be granted on a regular basis', an allowance for them should be made in the actuarial assumptions underlying the calculation of regular cost [*SSAP 24, para 35*]. Where allowance for realistic discretionary pension increases has been made in the assumptions used to calculate pension cost, the cost of an increase different to the assumed increase is treated as an experience surplus or deficit, and thus spread forward over the expected or average remaining service life.

In some circumstances, however, it may not be reasonable to treat the cost of a particular pension increase as an experience deficit, even where pension cost includes an allowance for increases, if the actual increase differs a great deal from that assumed. Where, for example, a policy of half RPI increases is allowed for by assuming 2% increases, and a 3% increase is granted following a year during which the RPI increased by 6%, it would be reasonable to treat the additional cost as an experience item. It would not be reasonable to adopt this treatment in a year when, for example, a special increase is granted, increasing all pensions in payment to restore their initial purchasing power, as the actuarial assumptions could not be considered to have allowed for this. In such circumstances it may be more appropriate to adopt the treatment set out in 6.13 below.

6.13 An employer may, however, grant pension increases, or grant a pension to someone in retirement or on the point of retirement, without having made any advance commitment or any advance provision for the cost.

The capital cost (i.e. the present value of all future payments resulting from the increase) of an *ex gratia* pension increase (or grant of a pension) which has not been allowed for in the actuarial calculations of cost must be recognised in the profit and loss account in the accounting period in which it is granted, unless it can be set off against a surplus [*SSAP 24 paras 84, 85*]. Where a surplus on the accounting basis (allowing for any balance sheet provision or prepayment) would cover all or part of the cost of granting such pensions or pension increases, the capital cost of the increase must be set against the surplus. Any remaining surplus continues to be spread, but any excess capital cost must be charged to the profit and loss account immediately. A surplus in one scheme should not be used to offset a discretionary increase or pension granted from another scheme.

The same principles apply whether the increase is granted at the time of a valuation, perhaps as a result of the surplus shown, or later. It is likely that an approximate review would be carried out at the date of the increase to check that the increase could be afforded.

Two situations where the treatment is not obvious may occur. The first is where a surplus at a valuation is allocated to pension increases over the following three years. It is suggested that the increases be treated as incurred at the valuation date and offset from the surplus immediately, even though in practice the decision to allocate the surplus in this way will be made somewhat after the valuation date.

The second situation will arise when a pension increase is granted between valuations, no previous allowance or allocation of surplus having been made. The capital cost of the increase would need to be charged in the profit and loss account for the period in which it is granted unless the actuary is able to say that there is sufficient surplus (in the accounting calculations) to meet the cost. This statement will often be possible without detailed calculations.

Thus if no provision is made for discretionary increases in pensions or for *ex gratia* pensions, the spreading rule does not apply. This requirement could cause problems in family-run companies where it is not unusual to find that directors are granted *ex-gratia* pensions on retirement. Without prior provision, SSAP 24 requires the whole of the capital sum to be charged to the profit and loss account at the time of granting the pension. Depending on the level of pension granted, this could have a material impact on the results for the year, and such companies may prefer to accept that their accounts will be qualified rather than comply with SSAP 24 in such circumstances.

Extraordinary events

6.14 The Statement requires that the pension cost associated with an extraordinary event must be recognised immediately and aggregated with the other revenue items associated with that event. This treatment applies even where the change in the employer's contributions in respect of that cost will occur over a longer period [*SSAP 24 para 81*].

This requirement is included in order to comply with the provisions of SSAP 6, 'Extraordinary items and prior year adjustments' and it thus overrules the usual spreading requirements of SSAP 24. While this may seem sensible, it does give rise to an anomaly as the treatment of pension costs depends on whether the closure of a business segment is regarded as exceptional or extraordinary. If treated as the latter, provisions for costs may be offset by the reduction of pension liabilities.

Where the amount involved is likely to be material, special actuarial calculations may be required on the accounting basis to identify it.

6.15 In the case of the closure of a business segment which operated its own stand-alone pension scheme, any existing provision (or prepayment) in the company's accounts in relation to that scheme would be written off immediately, the release or cost respectively being aggregated with other items involved in the closure. Where employees of the business segment are members of a scheme also covering other segments it will be necessary to identify any variation arising from the closure.

6.16 There may be a problem of timing in relation to extraordinary events (as defined by SSAP 6) where the related pension cost must be identified for the accounts relating to the financial year of the event. Often, full data relating, for example, to the sale of a subsidiary near a year-end, may not be available in time for a calculation of the relevant cost. In such cases, the actuary's best estimate will be required based on whatever data is available in time. If this estimate turns out to be reasonable any difference between the actual amount and the estimate will be allowed to emerge as part of the experience surplus or deficit. If the difference is material, it will appear in the accounts in a subsequent year, again as an extraordinary item. In practice, there may be several items relating to the extraordinary event which have to be estimated, not just the pension cost, and many of these may have similar margins of error.

Variations accounted for as reduction in contributions occurs

Significant reduction in the workforce not related to an 'extraordinary event'

6.17 The treatment of a variation arising from a significant reduction in the workforce which is not treated as an extraordinary event depends on whether or not there is a consequent adjustment to contributions.

SSAP 24 para 81 states that where an adjustment is made, the effect of the variation in cost should not be spread over the remaining service lives of employees in the scheme but should be recognised when the reduction in contributions occurs. The rationale for this is that the redundant employees have no future service with the employer and it is thus illogical to spread forward any variation associated with their departure over the service lives of those who remain. This does, however, mean that there is considerable flexibility for an employer in such circumstances because the reduced funding can be taken as:

(a) a pension holiday;

(b) a short-term reduction of contribution rate; or

(c) a long-term reduction of contribution rate at the next actuarial valuation.

If actual funding contributions are adjusted for a period shorter than the expected remaining service life, then the accounting variation attributable to the reduction in workforce should operate over the same shorter period. The funding calculations are relevant only in determining the spreading period. The accounting surplus or deficit which will be spread as a variation is identified in the usual way. Where, for example, there is to be a contribution holiday to eliminate surplus in the fund arising from both a significant reduction in the workforce and better than expected investment returns it is acceptable to spread the accounting surplus from the former source (but not the latter) over the period of the holiday.

SSAP 24 provides no definition of 'significant reduction', though it should clearly have some impact on pension cost. Such a reduction could comprise the consolidation of numerous small reductions or one or two major ones, and the views of the actuary and auditors should be taken into account.

Where no adjustment to contributions is made the surplus or deficit will be spread over the expected or average remaining service life. The treatment is therefore the same as it would have been on the pre-SSAP 24 basis, i.e. a funding one.

Recognition of a material deficit over a short period

6.18 SSAP 24 para 82 states that in strictly limited circumstances prudence may require that a material deficit is recognised over a shorter period than normally required. The situation given as an example in the explanatory note to the Statement of where this might apply is where there has been a major mismanagement of the scheme assets. It is expected that this will arise only very rarely.

Thus, provided:

(a) a major event or transaction has occurred which has not been allowed for in advance and is outside the scope of the normal assumptions; and

(b) this necessitates the payment of significant additional contributions to the pension scheme; and

(c) prudence requires recognition of the deficit over a short period

then the accounting deficit should be recognised over that period. The company, in consultation with its auditor, will decide the period of recognition, which will not necessarily be the same as the period over which the additional contributions are made.

Refunds of surplus

6.19 Where a company receives a refund of surplus from a scheme in accordance with the provisions of the *Finance Act 1986* (now consolidated into the *Income and Corporation Taxes Act 1988*), the company may choose as an alternative to the normal treatment to recognise the equivalent accounting surplus immediately.

SSAP 24 paras 29 and 83 refer to this option in relation to refunds subject to tax. Such refunds are subject to 40% tax at source and the tax cannot be offset or refunded. The employer receives only the net payment, the tax having been paid to the Inland Revenue by the scheme administrator.

This option to recognise a surplus immediately applies where a refund is paid and only to the extent of the refund. It does not apply to any contribution reduction or holiday agreed under the legislation as part of a plan to reduce the surplus. It is debatable as to whether there is any conceptual merit in this exception to the basic spreading rule, but where an employer is anxious for rapid recognition of a surplus, this will make a refund more attractive relative to a contribution reduction or holiday than previously, although it should be remembered that the taxation charge is higher than corporation tax rates in 1990-91 (25% or 35%).

If a refund is due to the reduction in the number of employees, then it is appropriate to credit the refund to the profit and loss account. The treatment of a reduction in the number of employees is, as described in 6.17 above, effectively dealt with on a cash basis. The logical extension to this is to treat a refund for such a reason as an immediate credit.

6.20 The problem often arises as to whether a refund should be treated as an extraordinary or exceptional item. This distinction might be difficult to determine. If a refund is the result of an extraordinary event, then the SSAP clearly requires it to form part of the extraordinary item (see 6.14 above). If the the refund is the result of a diminution of numbers in the workforce, the issue becomes more complex. SSAP 6, paras 2(a) and 4(a), states that redundancy costs relating to continuing business segments are to be regarded as exceptional while those relating to discontinuance of a business segment are extraordinary.

If the refund is treated as exceptional, the gross amount of the refund should be shown, with the tax deducted forming part of the taxation charge for the year. If it is regarded as an extraordinary item, it will be shown in the profit and loss account net of tax, the taxation charge being disclosed in the notes to the accounts. Treatment as an extraordinary item will mean that the refund is excluded from earnings per share.

6.21 Because of the formalities which have to be completed before a refund is payable to the employer, it is quite possible that the amount of the refund will be finally determined and paid in an accounting period after that in which the application to the relevant authorities has been made. However, SSAP 24, para 83, makes it clear that a refund under the *Finance Act 1986* may only be credited to the profit and loss account (if this is the preferred treatment) when it is received. This should be interpreted in a very restricted way. It is not acceptable to anticipate the amount as a debtor. However it may be necessary, in order to present a true and fair view, to mention the matter of a refund and its amount in the pensions note if a refund of a significant amount has been applied for and is expected to be credited in the following accounting period.

6.22 A scheme's trust deed may not permit the payment of a refund of surplus to the employer whilst the scheme is in an on-going situation, and winding-up may be seen as a way of releasing a surplus. Frequently, a winding-up is part of a process of rationalisation of schemes within a group of companies. This may be accompanied by the transfer of employees within the scheme to another group scheme. In either of these circumstances, it may be argued that the refund does not fall within the scope of SSAP 24, para 83 because it does not relate to the *Finance Act 1986*. This means that there may be more flexibility for the recognition of the refund in an accounting period other than when it occurs. Provided that the amount due is clearly quantifiable, it may be credited in an accounting period prior to its payment provided that winding up has been commenced and the receipt is certain.

Calculating the variation from regular cost

6.23 In general, variations from regular cost have to be spread over the expected remaining service life with the employer of the present members of the scheme.

SSAP 24 does not address the details of how the spreading of a variation should be calculated. In particular, it does not directly answer the following questions.

(a) Should it be a level amount or increase with earnings?

(b) Should it allow for interest on any balance sheet provision or prepayment?

(c) If interest is allowed for, should it be included within or additional to the variation which is calculated?

The variation, like the regular cost, may be expressed as a substantially level percentage of pensionable pay from year to year. This treatment is within the spirit of SSAP 24. However, in their computations of pension cost, it is common to see actuaries amortise variations from regular cost in a number of different ways. Three main approaches may be identified:

(i) spreading variations as a percentage of payroll;

(ii) straight line amortisation of the capital amount with interest on the reducing balance;

(iii) the mortgage method whereby equal amounts of interest and capital are charged or credited each year.

SSAP 24 states that regular cost should be a substantially level percentage of current and future payroll. However, it does not specify in the explanatory note or in SSAP 24, para 80, how variations (other than those subject to SSAP 24, paras 81-83) should be allocated. SSAP 24, para 80 states that variations from regular cost should be allocated over the expected remaining service lives of employees in the scheme. SSAP 24, paras 22-32, refers to 'spreading' and 'released over the expected remaining service lives' without specifying a method. Thus variations may be amortised on a basis other than as a percentage of payroll.

On a theoretical basis, it can be argued that amortisation of a variation as a percentage of payroll is to be preferred. Regular cost is calculated on this basis and it is therefore logical to calculate the variations in the same way. However, whichever method of amortising variations is applied, it is important to consider the long-term effects on pension costs, as a short-term advantage by the use of a particular method may have fluctuations in the cost profile which are not acceptable to the auditor. In particular, auditors may be unwilling to accept a pension cost which fluctuates from negative to positive. Whichever method of amortisation is applied, it is recommended that it be disclosed.

Calculation of the variation

6.24 The variation will be determined by dividing the total amount of surplus (deficit) to be spread by an 'actuarial factor'. This factor will be less than the number of years over which the surplus (deficit) is to be spread to allow for interest on payments in years after the current one (see 6.26 below).

The practical effects of different methods of amortisation

6.25 A detailed example, included as Appendix H, illustrates the calculations of the variations under the three different methods of amortisation outlined above. Extracts from this example are given below.

Example

A pension scheme has a surplus of £5 million, to be amortised over 10 years, and the interest rate is 10%. Initial payroll is £10 million, rising at 8% p.a. and the regular pension cost is 10%. Pension cost is as follows.

Year	% of payroll	Straight line	Mortgage method
1	457,716	54,228	240,501
2	494,333	148,218	303,118
3	533,879	254,692	375,082
4	576,590	375,145	457,575
5	622,717	511,243	551,915
6	672,534	664,837	659,576
7	726,337	837,988	782,201
8	784,444	1,032,987	921,622
9	847,199	1,252,382	1,079,880
10	914,975	1,499,005	1,259,253
11	2,158,925	2,158,925	2,158,925
12	2,331,639	2,331,639	2,331,639

Spreading the variation as a percentage of payroll gives the smoothest profile of costs over the period of amortisation. Where the variations have led to a surplus, the straight line method has the advantage of a low pension cost in earlier years when the effect of interest is taken into account (see 6.26). In some cases this may result in a negative cost in earlier years followed by a period of positive costs. However, the overall cost will be the same, as is demonstrated by the calculations in Appendix H, if the funding pattern is identical. If the funding pattern changes, then pension cost will correspondingly change, even if the same amortisation method is applied. This is because of the time value of the monetary contributions (see 6.26 and Appendix H (i) – (v)).

Interest

6.26 SSAP 24, para 40, mentions that actuaries make allowance for interest but that financial statements normally include items at face value without discounting them. It adds that interest effects arising from short-term timing differences between the payment of contributions and the recognition of cost are unlikely to be material and can be ignored, but implies that if the difference is long-term, interest should be recognised.

The actuarial calculation of pension cost will implicitly assume that the assets of the scheme will earn interest. Where variations are spread forward as a percentage of payroll and the payment of contributions is adjusted so that funding equals pension cost, no surplus or deficit arises, provided that the amortisation of the surplus recognises the effect of interest. Referring to the data in Appendix H(vi), the total of the variations from regular cost (£7,855,838) exceeds the surplus (£5,000,000), i.e. an amount in excess of the surplus is credited to the profit and loss account. This is because the surplus is a discounted amount. The run-off of the surplus, crediting the outstanding surplus at the beginning of each year by 10%, is as follows (note that some figures have been rounded).

Year	Surplus at beginning of year	Variation from regular cost 5.42% of payroll	Balance	Interest at 10%	Surplus at year end
0					5,000,000
1	5,000,000	542,284	4,457,716	445,772	4,903,487
2	4,903,487	585,667	4,317,820	431,782	4,749,602
3	4,749,602	632,521	4,117,081	411,708	4,528,789
4	4,528,789	683,122	3,845,667	384,567	4,230,234
5	4,230,234	737,772	3,492,462	349,246	3,841,708
6	3,841,708	796,794	3,044,914	304,491	3,349,405
7	3,349,405	860,537	2,488,868	248,887	2,737,755
8	2,737,755	929,380	1,808,375	180,837	1,989,212
9	1,989,212	1,003,731	985,481	98,548	1,084,029
10	1,084,029	1,084,029	0	0	0
11	0	0	0	0	0
12	0	0	0	0	0

If interest is not imputed on the balance of the surplus the result is as follows.

Year	Surplus at beginning of year	Variation from regular cost 5.42% of payroll	Balance	Interest ignored	Surplus at year end
0					5,000,000
1	5,000,000	542,284	4,457,716	0	4,457,716
2	4,457,716	585,667	3,872,049	0	3,872,049
3	3,782,049	632,521	3,239,528	0	3,239,528
4	3,239,528	683,122	2,556,406	0	2,556,406
5	2,556,406	737,772	1,818,634	0	1,818,634
6	1,818,634	796,794	1,021,840	0	1,021,840
7	1,021,840	860,537	161,303	0	161,303
8	161,303	929,380	(768,077)	0	(768,077)
9	(768,077)	1,003,731	(1,771,808)	0	(1,771,808)
10	(1,771,808)	1,084,029	(2,855,838)	0	(2,855,838)

Failure to account for interest leads to a much more rapid unwinding of the surplus, and causes distortion because the surplus is discounted. If however, the undiscounted surplus is amortised, then it does unwind over the 10 years as the following table demonstrates.

Year	Surplus at beginning of year	Variation from regular cost 5.42% of payroll	Surplus at year end
0			7,855,838
1	7,855,838	542,284	7,313,554
2	7,313,554	585,667	6,727,887
3	6,727,887	632,521	6,095,366
4	6,095,366	683,122	5,412,244
5	5,412,244	737,772	4,674,472
6	4,674,472	796,794	3,877,678
7	3,877,678	860,537	3,017,141
8	3,017,141	929,380	2,087,761
9	2,087,761	1,003,731	1,084,029
10	1,084,029	1,084,029	0

As mentioned above, the actuarial calculation of pension cost will implicitly assume that the 'assets' of the scheme will earn interest. For accounting purposes, the assets include any SSAP 24 provisions in the balance sheet. Again referring to the example in Appendix H, if contributions paid diverge from cost, as is the case where contributions are paid on the basis of percentage of payroll, but the variation for SSAP 24 purposes is spread on a straight line basis, then interest on the balance sheet provision (or prepayment) should be taken into account to avoid distortions. Failure to account for interest will lead to its emergence as a variation at the next valuation and being spread forward instead of being charged or credited in the year in which it arises. Therefore it is appropriate for interest to be added to these balance sheet items. In such circumstances interest should be included as part of the pension cost and not disclosed as interest receivable (a *Companies Act 1985* disclosure requirement). Where there is an accounting surplus, such interest is imputed to allow for the discounting approach adopted in calculating the surplus and is not receivable by the employing company.

Appendix H (v) graphically illustrates the effect of different funding approaches on pension cost.

Negative pension cost

6.27 It is possible for a negative variation to be so large as to exceed the regular cost, giving a theoretical negative pension cost. In practice, such a situation is most likely to arise where a scheme is substantially overfunded. While this commonly arises in the US under FAS 87, the UK auditing profession is divided in its views as to whether a negative pension cost is acceptable. The difficulty relates to the pension scheme being a separate legal entity outside the corporate structure, and is allied to the concept of realised profit under the *Companies Act 1985* and Statement of Standard Accounting Practice 2, 'Disclosure of Accounting Policies'. SSAP 2, para 14 states, in relation to prudence,

> 'revenue and profits are not anticipated, but are recognised by inclusion in the profit and loss account only when realised in the form either of cash or of other assets the ultimate cash realisation of which can be assessed with reasonable certainty....'

Under this interpretation, the surplus is seen as an overpayment in the past which will reduce the cost of providing employees' pensions in the future, but is not realised unless it is repaid as a refund of surplus. The view is that the surplus is tied up in the scheme's investments, and the profits and losses on those investments belong to (or are suffered by) the scheme. The employers' interest is what it costs to maintain the fund at an adequate level. If this view is taken, where the pension cost calculation is negative, the accounting cost is taken as zero on the grounds of prudence. As in such circumstances the company is very likely to be taking a contribution holiday, cost and funding will be the same. However, the alternative view is that the results of the scheme are part of those of the company, and negative pension cost is quite logical. In the absence of guidance from the Accounting Standards Committee, both approaches have been seen in published accounts (see Appendix I). When the effects of the Barber judgment and the provisions of the *Social Security Act 1990* are implemented, surpluses may be substantially reduced, thus making such arguments academic in many cases.

Subsidiary participating in a group scheme

6.28 Where a subsidiary company participates in a group scheme, pension cost need not be calculated as a 'best estimate' of the cost for the particular subsidiary company. Pension cost may instead be calculated as the best estimate of the common percentage of payroll for the whole of the scheme. (see 11.2, 11.3).

Foreign schemes

6.29 Where the pension cost charged in the accounts of a foreign company belonging to a UK group does not conform to the requirements of the standard, the pension cost should be adjusted when preparing the consolidated group accounts [*SSAP 24, para 41*].

However, no adjustment is appropriate where the employer's commitment is very different to that normal in the UK. For example, the employer's obligation may be limited to prescribed payments to a nationwide or industry-wide scheme with characteristics similar to those of the UK State scheme [*SSAP 24, para 42*].

Sometimes an adjustment to the pension cost on consolidation may be impractical due to cost or the difficulty of obtaining the necessary information. In such circumstances the amount of the charge and the basis on which it is assessed must be disclosed [*SSAP 24, para 43*] (see 11.4).

Which actuarial valuation?

6.30 In practice, it can be difficult to determine the most appropriate valuation for the purposes of SSAP 24, as it is possible that only outline results of the latest actuarial valuation may be available or the trustees have not made any decisions on benefit improvements when the accounts have to be prepared.

Pension scheme financial year ends are often co-terminous with that of the employer. Since the actuary will take account of the financial statements of the pension scheme at valuation date, and since the valuation may take some time to complete, the results may not be available until well into the subsequent financial year. The trustees then have to make their decisions on any benefit improvements in the light of the valuation, so that the time scale involved may be considerable. As an example, for a year end of 31 December 1990, the process may take until the following summer or longer. However, the company's accounts must be completed within four months if it is quoted on the The International Stock Exchange and public and private companies must file their accounts with the Registrar within seven and ten months respectively.

Clearly then pension cost may be calculated on the basis of an actuarial valuation which may have been based on scheme accounts of up to four years earlier. It may in certain circumstances be possible to use the interim results of a valuation if they are available, but this will depend on the judgment of the directors and the auditors, who respectively have the responsibility of preparing and reporting on the company's accounts. If there have been any events between valuations which have a significant bearing on pension cost, then clearly the actuary will have to examine the effects on the pension cost calculations with a view to assessing any changes in the cost for the purposes of the accounts (see 6.5).

Transfer of liabilities from company to a funded scheme

6.31 From time to time, unfunded liabilities which were previously borne by the employer (e.g. future pension increases to pensioners of an otherwise funded scheme) may, with the agreement of the employer and scheme trustees, become the responsibility of a funded arrangement.

A scheme surplus may sometimes be used to fund such liabilities. For example a company, in addition to operating a funded scheme, may pay out of revenue a number of pensions to employees who left service before the scheme was established. Following a valuation, surplus in the scheme could be used to fund the payments with liability for those benefits being transferred to the scheme.

On the introduction of SSAP 24, the liability for unfunded commitments will have given rise to a provision in the company's accounts through one or other of the permitted transitional treatments (see chapter 7). If it is subsequently agreed that the unfunded pensions are to become liabilities of a funded arrangement, part or all of the provision may no longer be needed. This will be the case if an accounting surplus is being used to fund the liabilities. The value of the liabilities offsets the surplus immediately. If there is no accounting surplus, the provision is still required.

The redundant part of the provision represents an accounting surplus in the unfunded arrangement. SSAP 24 states that this surplus should be written off over the 'expected remaining service lives of the current employees' [*SSAP 24, para 80*]. It is suggested that the expected remaining service life of the current members of the scheme which has assumed the liabilities should normally be used, for consistency with other accounting figures. There may, however, be other groups of employees (e.g. that to which the individuals entitled to unfunded pensions belonged) which could also be used. The whole workforce is one possible choice.

The remaining part of the provision now attaches to the funded scheme.

Members' contribution holiday

6.32 The accounting treatment of a members' contribution holiday is not specified by the Standard. There are clearly the following alternatives.

(i) Treat the cost as a past service benefit improvement.

Under this approach the cost of the holiday is calculated and then spread over the average remaining service life. Such treatment is appropriate where the employer treats the holiday as a past service benefit improvement (e.g. new members pay contributions as normal).

(ii) Recognise the cost over the period of the holiday.

The cost of a contribution holiday can be recognised by increasing regular cost by the amount of the members' contributions. Such treatment is appropriate where new members of the scheme benefit from the holiday and the holiday may be indefinite.

If approach (ii) is followed, the decrease in regular cost anticipated at the end of the period of the holiday must be disclosed.

Similar treatment might be applied to a temporary improvement in accrual rates.

The effects of subsequent actuarial valuations

6.33 Where a subsequent actuarial valuation reveals a surplus or deficit materially different from the actuary's estimate at the previous valuation, there are two accounting choices.

(a) To spread forward the surpluses or deficits at previous valuations on their original bases of amortisation, spreading any new variation which has arisen since the latest valuation over the estimated remaining service lives of employees at the latest valuation date. This means that the pension cost may include a number of variations being amortised.

(b) To assess the total surplus or deficit at the latest valuation date, combining the previous surpluses or deficits which have not been amortised with any which has arisen since the last valuation and spread forward the total variation over the expected remaining service lives of current employees.

The first basis is theoretically more correct, as under the second alternative the variation is constantly re-spread, such that the period of amortisation may be continually extended (rather like using a reducing balance basis). However, the first alternative means that the surplus or deficiency at each valuation must be separately spread over the expected remaining service lives of employees in the scheme at the time the variation arose. This results in greater complexity in the computations, because of the potential for having to amortise variations arising from three or four valuations. The second alternative is more likely to be adopted. The uncertainties inherent in assessing pension cost are such that it would be difficult to argue that the first alternative is superior.

2% Incentive

6.34 Under the *Social Security Act 1986*, occupational pension schemes which become contracted-out schemes during the period 1 January 1986 to 5 April 1993 and which have not previously been contracted-out for any part of that time, can qualify for the special incentive payments from the government. The incentive is available to a scheme which qualifies for each of the five years 6th April 1988-5th April 1993 under certain conditions. The payment is calculated each year from the earnings between the Lower and Upper Earnings Limits on which eligible employees have paid National Insurance Contributions during the year at the contracted-out rate. The amount payable is 2% of these earnings subject to a minimum of £1 for each week of the employee's contracted-out employment.

Under SSAP 24 there are three possible approaches to the treatment of this 2% incentive. Theoretically the most correct method would be to take the amounts receivable into account in the long-term calculation of pension cost. However, the incentive payments are only available for a limited period of time for a limited range of earnings and one option would therefore be to disregard them as immaterial. In this instance, the payments would emerge as a variation at the next valuation, having been credited to a pension provision in the meantime. Another option would be to credit the amounts received to pension cost in the year in which they are received, thus reducing regular pension cost in those years. If this route is taken, it is suggested that it be disclosed as pension cost will change when the payments are discontinued.

Treatment of death in service benefits and group permanent health insurance

6.35 Many employers provide death-in-service benefits for employees. Sometimes this is independent of pension scheme membership, but may be only available to scheme members. Employers often pay the annual premiums for this directly to insurers, though in an insured scheme, the employer's contributions usually cover the costs of life assurance within the percentage of payroll being paid as funding. The question often arises as to whether life assurance premiums should form part of pension cost. Where life assurance is linked with membership of the pension scheme, it would seem logical to include the cost as part of the overall pension cost, but there is no hard and fast rule. If an employing company rather than the pension scheme pays the premiums and does not wish to include such costs as pension cost, this is not unreasonable. It is important however, that once a particular approach has been taken, that it be followed consistently each accounting period.

The NAPF 1989 survey of occupational pension schemes revealed that a quarter of employers had group permanent health insurance (PHI) for some or all of their employees. Group PHI is a separate insurance policy taken out by the employer. Unlike death-in-service benefits, it is not linked with pension scheme membership and should not be included in pension cost.

Implementation of pension and benefit improvements part of the way through the financial year.

6.36 Once the results of an actuarial valuation are known, employers and their scheme trustees usually review the valuation and make decisions on the level of benefit improvements. Such decisions may be made some time after the effective date of the valuation. The question then arises as to when such decisions should impact on pension cost.

Example

A company with a financial year ending 31 December has decided to improve pensions in payment as of 1 July 1990. This decision was based on the latest valuation which was as at 31 December 1988. The pension improvements were expected to take £5 million of the estimated surplus of £10 million.

The company has the following choices.

(a) If the valuation were available by the time the 31 December 1989 accounts were being prepared and the trustees had agreed to improve pensions as from 1st July 1990, it could

either

spread the surplus after allowing for the pension increases, from 1st January 1989 (the usual choice)

or

it could spread forward the full surplus from 1st January 1989 until 30th June 1990 and thereafter spread the revised surplus, this revised surplus taking into account both the reduction between 1st

January 1989 and 30th June 1990 and the £5 million cost of pension improvements. This approach would mean that pension cost for the second half of the 1990 financial year would differ from that of the first half.

(b) If the valuation were available only after the completion of the 1989 company accounts,

either

the surplus could be spread after allowing for the pension increases from 1st January 1990 (the usual choice)

or

it could spread the full surplus of £10 million for the 6 months to 30th June 1990 and spread the revised surplus as at 1st July 1990, taking into account the reduction in surplus between 1st January and 30th June and the £5 million reduction due to the award of the pension increases. Again, the pension cost for 1990 would have two separate components.

Change from defined benefit to defined contribution scheme

6.37 Sometimes, an employer may decide to change from a defined benefit arrangement to a defined contribution scheme. This may have a number of consequences for pension cost. The winding up of a defined benefit scheme may result in a surplus being refunded to the employer or the employer being required to fund a deficit. In such circumstances, the surplus or deficit should be set off against any cumulative pension provision or prepayment recognised in the balance sheet. Any surplus or deficit not offset in this way should be credited or charged to the profit and loss account and not spread forward, as there is no relevant estimated future service life over which it can be spread. Pension cost then becomes the contributions payable to the defined benefit scheme.

If the surplus from a defined benefit scheme is not returned to the company but used to offset the contributions to the defined contribution scheme, then the employer can take advantage of SSAP 24, para 78, which states that the charge against profits for a defined contribution scheme should be the amount of contributions payable, and show a nil cost as long as the surplus is available in this way. Alternatively, (and theoretically more correctly), the notional surplus can be credited to the profit and loss account and debited to a pension prepayment. As the contributions to the defined benefit scheme are offset against the surplus, in the accounts of the employer the profit and loss account will be charged with the cost and the prepayment correspondingly reduced.

Financial resources computations under the rules of the Financial Services Act 1986

6.38 The *FSA 1986* has resulted in strict financial resources rules for businesses registered under this legislation. Where such a business has a large pension scheme surplus and is taking a contribution holiday, the application of SSAP 24 may result in a creditor being shown in the balance sheet. This may create difficulties in compliance with the relevant regulatory authority's financial resources rules. Any investment business in this situation should consult with its regulators as to the application of the rules in such circumstances, as it may be possible to exclude the effects of SSAP 24.

Chapter 7

Defined benefit scheme – transitional treatment on the implementation of SSAP 24

Introduction

7.1 Most companies operating defined benefit schemes will not in the past have accounted for pension cost in line with the principles of SSAP 24. A change in accounting policy will be necessary in order to comply. Such companies will need to decide how the difference between their past practice and the requirements of SSAP 24 should be reflected when implementing its requirements for the first time.

The provisions in the Statement concerning this transition require that a 'cumulative adjustment' arising from prior years must either be dealt with in accordance with the normal provisions of the SSAP 24 (which in most circumstances means spreading it forward), or be accounted for in accordance with the provisions of SSAP 6 'Extraordinary items and prior year adjustments' [*SSAP 24, para 53*].

7.2 Under SSAP 6, a prior year adjustment is dealt with by restating earlier years' accounts as though its provisions had applied in those earlier years. This gives rise to an adjustment to the balance sheet which reflects the difference between past and present practice.

By defining the 'cumulative adjustment' as broadly equal to the surplus or deficit at the start of the first accounting period for which SSAP 24 is applied (the transition date) the explanatory note to the Statement suggests an alternative approach to making a prior year adjustment, i.e. bringing the whole of the cumulative adjustment on to the balance sheet at the transition date.

The methods of dealing with the cumulative adjustment on transition

7.3 The following three methods are generally agreed as being acceptable. Method 1 deals with the cumulative adjustment in accordance with the normal provisions of SSAP 24. Methods 2 and 3 deal with it in two different ways as a prior year adjustment.

Method	*Treatment*
1	Parts of the cumulative adjustment which cannot be spread forward (i.e. those attributable to sources where a variation over future working lives is not permitted) are allocated to, attributed to or recognised in the current period's profit and loss account. The remainder of the cumulative adjustment is spread forward as a variation to regular cost from the transition date, without restating the prior year's figures.
2	Accounts for previous years (normally since the last valuation) are restated in accordance with SSAP 24. Parts of the surplus/deficit at the previous valuation which cannot be spread are recognised in prior years. The remainder is spread forward as a variation to regular cost from the valuation date.
3	The cumulative adjustment appears in the balance sheet at the transition date. There are no variations to regular cost.

The regular cost would be the same under methods 1 and 3, but might, for reasons of the timing of the valuations, be different under method 2. The total profit and loss account charge might be quite different under each of the three methods.

7.4 The Statement requires that the way in which the transitional provisions have been applied should be disclosed in the accounts for the accounting period in which SSAP 24 is first implemented [*SSAP 24, para 92*].

7.5 The *CA 1985* requires corresponding figures for the previous year to be shown against each item in the current year's accounts. Depending on the transitional treatment adopted, the previous year's profit and loss account may have to be restated, where practicable, in accordance with the new accounting policy, in order to be comparable with the current year's figure calculated under SSAP 24 (see 7.12).

Method 1

7.6 The cumulative adjustment to be spread is calculated as at the transition date as a broad estimate of the actuarial value of the accounting surplus or deficit on an ongoing basis. This means the approximate excess or shortfall of the actuarial value of the assets over the standard fund (see chapter 5).

The calculation of the adjustment may be based, where appropriate, on the results of the previous actuarial valuation in order to avoid undertaking a special valuation. The valuation may need to be updated to the transition date, allowing for contributions paid by the employer. In many cases this will have been done approximately, but allowing for significant changes which have occurred since the last valuation.

The cumulative adjustment is to be identified on the actuarial method and assumptions used for the calculation of the pension cost, which are not necessarily the same as those used for funding purposes. For example, if pension increases are not funded in advance, but the pension costs are to be calculated making allowance for the increases, the cumulative adjustment must be calculated in relation to liabilities including an allowance for the increases. In practice, it will usually be acceptable to carry out an approximate adjustment of the results of the previous valuation to the new basis.

7.7 Surpluses or deficits arising from some sources cannot be spread forward over the average remaining service life (see 6.11-6.22). In the same way, any part of the cumulative adjustment arising from such sources must be recognised immediately on implementation of the SSAP. It is necessary, therefore, to identify those parts of the surplus or deficit at the previous valuation date which fall into this category.

In practice, the split may be made on an approximate basis. Only major surpluses or deficits arising from sources for which spreading over the average remaining service life is not the appropriate treatment need be quantified (see also 7.15 below).

SSAP 24 does not make it clear whether the surplus (or deficit) which may not be spread forward should be treated as adjusted firstly by contribution reductions (or increases) in the interim period up to the transition date. To do so would appear to be in line with the spirit of the Statement. Any surplus or deficit at the transition date which may not be spread is set up as a prepayment or provision in the balance sheet. The remaining cumulative adjustment is spread from the transition date [*SSAP 24, para 53*].

Example – Method 1

7.8 The following example shows the effect of adopting Method 1. In the example actual contributions are given and the regular cost and the variation have been determined by the actuary. The remaining figures are derived as set out below.

Pension cost	=	Regular cost + Variation
New provision	=	Pension cost – Actual contributions
Year end provision	=	Provision at end of previous year + New provision

No account has been taken of inflation and interest so as to concentrate on the principles involved. Average remaining service life has been used instead of expected remaining service life.

£1 = £1m.
The regular cost is £100m p.a.
A valuation at 31.12.86 revealed a surplus of £500m.
The employer decided to take a 5 year contribution holiday from 1.1.87.
SSAP 24 is adopted from 1.1.89.
The cumulative adjustment at 1.1.89 is estimated to be £300m.

Cumulative adjustment is to be spread forward over average remaining service life; (say) 10 years. The revised pension cost is arrived at by using the formula:

$$\text{Regular cost} - \frac{\text{surplus}}{\text{average remaining service life}} = \text{pension cost}$$

The variation to regular cost is £300 million/10 p.a. = £30m p.a.

The pension cost is as follows:

$$\text{£100m (regular cost)} - \frac{\text{£300m (suplus)}}{\text{10 years (a.r.s.l)}} = \text{£70m p.a.}$$

7.9 *Defined benefit scheme – transitional treatment on the implementation of SSAP 24*

Year	Actual Contributions £	Regular Cost £	Variation £	Pension Cost £	New Provision (Pre-payment) £	Year End Provision (Pre-payment) £
1986	100	N/A	N/A	100	–	–
1987	–	N/A	N/A	–	–	–
1988	–	N/A	N/A	–	–	–
1988 Restated*	–	N/A	N/A	–	–	–
1989	–	100	(30)	70	70	70
1990	–	100	(30)	70	70	140
1991	–	100	(30)	70	70	210
1992	100	100	(30)	70	(30)	180
1993	100	100	(30)	70	(30)	150
1994	100	100	(30)	70	(30)	120
1995	100	100	(30)	70	(30)	90
1996	100	100	(30)	70	(30)	60
1997	100	100	(30)	70	(30)	30
1998	100	100	(30)	70	(30)	–
1999	100	100	–	100	–	–

Notes

(a) The comparative figures to be shown for 1988 in the 1989 accounts are the same as those in the 1988 accounts.

(b) Prepayments are treated as negative provisions.

(c) Negative amounts are shown in brackets.

Method 2

7.9 Under this approach, past company accounts are reworked to conform with SSAP 24, usually beginning at the previous actuarial valuation of the schemes. Regular cost and variations would have been recalculated at that date had SSAP 24 been in force all along and there is, therefore, normally no reason to look any further back. In particular, any unspreadable surplus or deficit is recognised in the year in which it arose, probably the year of the valuation. The remainder is spread forward as a variation to regular cost from the valuation date. There is, therefore, no need to calculate a cumulative adjustment at the transition date.

Example – Method 2

The facts are the same as in the previous example but Method 2 is applied.

Prior year adjustment – restatement of prior years' figures as if SSAP 24 had always applied.

The surplus or deficit disclosed at the 1986 actuarial valuation was all 'new', falling to be spread from that valuation.

The variation to regular cost running from 1.1.87:
£500m/10 years. = £50m p.a.

The pension cost (in millions) is as follows:

$$£100 - \frac{500}{10} = £50$$

Year	Actual Contributions £	Regular Cost £	Variation £	Pension Cost £	New Provision (Pre-payment) £	Year End Provision (Pre-payment) £
1986	100	N/A	N/A	100	–	–
1987	–	N/A	N/A	–	–	–
1988	–	N/A	N/A	–	–	–
1987 Restated	–	100	(50)	50	50	50
1988 Restated	–	100	(50)	50	50	100
1989	–	100	(50)	50	50	150
1990	–	100	(50)	50	50	200
1991	–	100	(50)	50	50	250
1992	100	100	(50)	50	(50)	200
1993	100	100	(50)	50	(50)	150
1994	100	100	(50)	50	(50)	100
1995	100	100	(50)	50	(50)	50
1996	100	100	(50)	50	(50)	–
1997	100	100	–	100	–	–
1998	100	100	–	100	–	–
1999	100	100	–	100	–	–

Method 3

7.10 The cumulative adjustment is calculated in the same way as for Method 1.

A balance sheet provision, if there is a deficit, or prepayment, if there is a surplus, equal to the cumulative adjustment is created and the retained profit brought forward is reduced or increased respectively to correspond.

Pension cost for the period following the transition date is equal to regular cost.

Example – Method 3

The facts are the same as in the example for method 1 but method 3 is applied.

Year	Actual Contributions £	Regular Cost £	Variation £	Pension Cost £	New Provision (Pre-payment) £	Year End Provision (Pre-payment) £
1986	100	N/A	N/A	100	–	–
1987	–	N/A	N/A	–	–	–
1988	–	N/A	N/A	–	–	–
1988 Restated	–	100	–	100	100	(300)
1989	–	100	–	100	100	(200)
1990	–	100	–	100	100	(100)
1991	–	100	–	100	100	–
1992	100	100	–	100	–	–
1993	100	100	–	100	–	–
1994	100	100	–	100	–	–
1995	100	100	–	100	–	–
1996	100	100	–	100	–	–
1997	100	100	–	100	–	–
1998	100	100	–	100	–	–
1999	100	100	–	100	–	

Comparison of the three Methods

7.11 Method 1 gives lower pension costs and hence higher company profits over the years 1989 to 1998 than Method 3 but at the expense of a weaker balance sheet. Method 2 reduces pension cost even more in the initial year, but weakens the balance sheet further.

The graphs on the following page compare respectively the total pension cost and the end year provision (prepayment) under each approach.

Method 3 results in the largest initial item in the balance sheet and an ongoing pension cost equal to regular cost. Methods 1 and 2 will result in smaller initial balance sheet items, but pension cost will vary from regular cost and is dependent on the surplus and the average remaining service lives.

Pension cost affects company earnings, whereas balance sheet items do not.

Comparative figures in the year of implementation

7.12 SSAP 6, para 46, points out that the *CA 1985 sch 4*, 4 sch. 4 requires that where the corresponding amount of an item for the preceding year is not comparable with the amount in the financial year to which the accounts relate, the former should be adjusted and the particulars of the adjustment and the reasons for it to be disclosed in a note to the accounts. SSAP 24 does not not explicitly address this issue. It is clear that Method 2 provides a prior year figure which conforms to the requirements of both SSAP 6 and the *CA 1985*. For Methods 1 and 3, the earlier year's figure should in theory be calculated by the actuary if a correct comparative figure for the previous year is to be shown. This may be a relatively straightforward exercise if the relevant actuarial valuation is as at the beginning of the previous financial year, but more complex if earlier or later or if there have been any events which have a significant effect on pension cost in the previous year. If this approach is taken, the pension cost for the previous year is restated if necessary, with the corresponding adjustment being made to opening reserves in the year SSAP 24 is implemented.

Example

A company implements SSAP 24 as at 1 January 1989. The actuary undertakes a special valuation to assess the surplus as at that date, the surplus being spread forward over the employees' estimated future service lives. The actuary estimates that pension cost in the financial year 1988 would have been £8 million if SSAP 24 had then applied. Pension cost actually charged in the accounts was nil, as the company taking a contribution holiday. The profit and loss account reserve at 31 December 1988 was £396 million.

7.12 *Defined benefit scheme – transitional treatment on the implementation of SSAP 24*

Pension cost charged in accounts for the year

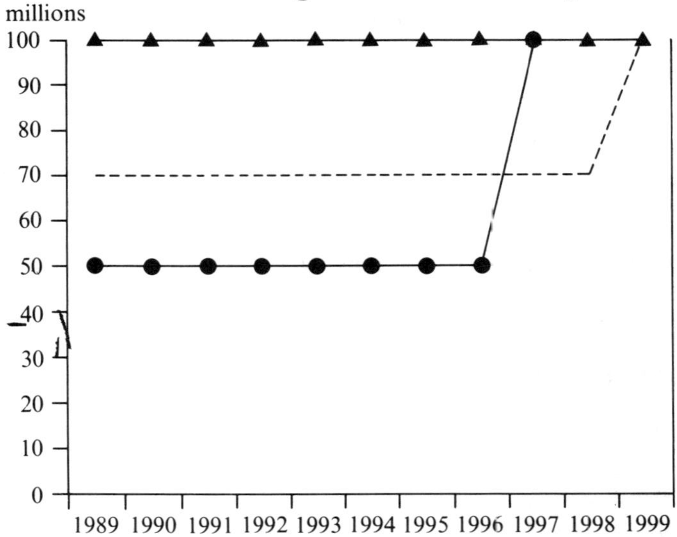

Provision (prepayment) in accounts at year end

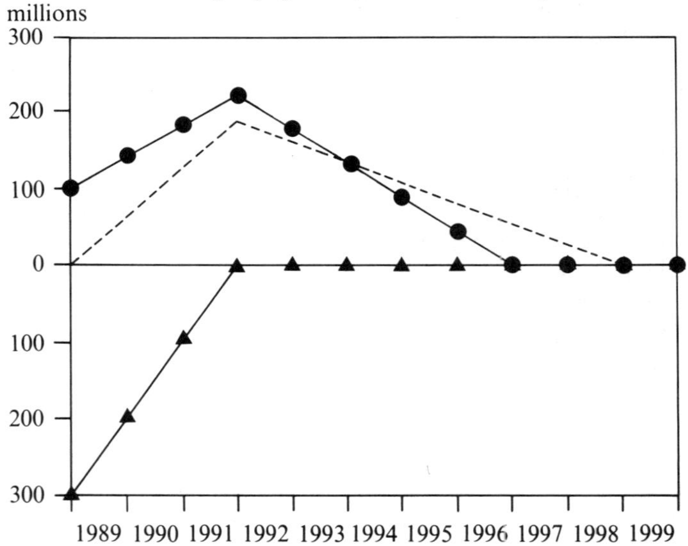

Method 1 spread from 1989	Method 2 restated, spread from 1987	Method 3 balance sheet adjustment
- - - - -	—●—	—▲—

Ignoring interest, the prior year comparative pension cost is therefore to be adjusted to £8 million, and the reserves at 31 December 1988 are reduced by that amount to £388 million by debiting reserves and crediting pension provision.

Note that such a prior year adjustment will result in a different future pension cost from that which would have resulted if no adjustment were made.

In practice, a number of companies have not adjusted comparatives, either because their schemes are neither markedly over- nor under-funded, in which case there is unlikely to be a material difference, or because overall the pension cost is not material in the accounts. Where companies have adopted Method 1, they have frequently not adjusted the prior year's figures, the transitional method being interpreted as not requiring such an adjustment. Where a company has adopted Method 3 and taken the transitional surplus on to the balance sheet, (few listed companies appear to have done so), in practice the prior year's pension cost figure often has not been adjusted and the company has tended to show the surplus as an adjustment to opening reserves.

Appendix I, paras I.10 and I.11, includes examples from quoted companies' accounts of these transitional treatments.

Historical summaries

7.13 SSAP 6, para 18 states:

> 'If an historical summary is published, amounts relating to past years will normally be restated to ensure that they are stated on a consistent basis. If, for reasons of practicality, prior years have not been restated in such a summary, to reflect a subsequent change in accounting policy, this should be stated. It should also be made clear which years, if any, have been restated.'

The transitional arrangements of SSAP 24 were designed to assist employers overcome the difficulties of restating prior years and many companies have taken advantage of these provisions by spreading forward pension scheme surpluses from the date the SSAP was first applied. The International Stock Exchange recommends that listed companies include historical summaries in their annual accounts, and although many listed companies do so, there is little evidence at present that restatement for the effects of SSAP 24 has been undertaken. For prospectuses, a five-year historical summary is required and any material difference between pension cost charged and the SSAP 24 cost should generally be adjusted.

Valuations on the implementation of SSAP 24

7.14 SSAP 24, para 53, does not require a special valuation on implementation, so long as the latest valuation was carried out on a basis broadly consistent with the requirements of the Statement. However, many employers have chosen to ask their actuaries to undertake a detailed review. In some circumstances this will have been necessary as a result of events since the last valuation, such as takeovers and redundancies. This is in effect no different from changes in the intervaluation period described in 6.5. However, a special valuation may be required because the actuarial method and funding assumptions of the latest valuation were chosen with a particular funding approach in mind and are not therefore the actuary's 'best estimate' required by SSAP 24, para 79.

Restrictions on the use of the transitional methods

7.15 SSAP 24, para 53, which deals with the transitional provisions, states the following in relation to the cumulative adjustment on transition.

> 'To the extent that the adjustment relates to a variation from regular cost (i.e. a surplus or deficit) that, in accordance with the provisions of paras 81 and 82, would not be eligible to be spread over the remaining service lives it should be accounted for as a prior year item. (An example of such an adjustment would be one arising from a significant reduction in the number of employees covered by a company's pension scheme arrangements.)'

This should be interpreted with some care however. If a company is in the middle of a contribution holiday which is the result of a significant reduction in the number of employees, it would be inappropriate to treat the surplus as a prior year item as this would mean that the pension cost in the year of implementation of the SSAP (and indeed in any subsequent year when reduced contributions were attributable to the reduction in the number of employees) would be regular cost. This is not in line with SSAP 24, para 81. Similarly, if a material deficit were being recognised over a period shorter than the expected remaining service lives at the time of the introduction of the Statement, it may be justifiable to continue this approach rather than estimating the deficit at the implementation date and debiting it to the profit and loss account reserve; the latter option may appear rather more attractive however, as the pension cost charged to the profit and loss account in the future would be lower.

Chapter 8

Timing differences and deferred tax

Introduction

8.1 For a defined benefit scheme the pension cost charged to the profit and loss account will be the aggregate of the regular pension cost and any variation therefrom, determined in accordance with the principles discussed in chapter 6. In many cases this cost will be different to the amount of contributions actually paid during the year by the employer. For example, if a fund has a surplus the employer may elect to take a contribution holiday. During the period of the holiday no contributions will be paid but a pension cost will still be charged to the profit and loss account. SSAP 24 requires that any excess of pension cost charged over contributions paid should be recognised in the balance sheet as a net pension provision and so, in this case, there will be an increasing provision building up in the balance sheet each year of the holiday [*SSAP 24, para 86*]. When the holiday has finished the amount of contributions subsequently paid would normally be higher than the net pension cost charged to profit and loss, reflecting the fact that the cost was spread over a longer period than the actual payments. This results in the net pension provision in the balance sheet being reduced each year until it is eliminated. A simple example will illustrate this.

Example

A scheme has assets of £10 million, a surplus of £2 million, regular pension cost of 10% of pensionable earnings and pensionable earnings of £10 million per annum. Average remaining service life of the membership is five years. Ignoring interest and salary inflation, if the employer takes the option of a contribution holiday lasting two years, the costs and contributions are calculated as follows:

Year	**Regular cost £m**	**Variations £m**	**Total cost £m**	**Employer contri-butions £m**	**(Over)/ Under Payment £m**	**Provision £m**
0						
1	1.0	(0.4)	0.6	–	0.6	0.6

example continued overleaf

Year	Regular cost £m	Variations £m	Total cost £m	Employer contri-butions £m	(Over)/ Under Payment £m	Provision £m
2	1.0	(0.4)	0.6	–	0.6	1.2
3	1.0	(0.4)	0.6	1.0	(0.4)	0.8
4	1.0	(0.4)	0.6	1.0	(0.4)	0.4
5	1.0	(0.4)	0.6	1.0	(0.4)	–

8.2 In some cases there may be an excess of contributions paid over cumulative pension cost charged, for example when a deficit in the fund is made up by increased contributions by the employer over a shorter period than the expected or average remaining service lives of employees in the scheme. SSAP 24, para 86 requires that these excesses should be recognised in the balance sheet as a net pension prepayment. This balance will be eliminated in the future periods when contributions paid become lower than pension costs charged.

8.3 The build up and elimination of net pension provisions or prepayments, as described above, assumes that there are no further events giving rise to variations in regular cost over the expected or average remaining service lives of the employees from the date of the original variation. In practice it is likely that there will be more variations, determined each time the fund is valued. The contributions required will be recalculated, resulting in adjustments to the provision or prepayment balances causing them to be extended, eliminated sooner than expected or reversed.

This treatment will have deferred tax implications because the employer receives tax relief in respect of contributions and pensions paid, not the amount charged in the profit and loss account. The pension prepayment or provision in the balance sheet will generally represent the cumulative timing difference between funding and cost. This is discussed in further detail in 8.4 below.

What is deferred tax?

8.4 Deferred tax is defined as the tax attributable to timing differences. Timing differences are differences between profits or losses as computed for tax purposes and as stated in financial statements, which arise from the inclusion of items of income and expenditure in tax computations in periods different from those in which they are included in financial statements. Timing differences originate in one period and are capable of reversal in one or more subsequent periods. SSAP 15 (Revised),

'Accounting for deferred tax', paras 26 and 27 state that tax deferred or accelerated by the effect of timing differences should be accounted for to the extent that it is probable that an asset or liability will crystallise and should not be accounted for to the extent that it is probable that an asset or liability will not crystallise. An asset or liability crystallises when the reversal of a timing difference is not replaced by a new timing difference of at least the same tax effect with the result that there is a decrease or increase in the amount of the taxation liability.

Method of calculation

8.5 SSAP 15 (Revised), para 24, specifies that deferred tax should be computed under the liability method, i.e. the tax is calculated using the corporation tax rate which is expected to apply when the timing differences reverse and a deferred tax asset or liability crystallises. The amount of the provision for deferred tax is usually calculated at the current tax rate unless there is a known change in the rate of corporation tax expected to apply.

Deferred tax and timing differences arising under SSAP 24

8.6 SSAP 24 can potentially give rise to a deferred tax asset or a deferred tax liability when funding diverges from cost.

Under *ICTA 1988, ss 592(4)* to *(6)*, contributions to Inland Revenue approved pension schemes are tax deductible. Such tax relief is usually granted on the basis of contributions paid. If there is a deficit in a scheme and an employer pays a lump sum to meet it, the tax relief may be spread over a period of up to five years. Up to the inception of SSAP 24, it has generally been the case that the pension charge for the financial period has been equal to the contributions payable. With the introduction of SSAP 24, the charge in the accounts could differ substantially from the funding arrangements. For example, if a scheme is overfunded, a variation from regular cost is calculated and reduces the net pension cost figure. The employer may have a number of funding options. Often the choice is either a contribution holiday for a short period followed by a resumption of the usual level of contributions or alternatively, contributions may be continued but at a lower level over a longer period. The latter choice may mean that funding continues to match cost and the tax effect is neutral, but Inland Revenue limits on overfunding may mean that the surplus has to be unwound over a period rather shorter than the expected remaining service lives of the employees, such that it is necessary to take a contribution holiday. During a pension contribution holiday, any pension cost charged in the profit and loss account is credited to a pension provision and is not tax deductible. The employing company has to add back the cost to profits assessable for tax. In subsequent accounting periods, the amount contributed to the scheme is likely to be above the accounting pension cost. The difference between the cost and funding is debited to the pension provision, but because the amount funded is above the cost in the profit and loss account, additional tax relief is available. To compensate for these timing differences, it may be appropriate to set up a deferred tax asset when creating the pension provision, which then unwinds as the associated reliefs become available when funding resumes. This scenario is reversed when a scheme is underfunded, that is, the variation from regular cost is an addition to it.

8.7 Further timing differences may arise in future as a result of the provisions of the *Finance Act 1989*. This introduced a ceiling on earnings for the purpose of tax reliefs available for contributions to prefunded occupational schemes (see 2.5 and Appendix C). If the excess cost is funded, the employer's payments to an unapproved scheme may generally be allowed for tax in the periods in which they are paid but will be assessed as the income of the employees concerned and in addition, an unapproved scheme does not benefit from tax exemption in respect of its income and capital gains. Advance funding is therefore improbable. A much more likely scenario is that the excess amount is unfunded, in which case the excess cost of pensions relating to new employees earning over the limit is not tax deductible until the pension is actually paid. Whilst in these circumstances the accounts will reflect the pension cost relating to such employees, because such costs are not deductible for taxation purposes, a timing difference will arise. It may be a very long time before the associated pension is paid and the associated tax relief obtained. Bearing in mind that payment of the pension may itself may extend over many accounting periods, the timing differences may turn out to be very long term.

Assessing the effect of timing differences

8.8 To assess the extent to which assets or liabilities arising from timing differences will crystallise, it is necessary to make reasonable assumptions as to future events, in particular as to the new timing differences which are likely to arise to replace the existing differences as they reverse. These assumptions should be based on all relevant information available including the intentions of management and ideally will be based on financial plans and projections covering a period of years. There is little formal guidance on instances where financial plans and projections are not available, but SSAP 15 (Revised) states that a prudent view should be taken.

Reconciling the provisions of SSAP 15 (Revised) with SSAP 24

8.9 Timing differences in relation to pension cost are likely to extend for several years i.e. the expected future service lives of employees for which the usual range is between 10 and 15 years.

Nevertheless, if a pensions contribution holiday is taken in respect of prefunded schemes, there is clearly a charge in the profit and loss account for which no tax relief is immediately available. As funding in later years is planned to be in excess of accounting cost it may be argued that it is appropriate to set up a deferred tax asset. The fundamental principle for setting up a deferred tax asset is whether the asset will crystallise. SSAP 15 (Revised) states that deferred tax debit balances should not be carried forward as assets, except to the extent that they are expected to be recoverable without replacement by equivalent debit balances ('partial provision'). For prefunded schemes maintained within Inland Revenue limits, cost and funding are likely to coincide over the long-term, so that a deferred tax asset is permissible within the terms of the standard.

Example

Using the same data as in the example in 8.1 and applying a tax rate of 35%, the associated deferred tax balances are as follows:

Year	Pension cost £m	Employer contri- butions £m	(Over)/ under payment £m	Provision £m	Deferred tax asset £m
1	0.6	–	0.6	0.6	0.21
2	0.6	–	0.6	1.2	0.42
3	0.6	1.0	(0.4)	0.8	0.28
4	0.6	1.0	(0.4)	0.4	0.14
5	0.6	1.0	(0.4)	0	0

8.10 However, for unfunded schemes, this particular principle may cause considerable problems. At present, unfunded liabilities are more likely to arise in respect of overseas schemes but will undoubtedly become more common in the UK as a result of the *Finance Act 1989*. Under the requirements of SSAP 24, companies must recognise a pension liability or asset even if on settlement of an asset or liability it is replaced by another, that is, full provision is required. The provisions of SSAP 15 (Revised) require only partial provision, such that in the case of an unfunded liability the company should not set up the appropriate deferred tax asset.

Although the asset will be recoverable, it will, if the scheme continues, be replaced by equivalent debit balances. This conflicts with the principle of matching although it undoubtedly complies with the principle of prudence. The arguments against setting up a deferred tax asset are reinforced by the very long-term nature of the commitment. Timing differences could literally last for decades, and it is clearly very difficult to predict the course of future events over such a time span.

8.11 There has been considerable debate in the UK accounting profession as to how to deal with this dilemma of partial provision under SSAP 15 (Revised) and full provision under SSAP 24, but at present there is no firm ruling on the matter. In June 1990, the Technical Committee of the Institute of Chartered Accountants in England and Wales issued a Technical Release, TR 794, which reviews the issue. It states that two main problems are appearing in practice.

(a) The fact that the two statements use different criteria for the recognition of profit and loss account charges and related assets and liabilities, giving rise to the full and partial provision problem outlined above.

(b) The extent to which it is reasonable to make assumptions about events during the long time within which pension timing differences may reverse, particularly in relation to unfunded schemes.

The paper considers that the most appropriate presentation is for the company to show the pension charge/liability in the accounts 'gross' rather than 'net' of attributable tax relief. It discusses the recognition criteria for tax relief on future payments and expresses the view that in calculating the pension cost of a funded or unfunded scheme, assumptions about the tax relief receivable on future payment should be dealt with in a similar way to the actuarial assumptions made relating to the long-term future. It emphasises the importance of whether or not tax will be recoverable and points out that the further apart the accounts charge and the first opportunity for obtaining tax relief are, the more difficult it is to estimate whether or not the employer will have taxable profits and thus receive the relief. The paper further suggests that the estimated tax relief receivable should be reviewed in relation to the level of profit that prudently appears to be sustainable in future. It points out that SSAP 15 (Revised) and SSAP 24 are not based on the same principles, and takes the view that companies should apply SSAP 24 principles when accounting for the effects of pension cost. SSAP 24 cannot be isolated from SSAP 15 (Revised) however, because deferred tax arising from sources other than pensions may enhance the prospective recoverability of tax in respect of pension payments.

Whichever approach is taken, it is clearly important to identify it in the notes to the accounts if the amount involved is material. It is suggested that the issue be explained and the amounts involved be disclosed. It is interesting to note that European practices in this area often differ from that of the UK, but that at least one UK multinational in its 1989 accounts complied with SSAP 15 (Revised) and did not set up a deferred tax asset in relation to its unfunded overseas schemes.

Pension costs relating to pensions in excess of the Inland Revenue limits may be funded or unfunded. In both cases the principles of the preceding paragraphs apply.

Discounting of the deferred tax balance

8.12 In calculating pension cost and any related assets or liabilities, future payments are effectively discounted. It is logical therefore to discount any related deferred tax balances in the same way. The Technical Committee's paper referred to above suggests two alternatives.

(a) Applying the appropriate tax rate to the amount of the discounted pension asset or liability not already allowed for or charged to tax.

(b) Explicitly estimating the timing and amounts of the gross (undiscounted) tax consequences of the pension arrangements and discounting these to net present value.

It is likely that (a) will be used in practice, being more straightforward to apply.

Chapter 9

Defined benefit scheme – Items to be disclosed

Introduction

9.1 As well as laying down the approach to the calculation of pension cost, SSAP 24 requires disclosure of an extensive range of information about the nature and finances of the company's pension arrangements in a defined benefit scheme. The information to be disclosed goes well beyond the method and assumptions used in calculating pension cost.

The disclosure requirements of SSAP 24 are comprehensive and are set out in paras 88 and 92. They consist, *inter alia*, of:

(a) the nature of the scheme (i.e. defined benefit);

(b) whether it is funded or unfunded;

(c) the accounting policy and, if different, the funding policy;

(d) whether the pension cost and provision (or asset) are assessed by a professionally qualified actuary and, if so, the date of the most recent valuation or review, and whether the actuary is an employee or officer of the company or group;

(e) the pension cost for the period together with explanations of differences from that of the previous year;

(f) any provisions or prepayments shown in the balance sheet;

(g) the amount of any deficiency and the way in which it is to be resolved;

(h) an outline of the valuation or review results (for details see SSAP 24 para 88(h)(i)-(iv));

(j) any commitments to make additional payments over a limited number of years;

(k) the accounting treatment adopted in respect of refunds;

(l) details of the expected effects on future costs of any material change in the pension arrangments of the company or group;

(m) in the first year of implementing SSAP 24, the way in which the transitional provisions have been applied.

Many of these requirements are similar to those contained in ED 32 'The disclosure of pension information in company accounts' but SSAP 24 contains more requirements with respect to actuarial information. However, the requirement to disclose self-investment by the pension fund in the company has been dropped, although particulars of self-investment in excess of 5% of the value of the net assets of the scheme are required in pension scheme accounts under the 1986 Disclosure Regulations.

In addition to the specific disclosures, sufficient further information should be disclosed where necessary to give a proper understanding of the impact of the pension arrangements on the accounts [*SSAP 24, para 45*]. Figures relating to the latest valuation or review may need to be amplified by a discussion of subsequent events or changes. In particular, this may lead to comment on the market value of the assets, the level of funding and any accrued benefits deficit at the date of that valuation.

The disclosure requirements of the Statement have been drafted from the perspective of a company using the same actuarial assumptions and method for both pension cost and funding purposes (see 9.17). SSAP 24 has examples of the disclosures for a small company and a large group.

In this chapter, the items have been divided between those which relate directly to the company accounts and those which relate to the funding of the scheme, although SSAP 24 itself does not make such a distinction.

Accounting Information

9.2 SSAP 24, para 88, sets out the required disclosures for a defined benefit scheme. Where these are amplified elsewhere in the Statement, or in the explanatory note, a cross-reference is given below.Information regarding the accounts is dealt with in 9.3-9.7 below.

Accounting policy

The statement of the accounting policy should be a brief description such as:

> 'the pension cost charged to the profit and loss account is such as to spread the cost of pensions over employees' working lives with the company as a constant percentage of pensionable payroll'.

The statement could, perhaps, go on to comment that the cost charged might not always equal the contributions paid.

Accounting treatments

9.3 These can be divided into transitional provisions and refund of any surplus.

(a) A requirement for disclosure regarding transitional provisions is set out in SSAP 24, para 92. In the accounts for the financial period in which SSAP 24 is first implemented, the way the transitional provisions have been applied should be disclosed. Where parts of the cumulative adjustment have been treated differently, this should be disclosed.

(b) A requirement for disclosure regarding refunds of surplus to a company is set out in SSAP 24, para 29. The treatment of a refund of surplus must be disclosed in financial statements in which a credit appears, i.e. in the year of the refund if the surplus is recognised immediately or throughout the spreading period otherwise.

Pension cost charge

9.4 The pension cost charge for the period together with explanations of significant changes in the charge compared with that of the previous accounting period must be disclosed [*SSAP 24, para 88(e)*].

(a) The amount of pension cost for the accounting period must be disclosed.

(b) Explanations should be given of significant changes in the charge compared with that shown for the previous accounting period.

Discussions between the company and its auditor may be needed to establish what changes are 'significant'. Only the sources of change need be disclosed: the Statement does not require the amount relating to each cause to be identified but companies may wish to be more explicit in some circumstances.

Circumstances that might lead to a significant change in pension cost include the following:

(i) closure, sale or purchase of a subsidiary company or business;

(ii) reduction in membership;

(iii) actuarial calculations for accounting purposes disclosing an experience surplus or deficit;

(iv) refund of surplus;

(v) grant of a discretionary pension increase;

(vi) change in actuarial method (specific disclosure required, see (f) below) or assumptions used for assessing pension cost; and

(vii) benefit improvements.

(c) Future changes must be disclosed [*SSAP 24, para 47*]. An indication should also be given of any significant changes in future pension cost expected under the particular actuarial approach used.

Often, an event listed under (b) above giving rise to a significant change in costs would lead to a corresponding future change.

(d) Actuarial method and assumptions must be disclosed [*SSAP 24, paras 7,48]*.

The actuarial method and significant assumptions used in calculating pension cost must be disclosed and, in particular, the assumption made about new entrants should be made clear. This may be obvious from disclosure of the valuation method used.

The principal actuarial assumptions are usually taken to be as follows:

(i) rate of return on investments;

(ii) rate of increase in salaries;

(iii) rate of increase in pensions; and

(iv) new entrants.

(e) The asset valuation method and assumptions should also be disclosed, together with the market value of the scheme assets at the date of valuation [*SSAP 24, para 49*].

(f) If the actuarial method used for assessing pension cost is changed, the fact of a change should be disclosed and the effect quantified [*SSAP 24, para 18*].

Provisions and prepayments

9.5 Any provisions or prepayments at the balance sheet date should be disclosed [*SSAP 24 para 88(f)*]. The Statement does not require any explanation of the provision or prepayment, but a brief explanation of the main reasons assists in the understanding of the figures.

9.6 *Defined benefit scheme – Items to be disclosed*

Actuarial advice

9.6 SSAP 24 requires the following disclosures on actuarial advice.

(a) It should be stated whether the pension cost and any prepayment or provision are assessed in accordance with the advice of an actuary and, if so, the date of the most recent formal actuarial valuation or later formal review used to calculate them should also be stated [*SSAP 24 para 88(a)*].

The SSAP does not give any further clarification of how formal a 'formal review' must be. The criterion appears to be whether or not the review is used to calculate the pension cost.

(b) If the actuary is an employee or officer of the company or its controlling group, this must be disclosed [*SSAP 24, para 88 (d)*].

Changes to pension arrangements

9.7 Details of the expected effects on future pension costs of any material changes in the pension arrangements should be given [*SSAP 24, para 50,*] (see 9.4(c) above).

Funding information

9.8 Information on funding and contributions must be disclosed as follows.

Funding policy

(a) Whether or not the scheme is funded must be stated [*SSAP 24, para 88(b)*].

(b) If the funding policy differs from the accounting policy the funding policy should be disclosed [*SSAP 24, para 88(c)*].

Differences between the funding and accounting policies might, for example, result from the funding policy being based on a discontinuance actuarial method, not funding for discretionary pension increases, or spreading variations over different periods or by different methods.

(c) Apparent differences between the funding and accounting policies may, in practice, be differences in actuarial assumptions and method. The distinction between differences of policy and different actuarial assumptions will not always be clear cut. This matter should be considered in the light of the requirements for spreading variations. Hence the actuarial method used is required to be disclosed [*SSAP 24, para 88(h)*], (see 9.9 below).

Actuarial valuation

9.9 An outline of the results of the most recent formal actuarial valuation or later formal review of the scheme on an ongoing basis for funding purposes should be given [*SSAP 24, para 88(h)*]. This outline must include the following matters:

(a) The actuarial valuation method and significant assumptions used must be disclosed. The principal actuarial assumptions to be disclosed would normally consist of:

  (i) rate of return on investments;

  (ii) rate of increase in salaries;

  (iii) rate of increase in pensions; and

  (iv) future rates of inflation.

  The SSAP does not indicate whether absolute or relative percentages should be disclosed and both are therefore acceptable, though absolute numbers are to be preferred.

(b) Market value of assets. The market value of the scheme assets at the valuation or review date should be stated [*SSAP 24, para 49*]. The asset valuation method and assumptions should also be disclosed.

(c) The level of funding of the scheme on an ongoing basis should be quoted in percentage terms [*SSAP 24, para 49*]. The usual interpretation is that this should be expressed as follows:

$$\frac{\text{actuarial value of assets}}{\text{value of past service liabilities}}$$

  expressed as a percentage. SSAP 24 seems to permit the use of current or projected final earnings in the computation of level of funding (paragraphs 56 and 66). However, para 67 defines an ongoing actuarial valuation as 'a valuation in which it is assumed that the pension scheme will continue in existence and (where appropriate) that new members will be admitted. The liabilities allow for expected increases in earnings'. In view of this, some commentators have suggested that the intention of the Statement is that projected final earnings be used. To avoid ambiguity, the relevant note should state that the percentage given relates to the actuarial value of assets and not their market value, and indicate whether allowance has been made for pay increases in the calculation.

(d) Appropriate comments should be made if there is any material surplus or deficit i.e. the ratio differs materially from 100%. These comments might relate to any current or intended contribution adjustment intended to reduce the surplus or deficit, or perhaps that the funding policy adopted aims at a target different from 100%. Whether the surplus or deficit is material should be discussed with the company by its auditor.

The figures disclosed under (b), (c) and (d) may need to be amplified by a discussion of changes which have occurred since the appropriate review date, for example, due to:

(i) benefit changes;

(ii) pension increases;

(iii) sale, closure or purchase of a subsidiary;

(iv) movement in the market value of assets;

(v) additional or reduced contributions over the subsequent period; and

(vi) subsequent informal actuarial review.

Accrued benefits deficit

9.10 Accrued benefits deficit (otherwise termed a deficiency on a current funding level basis) is defined in SSAP 24, paras 56 and 59, which provide definitions for:

(a) accrued benefit and;

(b) current funding level valuation.

If there is a deficit in the scheme in relation to current accrued benefits, the cash amount of this deficit should be disclosed.

In assessing the deficit, if any, the market value of the assets will usually be compared with the value of pensions and deferred pensions and, for active members, the value of accrued benefits based on pensionable service to, and pensionable earnings at, the date of the valuation and whether or not the member has less than two years' service, including revaluation on the statutory basis or such higher basis as has been promised.

If there is a deficit the action, if any, being taken to deal with it, both now and in future, should be disclosed [*SSAP 24, para 88(g)*].

Additional payments

9.11 Any commitment by the employer to make additional payments over a limited number of years should be disclosed [*SSAP 24, para 88(i)*].

Where a company or group has more than one scheme

9.12 Where a company or group has more than one pension scheme, information should be combined, unless disclosure of information about individual schemes is necessary for a proper understanding of the accounts.

In general, separate disclosure need not involve setting out all the disclosure items for each scheme. Combined disclosure of most items together with separate comments for the few items where clarification is needed should suffice. Where the amount of any deficiency on a current funding level basis occurs in the case of a defined benefit scheme, it should not be set off against a surplus in another [*SSAP 24, paras 51, 89*] (see 11.3).

Although not specifically dealt with in SSAP 24, it would not be appropriate to combine information for a significant defined contribution scheme with that for a significant defined benefit scheme because the very different natures of the two arrangements might then prevent a proper understanding of the accounts.

Separate reference might also be necessary in relation to any unfunded arrangements. If liabilities for such schemes are responsible for a significant part of any pension provision in the balance sheet, then the directors may wish to disclose the amount separately.

In some circumstances, materiality considerations alone will mean that separate reference to each individual scheme would not be needed. For example, many companies have one or more large schemes for their general workforce together with a small senior executive scheme. There may be no need for explicit disclosure of the executive scheme in the accounts if it is not material.

Group Schemes

9.13 The requirement for disclosure for pension schemes relating to group companies are contained in SSAP 24, paras 52 and 90.

9.13 *Defined benefit scheme – Items to be disclosed*

Where:

(a) a subsidiary company is a member of a group scheme, and

(b) contributions are based on a group rate, and

(c) the holding company is registered in the UK or the Republic of Ireland

then the following reduced disclosures should apply.

(i) The accounts should disclose that the company is a member of a group scheme and the nature of the scheme and state that contributions are based on costs across the group as a whole.

(ii) There is no need to give details of any accrued benefits deficit or an outline of the latest actuarial valuation or review. Instead the name of the holding company should be stated and the holding company accounts should disclose the full information for the group scheme as a whole.

The pension cost need not be calculated as a 'best estimate' of the cost for the particular subsidiary company. Pension cost may be calculated as a common percentage of payroll for the whole of the scheme.

(See 11.2 for further details).

An example of disclosure under SSAP 24 for a defined benefit scheme is given below.

Example

(i) *Accounting policy*

The pension cost charged to the profit and loss account is such as to spread the cost of pensions as a percentage of payroll over the working lives with the company of employees who are members of the scheme.

(ii) *Note to accounts*

The company provides a final salary i.e. defined benefit, pension scheme for its employees. The assets of the scheme are held separately from those of the company. This fund is under the control of trustees, who have invested it in a wide range of stock exchange securities.

The company pays contributions to the fund in order to provide security for existing pensions and the accrued benefits of members. Increases to pensions in payment are not anticipated in the contributions made. When increases are granted, the company makes additional payments, if these are necessary, to meet the capital cost of the increases.

The pension cost charge for the period was £1,000,000 (1997 £1,100,000). This allows for a reduction of £250,000 (1997 £nil) in respect of the amortisation of surplus which is being recognised over 10 years, the average remaining service life of members at the time when the surplus arose.

The pension cost charge is determined by qualified actuaries who are partners of Bacon & Woodrow, consulting actuaries. The charge for 1998 is based on the most recent valuation, which took place as at 30th November 1997. The projected unit method was used. The most significant actuarial assumptions were:

> Rate of return on investments 9% p.a.
>
> Rate of increase in pay levels, including promotional increases, 7%p.a.
>
> Rate of pension increases 4% p.a.

Members retiring are assumed to be replaced by new entrants so that the average age of the membership remains constant.

The valuation as at 30th November 1997 also assessed the funding of the scheme and the contributions to be made by the company to the scheme. The same actuarial method was used as for assessing pension cost. The actuarial assumptions differed from those used for assessing pension cost in that no allowance was made for future pension increases.

A provision of £5,000,000 (1997 £4,800,000) is included in the balance sheet in respect of future pension increases for members of the scheme and existing pensioners.

The valuation showed that the actuarial value of the assets at 30th November 1997 represented 120% of the actuarial value of the accrued benefits. The accrued benefits include all benefits for pensioners and other former members as well as benefits based on service completed to date for active members, allowing for future pay rises. The excess of assets over liabilities has arisen because recent investment performance has been better than assumed. The company's contributions were reduced to 7% of earnings in order to eliminate the surplus. The contributions amounted to £700,000 (1997 £850,000) in the period.

The market value of the scheme's assets was £25,000,000 at 30th November 1997.

Legal requirements as to disclosure

9.14 The *Companies Act 1985* requires certain information regarding pensions to be disclosed in the annual accounts.

(a) A company must give details of any pension commitment included under any provision in the balance sheet and for any commitment for which no provision has been made *(CA 1985 4 Sch 50(4))*.

(b) Particulars of pension commitments to past directors of the company must be disclosed separately *(CA 1985 4 Sch 50(4)*.

(c) Pension cost incurred on behalf of all employees, together with separate disclosure of social security costs, must be given *(CA 1985 4 Sch 56(4)*. (See 9.15 and 11.4).

(d) The disclosure requirements set out in (a) above must include separately details of commitments undertaken on behalf of any parent company or fellow subsidiary undertaking of the company *(CA 1985 4 Sch 59A* inserted by the *CA 1989 1 Sch II (3))*.

(e) These requirements (a)-(d) above also apply to group accounts *(CA 1985, 4A Sch1 (l), 2(1)* inserted by the *CA 1989, s6(4), 4 Sch 37)*.

(f) Directors' remuneration, which must be disclosed, includes contributions paid in respect of each director under any pension scheme (*CA 1985 6 Sch1 (4)(c)* inserted by *CA 1989 s6(4), 4 Sch (3)*) Note that this does not include any payment in respect of two or more persons if the amount paid in respect of each of them is not ascertainable (*CA 1985 6 Sch 13(3)(c)* inserted by *CA 1989 s6(4))*.

(g) The total amount of pensions paid to directors or past directors, other than pensions funded substantially through a pension scheme must be given. The amount shown must distinguish between pensions paid in respect of his services as director and other pensions. References to pensions include benefits otherwise than in cash and in such cases estimated money values of the benefit must be given and its nature (*CA 1985 6 Sch 7* inserted by *CA 1989 4 Sch 3*).

Banking and insurance companies are exempt from these CA requirements [*SSAP 24, para 99* and *CA 1985 9 Sch*].

CA 1985 does not interpret or define what constitutes 'pension commitment' and consequently companies have given little detail where schemes have been adequately funded. The introduction of SSAP 24 with its detailed disclosure requirements broadens the narrow view taken up to now, and it is expected that compliance with SSAP 24 will ensure compliance with *CA 1985* in most respects.

Statutory disclosure in practice

9.15 As indicated in 9.14 (c) above, CA 1985 requires specific disclosure of pension costs incurred 'save in so far as those amounts ... are stated in the profit and loss account' (*CA 1985 4 Sch. 56(4)(c)*). Para 94(2) of the same schedule states that 'pension costs' includes any other contributions by the company for the purposes of any pension scheme established for persons employed by the company, any sums set aside for that purpose and any amounts paid by the company in respect of pensions without first being so set aside'.

The SSAP 24 pension cost note should provide the appropriate disclosure for this statutory requirement. This would include any costs relating to directors as they too are employed by the company. To exclude them would be contrary to the legislation and in any event would probably require actuarial calculation if the directors were not covered by a separate pension scheme.

Statutory disclosure – directors' pension contributions

9.16 As indicated in 9.14(f) above, *CA 1985* requires the inclusion, as part of the directors emoluments, of any contributions paid in respect of a director under any pension scheme . Pension scheme is defined in *CA 1985, 4 Sch. 33(3)(b)* of the same schedule as meaning 'a scheme for the provision of pensions in respect of services as director or otherwise which is maintained in whole or in part by contributions'. Contribution is defined in *CA 1985, 4 Sch. 33(3)(c)* as meaning 'any payment (including an insurance premium) paid for the purposes of the scheme by or in respect of persons rendering services in respect of which pensions will or may become payable under the scheme'. Effectively, any contributions paid or payable in respect of directors must be disclosed as part of their emoluments. However, this may not be the same as pension cost, so that the amount included as part of emoluments may not be the same as that included in the disclosure of pension cost. It should be noted that amounts paid into a directors' pension scheme are excluded from disclosure as directors' emoluments if the amounts are not separately identifiable. If, for example, a directors' scheme is underfunded and the actuary advises that lump sums be paid to restore reasonable funding levels, the payment in respect of each individual may not be ascertainable, in which case it will not fall within the definition of payment.

Payment of *ex gratia* pensions for directors is disclosable under directors'emoluments and such payments will be disclosed annually as the payments are made. Under SSAP 24 however, the capital cost of such a pension is charged to the profit and loss account in the year of award. If this is material, then it should be explained in the notes to the accounts, as indicated in SSAP 24, para 88(e). The earnings cap for highly paid employees may also affect directors. Where there is an unfunded arrangement, there is no statutory disclosure required under the heading of directors' emoluments as no payments are made, but a substantial liability could be building up in the company's balance sheet. If this is the case, SSAP 24, para 88(f) implies that disclosure should be made.

Which actuarial assumptions?

9.17 SSAP 24, para 88(h), requires an outline of the latest formal actuarial valuation or later formal review of the scheme on an ongoing basis, to include the actuarial method used and the main actuarial assumptions. If the valuation method and/or assumptions for SSAP 24 purposes are different from those for funding, the problem arises as to what disclosures should be made. For example, it might be misleading to disclose the actuarial assumptions for funding purposes where they differ from the SSAP 24 assumptions in the context of a note relating to pension cost. It is suggested therefore that the actuarial assumptions for both funding and SSAP 24 cost be given, or the assumptions used in the computation for pension cost be provided alone but clearly described as such.

Failure to disclose actuarial assumptions

9.18 A number of companies are reluctant to disclose the actuarial assumptions, particularly those relating to projected pay increases, on the grounds that the information is sensitive. However, the assumptions for funding purposes are already available to employees and unions under *The Occupational Pension Scheme (Disclosure of Information) Regulations SI 1986 No 1046.*

SSAP 24 states that 'sufficient information should be disclosed to give the user of the financial statements a proper understanding of the impact of pension arrangements on the group's and/or company's financial statements'. SSAP 24, para 47, emphasises this in the case of defined benefit schemes by stating that more extensive disclosures are needed because of the greater and more uncertain obligations of the employer. It adds that the disclosures should not only relate to the amounts in the financial statements for the periods presented but should also give an indication of the significant changes in future costs that are expected under the actuarial assumptions and method used.

With this in mind, SSAP 24, para 88 states that disclosures should include a brief description of the main actuarial assumptions. If a company refuses to comply with these disclosures, and the omission is in the opinion of the auditor concerned material in arriving at a true and fair view taking into account the requirements of SSAP 24, then the auditor may need to qualify his report, for example in the following terms.

> 'The main assumptions underlying the actuarial valuation/review of the company's employees' pension scheme as at (insert date) have not been disclosed as required by Statement of Standard Accounting Practice 24 'Accounting for Pension Costs'. They are that investment returns will be 9% per annum, that wages and salaries will increase by an average of 7% per annum and that present and future pensions will increase at a rate of 4% per annum.
>
> Except for the absence of this information, in our opinion........'

Balance sheet classification of pension liabilities and assets

9.19 Where funding diverges from cost and the cumulative pension cost recognised in the profit and loss account has not been completely discharged by payment of contributions or directly paid pensions, SSAP 24, para 86, states that the excess should be shown as a net pension provision. The *CA 1985* balance sheet formats have, under the heading 'provisions for liabilities and charges', (I in format 1 and B in format 2) the appropriate sub-heading entitled 'Pensions and similar obligations'. Sub-heading 2 in the same category, 'Taxation, including deferred taxation', provides a suitable slot for any deferred tax liability (*CA 1985 4 Sch para 8*). There are no such convenient sub-headings under debtors, and SSAP 24, para 86, simply states the following.

> 'Similarly, any excess of contributions paid or directly paid pensions over the cumulative pension cost should be shown as a prepayment.'

This has led to some problems of definition, as in many cases the prepayment could unwind over a very long period of time, and to show a pension prepayment under debtors would include the prepayment as part of current assets, which are generally regarded as being turned into cash within a relatively short period. However, a pension scheme prepayment is clearly not a fixed asset nor is it an investment. In practice, companies have adopted a variety of disclosure, sometimes within the pension cost note, sometimes under the heading of prepayments. This prepayment has been generally analysed under prepayments or as a debtor due after more than one year.

Examples of disclosure

9.20 Appendix I includes numerous examples of the way in which listed companies have dealt with the disclosure requirements of SSAP 24. The topics dealt with are listed in the contents page of this book and include groups, overseas schemes, actuarial methods and assumptions, accounting policies, transitional provisions, amortisation of variations, measures to deal with surpluses and deficits, pension surpluses on takeover, comparatives, post-retirement benefits other than pensions and even non-compliance with SSAP 24.

Chapter 10

Defined contribution scheme – Pension cost and disclosure

Pension cost charge

10.1 Scheme definition and attributes are discussed in chapter 4. The accounting cost is explained in SSAP 24, para 17, which states that:

> 'in the case of a defined contribution scheme, the employer's obligation at any point in time is restricted to the amount of the contributions payable to date. The pension cost is, therefore, the amount of the contributions payable in respect of the particular accounting period.'

Balance sheet items

10.2 In the context of a defined contribution scheme the only provision or prepayment likely to occur will represent contributions owing or prepaid at the year end. Contributions for a short period only are likely to be involved. It would generally not be appropriate to add interest to balance sheet items resulting from such short term timing differences.

Transitional treatment on the implementation of SSAP 24

10.3 It is unlikely that any change in accounting policy will be required on implementing SSAP 24.

Disclosure

10.4 The following disclosures should be made in the case of a defined contribution scheme.

(a) The nature of the scheme i.e. that it is a defined contribution scheme.

(b) The accounting policy, which should be a short (preferably one sentence) statement of the policy which has been adopted under SSAP 24 for pension costs. It should remain substantially unaltered from year to year and be independent of the particular financial situation of the employer and scheme at the time.

An appropriate statement would be as follows.

'The company operates a defined contribution pension scheme. The pension cost charge represents the contributions payable by the company under the rules of the scheme.'

(c) The pension cost charge for the period.

(d) Any outstanding or prepaid contributions at the balance sheet date. The contributions paid may not equal those payable during the year, and this would be reflected by including the difference between pension cost and contributions in debtors or creditors as the case may be [*SSAP 24, para 87*].

Disclosures relating to a number of schemes

10.5 Where a company or group has more than one pension scheme, disclosure may be made on a combined basis, unless disclosure of information about individual schemes is necessary for a proper understanding of the accounts [*SSAP 24, para 89*]. It would not be appropriate to combine information for a significant defined contribution scheme with that for a significant defined benefit scheme because the very different natures of the two arrangements would then compromise a proper understanding of the accounts. Disclosures could be combined and presented as disclosure relating to the defined contribution scheme in cases where the defined benefit scheme was not material in relation to the accounts as a whole. This might arise, for example, if an employer operates a money purchase scheme for most of his workforce, and a final salary scheme for a small group of senior executives. Another example is where an employer pays *ex-gratia* pensions to a closed group of former employees directly from revenue but operates a formal money purchase scheme for all his current employees.

If other material schemes have been combined with the main defined contribution scheme for disclosure purposes, specific comments may need to be made about individual schemes to give a clear understanding of the accounts.

Examples

10.6 Example (i) below gives an example of minimal disclosure for a defined contribution scheme. Example (ii) shows how additional information could be included.

(i) The company operates a defined contribution (money purchase) pension scheme. The assets of the scheme are held separately from those of the company. This fund is under the control of trustees, who have invested it with a U.K. insurance company.

The pension cost charge represents contributions to the fund payable by the company under the rules of the scheme. The total charge for the year amounted to £500,000 (1989 £450,000).

Contributions totalling £25,000 (1989 £15,000) were due to the fund at the year end and are included in creditors.

(ii) The company operates a defined contribution (money purchase) pension scheme. In addition to the money purchase benefits, the scheme pays salary related benefits on a member's death before retirement. The assets of the scheme are held separately from those of the company in a fund under the control of trustees.

The trustees have invested the fund with a U.K. insurance company. They have taken out insurance cover for the benefits payable on death before retirement.

The pension cost charge represents contributions payable to the fund by the company at rates specified in the rules of the scheme in respect of retirement benefits, together with the insurance premiums for death benefits. The total charge for the year amounted to £500,000 (1989 £450,000).

Contributions totalling £25,000 (1989 £15,000) were due to the fund at the year end and are included in creditors.

Chapter 11

Multi-employer schemes, takeovers and centralised schemes

Introduction

11.1 In practice, while there are many individual companies with a single pension scheme, it is very common to find groups of companies contributing to a single scheme, or to find an individual company contributing to more than one scheme. This chapter aims to examine two common situations where there is more than one contributing employer, group schemes, where companies under common ownership contribute to a scheme covering the group's employees, and centralised schemes, which cover the employees of a number of different employers. Any group of employers, perhaps in the same locality or industry, may band together to set up a pension scheme and many multi-employer schemes exist in the UK, for example in merchant shipping, construction, the legal profession and the motor trade. The chapter also reviews the issue of pension costs on takeovers.

Group schemes

11.2 These schemes can be defined as one of two types, single group schemes and groups with more than one pension scheme.

Single group schemes

As SSAP 24, para 52 points out, it is quite common for companies within the same group to contribute to a single group scheme. In such circumstances, the actuary usually examines the actuarial liability of the group as a whole rather than those of the individual companies. A contribution rate is therefore calculated as a percentage of payroll which applies to all group companies within the scheme and contribution rates on an individual company basis are not provided. The SSAP permits the use of a common group rate for pension cost applicable to sponsoring employers on the grounds that it may not be possible to estimate the pension obligations for which a particular group company is responsible. It also allows for reduced disclosure in the financial statements of subsidiaries which are members of group schemes (see 9.12 and 9.13).

A subsidiary undertaking which is a member of a group scheme should disclose this fact in its financial statements and disclose the nature of the group scheme indicating, where appropriate, that the contributions are based on pension costs across the group as a whole. Such a company is exempt from the disclosure requirements of SSAP 24, para 88 (g), (h), which require particulars of the actuarial valuation, and should instead state the name of the holding company in whose financial statements particulars these are contained. This exemption only applies to UK or Republic of Ireland companies [*SSAP 24, para 90*].

Group with more than one pension scheme

11.3 For groups with a number of schemes the situation is not so straightforward. Pension costs for companies under the control of the main holding company may well vary according to the particular scheme to which a participating subsidiary contributes. In effect, there may be common group rates not for the group overall but for sub-groups, determined by participation in the individual schemes. In such circumstances, pension costs should be determined for each sub-group and company with its own scheme. The full requirements of SSAP 24 should be applied to those companies and sub-group holding companies. Subsidiaries of the latter would disclose the common sub-group rate and comply with at least the SSAP's minimum disclosure for subsidiaries using the sub-group holding company as their point of reference.The consolidated accounts of the entire group will reflect the overall group situation, with disclosures on a combined basis (see 9.12).

SSAP 24, para 89, points out that a proper understanding of the accounts may require disclosure of information about individual schemes. (See Appendix I, para I.15, for an example of this in practice). In addition, a current funding level deficiency in one scheme must not be set off against surpluses in other schemes. Such a deficiency is determined by undertaking a current funding level valuation, which is defined in SSAP 24, para 59 as being a valuation which:

> 'considers whether the assets would have been sufficient at the valuation date to cover liabilities arising in respect of pensions in payment, preserved benefits for members whose pensionable service has ceased and accrued benefits for members in pensionable service, based on pensionable service to and pensionable earnings at, the date of valuation including revaluation on the statutory basis or such higher basis as has been promised.'

In such circumstances it is possible that the accounts may need to show both a pension prepayment and provision.

Pension schemes for overseas subsidiaries

11.4 Companies or groups with overseas subsidiaries must ensure that the pension cost in respect of foreign operations is dealt with in accordance with SSAP 24. This may necessitate an adjustment on consolidation unless the nature of the commitment is such that an adjustment is inappropriate. The example given by the SSAP of such a circumstance is where the employer's obligation is discharged by prescribed payments under a nationwide or industry-wide scheme with characteristics similar to those of the state scheme in the UK, i.e. with pensions being funded on a pay-as-you-go basis. In such cases, charging the contributions payable will satisfy the requirements of the Statement. SSAP 24 does recognise that even when pension commitments are similar, the costs and difficulties of obtaining the necessary actuarial information may mean that an adjustment is impractical. In such instances, the minimum disclosure in the consolidated financial statements should comprise the basis and amount of the charge [*SSAP 24, paras 41, 42* and *43*]. Examples of disclosure relating to overseas schemes are given in Appendix I, para I.18. Outlines of pension arrangements in some other countries and the accounting consequences are provided in Chapter 13, 'Overseas arrangements'.

It is important to remember the provisions of the *CA 1985* in relation to social security costs. In some countries, contributions are made to state-run industry-wide schemes. *CA 1985 4 Sch 94(1)* defines social security costs as 'any contributions by the company to any state social security or pension scheme, fund or arrangement'. This would appear to require contributions to such state schemes to be disclosed as social security rather than pension costs. To avoid ambiguity, and to comply with SSAP 24, it is suggested that such costs be disclosed as required by the *CA 1985* but that the pension cost note should refer to the matter and disclose the amount included under social security which comprises pension cost in relation to such schemes.

Takeovers and acquisitions

11.5 SSAP 24 provides no guidance in the area of takeovers and currently there are no specific requirements in any Statements of Standard Accounting Practice relating to pension costs on acquisition, merger or disposal of a company. The relevant paragraphs in ED 39, the exposure draft relating to pension costs, were not incorporated in SSAP 24. However, the ASC addressed the issue of pension assets and liabilities when one company takes over another in its discussion paper, 'Fair value in the context of acquisition accounting'. This paper was developed into ED 53, which was published in July 1990.

In a defined contribution scheme, because the employer's obligation is restricted to the amount of contributions payable, the situation on takeover is straightforward. If the contributions payable have not been paid, a liability exists, and if payments exceed contributions an asset exists. Thus determining the fair value to the acquiring company should present no problems (ED 53, para 44).

If the acquired company has a defined benefit scheme, ED 53, para 45 states that:

> 'the acquirer should determine the fair value of the pension scheme from its own perspective, employing the assumptions and methods of its own actuary to perform the valuation, recognising the resulting surplus or deficit at the acquisition date and, thereafter, charging the regular cost at the acquisition date to the profit and loss account'.

This policy was put forward as the preferred option in the original discussion paper. It treats the surplus or deficit at acquisition as the fair value of the scheme to the acquirer and eliminates distortion of post-acquisition results, because the regular charge will not be affected. The ED states that no provision should be made to account for changes in benefits on the grounds that this is a post-acquisition decision. An exception to this is where provision for redundancies has been made relating to the closure of a business segment in which case the related adjustment should be made for the effect on the fair value of the pension scheme (ED 53, para 46).

11.6 This approach does in fact appear to be emerging as current best practice. However, there are alternative views which may be acceptable in certain circumstances. Where a holding company has a policy of providing standard benefits for all group employees and takes over another with less generous provision, the application of the group policy to the new subsidiary's employees is arguably an expense related to the takeover. Just as the costs of redundancies may be taken into account in assessing the fair value of the assets acquired, so should additional pension costs. This would mean that the cost of standardising benefits for the employees in the newly-acquired company should be provided at the time of acquisition and the surplus or deficit in the pension scheme should be assessed after due allowance for the intended benefit improvements. It should be noted that pension provision and the accounting practices in overseas countries can be very different from those in the UK, and particular care should be taken in the fair value exercise to investigate the costs, assets and liabilities of overseas schemes (see 13.1).

The lengthy timetable for comment and review coupled with the replacement of the ASC by the Accounting Standards Board (ASB) mean that it is likely to be quite some time before any definitive guidance is issued. In the meantime, the recommendations in ED 53 will be regarded as being persuasive until a new standard is issued. These are based on the view that a pension fund represents a positive or negative off-balance sheet resource of the employer and that post-acquisition results will be distorted unless recognition is given to the existence of a surplus or deficit at the time of acquisition.

11.7 Past practice, according to the original discussion paper, has generally been to ignore the pension scheme in the fair value exercise. The practical consequence of including pension scheme surpluses or deficits in the fair value exercise is that the consolidated accounts will include a pension prepayment or provision at the level of the surplus. This treatment is analogous to the recognition of surpluses and deficits at the date of implementation permitted by the transitional treatment of the SSAP (described as Method 3 in para 7.10).

ED 53, para 45, states that the asset or liability will be reduced by the difference between the regular charge and the funding payments. In practical terms, any prepayment is an asset which has been paid for and its amortisation will depend on the group's decisions and the actuary's professional judgment of its source and how it is being used. If, for example, the group decides to take a pension contribution holiday in the subsidiary on actuarial advice, the prepayment will be written down at group level as the holiday occurs, although in the accounts of the subsidiary there may be a pension cost and an associated pension provision. On consolidation, the provision will be netted against the prepayment. If the subsidiary acquired continues to fund the scheme at the rate the actuary determines as the pension cost, then the prepayment may take considerably longer to unwind, though in any event it should be amortised over a period not exceeding the expected or average remaining service lives of the employees in the acquired company. Note that if such a scheme is subsequently merged into a group scheme, it may be necessary to adopt the estimated remaining service lives of group employees on the grounds of practicality. Any resulting refund should be netted against the pension prepayment set up on acquisition.

The reverse treatment applies to any provision arising from the fair value exercise.

Depending on the accounting policy for goodwill, the reduction of goodwill by setting up a pension prepayment may result in a lower goodwill amortisation charge to the profit and loss account than would otherwise be the case in the alternative option of ignoring the pension surplus, in which case the surplus would be spread forward in the usual way in the accounts of the subsidiary only. Where the fair value exercise results in a provision, the effect on goodwill is to increase the amount and if goodwill is amortised through the profit and loss account, to increase the charge.

Pension cost in the accounts of the company being taken over will not be affected unless the accounting policy is changed to bring it into line with group practices.

Centrally imposed contribution rates by holding companies

11.8 It is not unusual for holding companies to impose a standard contribution rate on subsidiaries whose employees belong to a group scheme. The standard charge is unchanged by any variations from regular cost advised by the scheme's actuary. This is common in manufacturing industry where it is important for costing and management accounting purposes to avoid variances in unit costs caused by fluctuations from regular pension cost.

In such circumstances, as far as the individual companies are concerned, a corresponding standard rate for pension cost is likely to satisfy the requirement of SSAP 24. However, where the scheme is in surplus or deficit the actuary will advise that there is a variation from 'regular cost' which will need to be reflected in the group accounts. Where a pension scheme is in surplus and the actuary recommends a reduction in funding, the holding company may require the subsidiaries to continue to pay the standard rate. The difference between the pension cost as a percentage of payroll for the group as recommended by the actuary for SSAP 24 and the sum collected from subsidiaries as pension contribution would, if payments are routed via the holding company, constitute a profit in the holding company. Conversely, if the scheme is in deficit, and the holding company effectively pays more to the scheme than the pension cost being charged to the subsidiaries as regular cost, the difference would constitute a loss to the holding company.

In practice, such an approach could create considerable tax problems. Tax relief is given by statute to contributions to a pension fund. If a trading company makes a payment to its parent company it is not making a payment to a pension fund. Furthermore, if a scheme is overfunded, companies paying more than the rate recommended by the actuary may suffer tax consequences In these circumstances, great care should be taken and professional advice may be required to ensure that tax reliefs are not lost. In some groups, this results in payments over and above those recommended by the actuary being reversed. The variation advised by the actuary will be then be reflected in the subsidiary's accounts as well as in the group's, although the management accounts may continue to reflect a standard charge. Where this occurs and a standard costing system is in operation, the amount of pension cost overhead in stock at the year end needs to be reviewed along with other variances.

Groups with schemes which are not exclusive to particular group companies

11.9 Some groups, particularly those which have grown by merger and acquisition, operate several group schemes which, for a number of reasons, are not exclusive to particular group companies or sub-groups. The result is that employees in any particular company may not all be in the same group scheme. In certain cases, a subsidiary may pay contributions to three or four different schemes, perhaps reflecting restructuring whereby employees have moved to different companies within the group but retained membership of their original schemes. Whatever the origins of this type of situation, it can cause difficulties in determining pension cost for the individual company, particularly where the level of funding in the different group schemes varies.

In such circumstances, the employing company will need to examine the pension cost in relation to the numbers of employees belonging to particular group schemes and the funding of those schemes. In extreme cases it may be necessary in the accounts of subsidiaries to take a pragmatic view that contributions payable constitute cost since the individual company does not control costs but has to pay what is required by the various schemes. It is suggested, however, that if this approach is taken that the notes to the accounts should explain the matter clearly. In the consolidated accounts, it should be possible to calculate the overall pension cost satisfactorily.

Post-retirement costs other than pensions

11.10 Post-retirement costs other than pensions are at present rare in the UK. In the US however, where there is no national health service, it is very common for the health insurance cover for employees paid by employers to continue into retirement and the unfunded liability can be very high. The US Financial Accounting Standards Board issued an exposure draft on the subject in 1989 along the lines of its accounting standard for pension costs and it is intended that this should become an accounting standard. In the UK there are no plans for such a standard although the Accounting Standards Committee did pronounce that the principles of SSAP 24 may be equally applicable to other post-retirement benefits (see 3.15). A problem arises in the UK when a UK holding company is consolidating the results of its US subsidiaries which may well have large, unfunded liabilities for the health care cost of its retired employees. The ambivalence of the ASC announcement has led to a dichotomy in the treatment of such costs in UK accounts. Some listed companies have provided for the liability, whilst others have not (see Appendix I, para I.12). It is suggested that provision should be made, since such costs are just as much a liability to retired employees as are pension costs.

Pension cost in joint ventures

11.11 Where joint ventures are set up by companies, the new company may set up its own pension scheme or the employees may join the scheme of one of the participating companies. If this latter is the case, the scheme may charge a standard contribution rate for such members, rather than the contribution rate being paid by companies which are subsidiaries rather than associates. This is logical in that the joint owners of the venture company should not participate in the benefits of a surplus built up in the scheme to the detriment of the company or group whose scheme it is. In such circumstances, pension cost will be based on the contributions required. Full disclosure is required in the associate's accounts. SSAP 24 permits reduced disclosure for subsidiaries which are members of group schemes, but not for associates, even those 50% owned [*SSAP 24, para 90*].

Centralised and industry-wide schemes

11.12 SSAP 24 is directed towards the employing companies, with the implicit assumption that the actuarial valuation will cover the employees of the employing company or group of companies. It does not address the issues where the employer participates in a centralised scheme, i.e. a scheme operated on behalf of several unrelated employers, or in an industry-wide scheme, where a centralised scheme for non-associated employers in a particular industry exists.

Defined contribution schemes

11.13 Many centralised and most industry-wide schemes are operated on a money purchase basis. In these circumstances the pension cost charge represents contributions payable by the company to the fund in the same way as for any other defined contribution scheme.

Defined benefit schemes

11.14 Sometimes, centralised schemes are defined benefit schemes where contribution rates are calculated separately for each employer. In such circumstances, the employer's pension cost is easily identifiable because the contribution levels are actuarially assessed on the basis of the individual contributor's workforce. However, some centralised schemes operated on a final salary basis have a number of features which distinguish them from the usual single employer or group scheme. The individual employer is in a participating situation but does not control the funding rate nor directly influence the benefits. Most importantly, the actuarial liability will normally be determined as being that of the scheme as a whole and will not reflect the cost of providing pensions to the employees of the individual participating employers, which might be very different. The practical implications of this situation are that the actuarial liability will not be what it would have been if the employing company funded its own scheme. Thus the amounts paid to the scheme in respect of the employees of a participating employer do not necessarily coincide with that employer's true actuarial cost.

11.15 As a result of the absence of actuarial valuations relating to individual employers and the imposition of a centrally calculated contribution rate, in the case of some members of the scheme the charges being paid may be in excess of the actuarial cost while for others they will be less. However, for the participating employers' accounts, in practical terms the contributions payable to the scheme will normally represent, for the purposes of SSAP 24, the pension cost to the employing company. Only if the scheme as a whole is subject to variation will funding and cost differ.

The rationale for this essentially pragmatic approach is provided by the practices of such schemes. It is often the policy of the trustees to take a long-term view of contribution rates and not to refund surpluses or take holidays, or if there were to be a shortfall, to require that it be made good in the short term, as such decisions could benefit certain employers at the expense of others. For example, if there were a substantial surplus and a contribution holiday were to be given, employers new to the scheme would benefit from funding built up by long-standing members. Where it is the policy of the trustees not to refund surpluses to participating employers, then they are usually spread over a number of years by reducing the employers' and/or employees' contributions. The contribution rate is reviewed at each actuarial valuation and if the situation changes, a new contribution level is calculated. In practical terms, this is a new 'regular cost'. Periodic valuations allow the trustees to keep the situation under regular review and they regard such changes of rate of contribution as being permanent changes which would fall within the definition of 'regular pension cost'. This approach undoubtedly provides regular pension cost as a substantially level percentage of the current and expected future pensionable payroll in the light of current actuarial assumptions for the overall membership.

It is possible that individual employers might differ in their views as to the time periods over which to take into account any surpluses or deficits because they consider that the expected service lives of their employees differs from the period used by the scheme actuary. However, if the expected or average service lives were longer, then the share of the liabilities is also likely to differ from the average implicitly applied by the scheme actuary. The costs and complexity of not accepting the pragmatic approach outlined above are generally not justified. For practical purposes, the contributions payable, whilst not strictly meeting the 'best estimate' criteria of SSAP 24, will probably provide a satisfactory figure for pension cost.

Disclosure

11.16 It is important for all participating employers to obtain from the administrators and trustees of centralised schemes sufficient information to demonstrate that the contribution rate is the 'regular cost' for the purposes of their accounts and to ensure that the disclosure requirements of SSAP 24 are satisfied. As participating employers presumably receive details of the actuarial report, confirmations of contributions paid and all the other information required by SSAP 24, this will not usually impose any extra burden on the scheme's administrators. For some employers, the contributions paid to an industry-wide scheme will be immaterial in the context of the company's or group's accounts because only part of the workforce belongs to such a scheme.

Discretionary payments

11.17 SSAP 24 requires that where allowance is not made for discretionary payments in the actuarial assumptions, the capital costs should, to the extent not covered by a surplus, be recognised in the profit and loss account in the accounting period in which they are initially granted. As with any other schemes, discretionary benefit increases may be made by a centralised scheme. The provisions for this would be contained within the trust deed. In general it is likely that such payments would only be made on actuarial advice and when there was a surplus. As SSAP 24 only prescribes the accounting treatment of such increases where there is no surplus, participating employers are unlikely to have the problem of recognising in the company accounts increased pensions to ex-employees in respect of participation in a centralised scheme.

Refund of surpluses

11.18 It is considered unlikely that any surplus in a scheme of this nature would be repaid to participating employers, as it is usual that the trust deed of the scheme would not permit such an option except on winding up of the scheme. If a surplus could be refunded, then it would be treated by the participating employer in the way stipulated in SSAP 24, para 83, i.e. either by taking a credit to the profit and loss account in the period in which the refund is made or by spreading it forward.

Overseas employers

11.19 Following the arguments outlined above, the position of non-UK employers will be the same as those in the UK if they are reporting under UK generally accepted accounting principles (GAAP). For any participating employer who reports under US GAAP, Statement of Financial Accounting Standard 87 (FAS 87) does not require changes in the accounting for 'multi-employer' plans, a term which would include UK industry-wide schemes.

Disclosure of market value of assets

11.20 Where a company participates in a centralised or an industry-wide scheme, the assets of the scheme relating to the individual employer cannot be identified. If the pension cost relating to the scheme is material in the context of the employing company's pension costs, it is suggested that disclosure be made of the total assets of the scheme and the proportion of members which the company's employees constitute. Where the employer's actuarial liability is separately calculated, it may be possible to apportion the assets of the scheme for the purposes of disclosure of market value of assets, at least on an actuarial basis.

Chapter 12

Payments other than contributions to occupational pension schemes

Introduction

12.1 Occupational pension schemes are by far the most important way of private pension provision in the UK. However, the *Social Security Act 1986* and recent *Finance Acts* have led to many changes in the field of pension provision by:

(a) ending compulsory occupational scheme membership;

(b) permitting money-purchase contracted out schemes;

(c) offering financial incentives to join personal pension plans by offering a contracting-out rebate;

(d) imposing ceilings on the maximum pension benefits which can be derived from occupational pension schemes; and

(e) encouraging unapproved pension schemes.

The effects of this legislation are still in their early stages, but it will undoubtedly impact on pension cost in some employers' accounts.

Personal pension schemes

12.2 Employees who are not members of an occupational pension scheme have always been able to purchase additional benefits and obtain the relevant tax reliefs by the purchase of what was termed a section 226 policy. This referred to pension arrangements made under ICTA 1970, s226 (*now ICTA 1988, ss619(1),620* and *621)*. From 1 July 1988, the government introduced personal pension plans, for people who do not belong to an occupational pension scheme. Some personal pension schemes allow the individual to contract out of the SERPS. These are 'appropriate personal pension plans', where full national insurance contributions are paid by employer and employee but the Department of Social Security (DSS) pays to the plan a rebate of the difference between the contracted-in and contracted-out rates. For those who have not been in contracted-out employment for more than two years before starting the plan, the DSS makes an incentive payment of 2% of earnings between the lower and upper limits for national insurance. This is offered to all new contracted-out pension arrangements, not only personal pension plans.

Contributions are subject to Inland Revenue limits, but it is possible for employers to contribute. In practice, very few employers do contribute to such schemes. The National Association of Pension Fund's 1988 survey revealed that in less than 3% of schemes responding did the employer do so. Where an employer contributes, these schemes are money purchase and not final salary. Therefore the charge against profits in the accounts of the employer will simply be the amount of contributions payable to the scheme in respect of the accounting period.

Unfunded pension arrangements

12.3 It is unusual for pension schemes in the UK to be unfunded. Successive governments have treated the prefunding of occupational pension schemes very favourably, allowing generous tax relief on both employer and employee contributions. Unfunded arrangements attract neither formal recognition nor relief.

The *Finance Act 1989* introduced a ceiling on earnings of £60,000 in 1989-90 in relation to contributions and benefits for occupational pension scheme purposes for those joining an existing occupational scheme on or after 1st June 1989 and for new schemes from 14 March 1989. The ceiling is linked to price rather than earnings inflation (see 2.5) which means that companies may look at alternative methods of pension provision for highly paid staff subject to this restriction. Prefunding amounts in excess of the *Finance Act's* limits is unlikely (see 8.7) and as no taxable benefit is assessed on an employee in respect of an unfunded scheme, (the legislation which did this having been repealed in 1989), unfunded arrangements are becoming more popular. Nevertheless, whether it is funded or unfunded, any commitment to pay a pension in excess of Inland Revenue limits will be part of the employer's pension cost, even though it is outside the tax-approved pension scheme. Clearly actuarial advice will be necessary to establish the cost of any such arrangements if material amounts are likely to be involved, not only to assess the costs for SSAP 24 purposes but to comply with *CA 1985, 4 Sch* which requires the statement of pension costs (see 9.14).

An issue of particular relevance to unfunded schemes is the measurement of the unfunded liability Clearly this is a matter for the employer's actuary. The frequency with which the actuary will need to examine the liability will depend on a number of matters, including the number of employees involved, the materiality of the amount and whether there have been any material events in pension terms. It may be possible to value the liabilities triennially along with those of any funded schemes, but circumstances may require a shorter inter-valuation period. The provision established for unfunded pension costs will be assessed on a discounted basis, so that the pension cost will comprise two main elements,

(a) the charge for the year (regular cost plus variations) and

(b) an interest charge on the unfunded liability.

The cost will be calculated in much the same way as for a funded scheme, except that there will be no variations relating to investment performance of scheme assets, because there are none.

Ex gratia arrangements

12.4 Where an employer pays an *ex gratia* pension, i.e. one which he is neither legally nor contractually required to provide, SSAP 24 states that the capital cost, to the extent not covered by a surplus, should be recognised in the profit and loss account in the accounting period in which it is granted. If the *ex gratia* pension is not granted by the trustees of the employing company's occupational scheme but is funded from the company's own resources, either by the purchase of an annuity or the regular payment of a pension by the company's own resources, it is arguable that the capital cost should be recognised in the profit and loss account when it is granted and not offset against a surplus in the pension scheme. This might apply, for example, in the case of an *ex gratia* pension to a former director.

A few employers do not have any formal pension arrangements but nevertheless regularly grant *ex gratia* pensions to retiring employees, such that in effect there is an informal but implicit commitment to pay a pension (see 3.1). Where this occurs, the pension cost should be computed on a full SSAP 24 basis, as it is a regular ongoing cost.

Discretionary pension increases

12.5 A similar problem arises in the treatment of discretionary and *ex gratia* pension increases. Many employers do not contractually provide for pension increases and do not provide for them in the funding plan. They nevertheless do regularly increase pensions in payment. In such circumstances, the increases anticipated should be incorporated into the actuarial calculation of pension cost (see 6.12, 6.13). The *Social Security Act 1990* has now introduced compulsory increases to pensions in payment so that in future there will have to be an allowance for increases.

Chapter 13

Overseas arrangements

Introduction

13.1 Historical and cultural differences mean that each country has developed its own social security and pension legislation. Whilst developed countries generally maintain state pension schemes, the level of benefits provided varies from country to country. As a result, private pension arrangements made by employers for their staff are also very different and this is reflected in the methods of financing and accounting for pension costs.

The major areas of difference are set out below.

(a) Obligations may be financed outside the company through insurance companies or in separate funds (externally funded pensions); alternatively, reserves may be set aside with the assets within the company (internally funded pensions), or pensions may be charged to the profit and loss account as they are paid to the employee (unfunded pensions).

(b) The basis of calculating charges to the profit and loss account.

(c) The basis of calculating payments, if any, to externally funded schemes, and the extent to which these may vary from the charge against profits.

This chapter aims to provide an outline of the pension arrangements in Australia, Japan, Germany, France and North America, the accounting consequence of those arrangements and the accounting practices currently in force.

Australia

Company Plans: Benefit structure

13.2 Multinational companies and medium to larger local companies usually provide final average salary related defined benefit schemes. Benefits are normally defined in lump sum form. However, defined contribution schemes are still prevalent among smaller local companies and favoured by unions who are playing a more active role in promoting industry-wide schemes as part of the collective bargaining process.

Normal retirement age is 65 for men and either 60 or 65 for women.

Company Plans: Contributions and funding methods

Funding methods are generally similar to those in the UK, with a mix of insured and self-administered plans.

Taxation and regulation

Recent legislation has been introduced which has fundamentally changed the taxation treatment of superannuation funds.

Employer contributions to approved schemes are tax deductible. Employee contributions to employer sponsored approved schemes are not generally tax deductible; the extent to which employee contributions may be deducted depends on the employer's level of support.

Pension fund income (including employer contributions) is taxed at 15%.

Accounting treatment

Contributions are generally charged to the employers' profit and loss accounts when they are payable. Listed companies and certain other companies are required to make certain disclosures under the Companies Code. These include an indiciation that the plan exists, the principal type of benefit, the basis of contribution, the date of the last actuarial valuation (with the name and qualifications of the actuary) and any surplus or deficit in relation to vested benefits.

Japan

Company Plans: Benefit structure

13.3 Most company schemes provide defined benefits in lump sum form, both on normal retirement and on termination of employment for any other reasons. The benefit is normally calculated by reference to years of service, final monthly basic salary (sometimes plus some of the various allowances) and whether the termination of employment is voluntary or involuntary.

13.3 *Overseas arrangements*

Benefit levels vary but normally would be lower for voluntary than for involuntary termination, other than when the employee nears normal retirement age.

Normal retirement age is usually 60 for men and women.

While there are no minimum legal vesting conditions, it is customary for Japanese schemes to provide benefits on voluntary termination after not more than three years' service. For involuntary termination, the period is generally one year or less.

Company Plans: Contributions and funding methods

The majority of schemes are non-contributory.

For taxation reasons (discussed below), benefits are often expressed in pension form with a full commutation option. These schemes can be operated on a funded basis subject to a minimum of 15 employees being covered. The scheme must be insured unless there are a minimum of 100 employees, in which case a trust bank may be used.

Taxation and regulation

Appropriations to book reserves for the purposes of providing retirement or termination of employment allowances are tax deductible within certain limits. For an externally funded plan to be tax approvable, it must be established in pension form; this approach usually leads to a larger tax deductible employer contribution.

Employees' contributions are tax deductible up to a certain amount including life insurance premiums.

Accounting treatment

For pension plans, the charge to profit and loss accounts is made on the basis of contributions paid.

For unfunded lump-sum retirement indemnity plans the accounting and tax treatment usually coincide, and when the employee becomes eligible for benefit there is usually an additional charge to the profit and loss account of the balance of the unrecognised cost. For directors, however, pension cost is not accrued at all, but charged in the year in which the shareholders approve the pension. Clearly, pension costs for Japanese companies can fluctuate considerably from year to year.

Federal Republic of Germany

Company Plans: Benefit structure

13.4 Multinational companies tend to provide pensions ranging from 1%–2% of final average salary per year of service on earnings above the Social Security ceiling (currently about £25,000); the rate below the ceiling ranges from 0.25%–1%.

Normal retirement age is usually 65 for men and women, but early retirement ages of 63 for men and 60 for women and severely disabled persons (following the flexible retirement ages in the Social Security system) are common.

Company Plans: Contributions and funding methods

Employees' contributions are not customary (and not possible under book-reserve financing methods).

The practical alternative funding methods for German companies are:

(a) Book reserves, possibly coupled with full or partial reinsurance of benefit liabilities.

(b) Support funds, which are established as separate legal entities from the employing company. The employer has some responsibility to ensure adequate financing.

(c) Direct insurance, in which case policies are 'owned' by the employees.

(d) Pension funds, established as separate legal entities and subject to strict supervision by the insurance authorities.

About two-thirds of all employees are covered by company schemes. Those financed through book reserve systems cover about 70% of all employees and about 78% of the total cost of company benefits. This unusual feature distinguishes Germany from most other European countries.

Taxation and regulation

The tax treatment of benefits and contributions depends on the method of funding adopted.

Appropriations to *book reserve* are calculated by a prescribed method (which may not reflect true cost) and, together with any reinsurance premiums, are tax deductible to the employer. (Employees cannot contribute to a book reserve plan.) Benefits payable to employees or dependants under the book reserve system are taxed as income subject to certain modest tax-free allowances.

Employers' contributions for *direct insurance policies* or to a *pension fund* are tax deductible but constitute additional taxable income to the employee. Employees' contributions to direct insurance policies or a pension fund are only tax deductible, up to a (low) ceiling. Lump sum benefits from direct insurance are tax-free. Pensions are taxed only on the interest content (24% of a pension commencing at 65).

Contributions by an employer to a *support fund* are tax deductible but unless the fund is reinsured, the maximum contributions and fund assets are very restricted in size. (Employees cannot contribute to support funds). Support fund benefits are taxed in a manner similar to book reserve system benefits.

Schemes financed under the book reserve or support fund system must effect insolvency insurance with a government agency (PSV).

Labour court legislation prescribes a triennial review of pensions in payment.

Accounting treatment

Charges made to the profit and loss accounts for internally funded arrangements are tax deductible if they comply with the method laid down by the authorities.

However, this method is not consistent with SSAP 24 as, for example, no allowance in the actuarial basis is made for salary and pension increases, and the interest rate is based on the levels permitted by the tax authorities.

Furthermore, past service costs arising from an increase in pension liabilities of more than 25% in comparison with that of the previous year, can either be charged against the profit and loss account immediately or be spread over three years if they are to be tax deductible. This can lead to marked short-term fluctuations in costs.

Clearly, separate calculations of cost for SSAP 24 compliance should be undertaken for German subsidiaries if their results are likely to be material in the context of the group as a whole. There is also a need for particular care in valuing pension liabilities in the case of an acquisition.

France

Company Plans: Benefit structure

13.5 Few employees in France are entitled to benefits other than those provided by the basic State scheme and the mandatory complementary pay-as-you-go schemes (principally ARRCO and AGIRC), the rate of contribution to which can be selected within specified bands.

Normal retirement age is 60 for men and women.

As spouses' and disability benefits payable from the mandatory systems tend to be inadequate (being based only on service completed), many employers provide insured death and disability pensions. Insured medical plans are also common.

Company Plans: Contributions and funding methods

Some companies pay defined contributions to funded (insured) arrangements to top up the ARRCO/AGIRC benefits. A few large companies guarantee a target final pay pension, the accrual rate being 1.7%–2% p.a. of final pay for each year of service, including State benefits and the proceeds from the complementary systems. Such schemes are normally confined to highly-paid employees.

Taxation

Employee and employer contributions to social security, the complementary systems and supplementary company arrangements are tax-deductible up to 19% of 8 times the social security ceiling (currently about £13,000).

Accounting treatment

Accounting for pension costs has for most companies been based on contributions paid to an outside agency.

The pension system in France parallels that described in SSAP 24, paragraph 42 which states:

> '..the employer's obligation may be discharged by prescribed payments under a nationwide or industry-wide scheme with characteristics similar to those of the State scheme in the UK. In such cases, charging the contributions payable will satisfy the requirements of this Statement.'

However, employers are also often require to provide employees with a lump sum on retirement, and are increasingly recognising the need to make provision for this liability, even though it is not allowable for tax purposes until paid unless it is externally funded.

Canada

Company Plans: Benefit structure

13.6 Most pension plans provide benefits related to final average salary, the most common pension formula being 2% per year of service, integrated with the State earnings-related scheme (CPP/QPP). However, defined contribution schemes are still prevalent among small local companies and are becoming more attractive with the increasing regulatory controls.

Normal retirement age is customarily 65 for men and women.

Recent legislation emanating from the various provinces has increased controls and disclosures; for example, Ontario requires increases to pensions in payment and vesting after two years' plan participation.

Company Plans: Contributions and funding methods

Most earnings-related schemes are contributory, with employees normally contributing 5%–6% of annual salary inclusive of contributions to CPP/QPP.

Funding methods are broadly similar to those used in the UK and may involve insurance and/or direct investment.

Pensions for employees earning more than the tax-approved salary 'cap' are normally unfunded.

Taxation and regulation

Employer and employee contributions to an approved pension scheme are deductible. For defined benefit plans within prescribed maximum pension limits (currently about C$60,000 p.a. after 35 years' service), both employee and employer contributions are deductible without limit. For defined contribution plans, the contributions up to a specified limit are deductible.

Accounting for pension cost is subject to the Canadian Institute of Chartered Accountants standard 3460. This is a complex standard which has a number of similarities to FAS 87 in the USA (see 13.7 below). The use of the projected benefit method is prescribed, and pension fund assets must be valued at market-related values i.e. either market value or a smoothed average over no more than five years. Experience gains and losses and benefit improvements are generally spread forward over the average remaining service life of the company's employees. However, the Canadian standard, issued some time after FAS 87, avoids one of the contentious areas of the US standard. It does not require the market-related assumptions relating to interest rates but allows the use of best estimate long-term actuarial assumptions.

The disclosure requirements for defined benefit plans are limited to the value of accrued liabilities and the value of assets, although more detailed information is encouraged.

USA

Company Plans: Benefit structure

13.7 Company plans are much influenced by ERISA (Employees' Retirement Income Security Act 1974), non-discrimination legislation and recent tax reform. Pensions practice is constantly changing and it should also be understood that it varies considerably between different industries and geographical areas.

Union-negotiated schemes are widespread and many are based on a fixed dollar pension amount per year of service. Such schemes, which are not normally contributory, are regularly reviewed as part of normal pay bargaining negotiations. For salaried staff, retirement benefits can be included in pension, profit-sharing or savings schemes; many companies operate more than one type of scheme.

Pension schemes for salaried staff normally provide final salary related benefits. Pension formulae range from around 1%–2% of final average earnings per year of service, including Social Security benefits. There are rules relating to eligibility, integration with Social Security, average benefit/contribution levels etc. to ensure that the scheme does not

discriminate in favour of 'highly compensated' employees.
Normal retirement age is currently 65 for men and women; this will eventually rise to age 67 in line with Social Security provisions.

Company plans: Contributions and funding methods

Most staff pension schemes are non-contributory but employees may be required to contribute to separate group insurance schemes, including death, disability and medical expenses benefits.

Pension scheme funding methods are similar to those available in the UK, although it is not essential to establish a separate trust for an insured scheme. Maximum and minimum tax-deductible funding levels are prescribed by legislation.

Taxation

Employers' contributions to a qualified pension plan are tax-deductible subject to certain maximum benefit and contribution limitations. Benefits for more highly paid employees are usually unfunded. Obligatory employees' contributions are not tax-deductible, but contributions to profit sharing plans and personal pensions (IRA's) are deductible within defined limits.

Accounting treatment

Accounting for pension costs is determined by the requirements of FAS 87 and FAS 88, which are examined below.

Background to Statements of Financial Accounting Standards 87 and 88

13.8 There have been professional pronouncements in the US relating to pension costs for many years. The subject was first dealt with in Accounting Research Bulletin (ARB) 43 in 1953 and subsequently in ARB 47 in 1956. It was given a more comprehensive treatment in Accounting Principles Board (APB) Opinion No 8 'Accounting for the cost of pension plans' issued in 1966. The Financial Accounting Standards Board (FASB) dealt with disclosure issues in its Statement of Financial Accounting Standards (FAS) 36 'Disclosure of pension information' in 1980 and later dealt with related topics in FAS 74 'Accounting for special termination benefits paid to employees' and FAS 81 'Disclosure of post-retirement health care and life insurance benefits'.

This topic of post-retirement benefits is presently being considered by the FASB but the topic is very complex and contentious due to the size and difficulty in estimating such benefits. The FASB's most recent pronouncements are FAS 87 'Employers' accounting for pensions' and FAS 88 'Employers' accounting for settlements and curtailments of defined benefit pension plans and for termination benefits'. These two FASs have superseded the earlier pronouncements on the subject.

Financial Accounting Standard Board's Statement 87

13.9 FAS 87 and FAS 88 were issued in the US in December 1985 and apply to US plans for accounting periods commencing after 15th December 1986, with compulsory application to non-US plans being deferred for two years and to apply to periods commencing after 15th December 1988.

FAS 87 requires a particular actuarial approach to be used for measuring cost and in the main prescribes tightly drawn rules as to the computation and disclosure of pension figures in the financial statements. The pension cost to be attributed to a financial period is that which accrues in respect of the period under the terms of the pension scheme i.e. it applies an accrued benefit approach to the allocation of costs to periods and for final salary schemes the cost must be calculated using the projected unit credit method (termed the projected unit method in the UK).

As with SSAP 24, the accounting objective is to recognise the expected cost of providing pensions on a systematic and rational basis over the period during which the employer derives benefit from the employees' services and not on the basis of funding. The FAS 87 approach is however, rather more complex. While SSAP 24 recognises two major components of pension cost, regular cost and variations, in FAS 87 the components are analysed in greater detail because the FASB concluded that an understanding of the accounting required is facilitated by considering the components separately. These six components are as follows.

(a) *Service cost* – The actuarial present value of benefits accruing during the accounting period, including, where appropriate, allowance for future salary increases – i.e. the regular cost.

(b) *Interest cost* – Interest on the projected benefit obligation, (allowance for the actuarial present value of benefits accrued to date including future salary increases).

(c) *Actual return on plan assets* – The difference between fair value of plan assets at the beginning and end of the period, adjusted for contributions and benefit payments.

(d) *Amortisation of unrecognised prior service costs* – The amortisation of benefit changes, which may be spread forward over future service periods or, if most of the participants are pensioners, over the remaining life expectation of participants, straight-line amortisation being expressly permitted.

(e) *Gain or loss* – Changes in the projected benefit obligations or plan assets resulting from the effects of experience or changes in assumptions. These do not have to be recognised immediately, but as a minimum the unrecognised net gain or loss (excluding asset gains and losses not yet reflected in market-related value) which is in excess of 10% of the greater of the projected benefit obligation or the market-related value of plan assets has to be amortised over the working life. The gain or loss component should also include the difference between the actual return on plan assets and the expected return on plan assets.

(f) *Amortisation of unrecogised net obligation or unrecognised net asset on transition* – A 'temporary' component to deal with the unrecognised surplus or deficit on transition, though the period of amortisation can be 15 years or more.

FAS 87 requires disclosures of the headings stated above and a reconciliation of the funded status of the scheme with the amounts which appear in the employer's balance sheet.

13.10 FAS 87 is very prescriptive in its approach to these components. It requires the application of the 'projected unit credit' actuarial method and a 'best estimate' must be made of each individual actuarial assumption. Discount rates are to reflect the rates at which the pension benefits could be settled and companies are expected to take into account current annuity rates and rates of return on reliable fixed-interest stocks, i.e. a market rate at each valuation is to be used rather than the long-term rate estimated by the actuary which is usual actuarial practice. The long-term rate of return on plan assets is to reflect the average rate of return expected on investments, and this may not be the same as the settlement rate.

The use of current market rates for annuities and fixed interest stocks to value liabilities has been much criticised on conceptual grounds as the liabilities are not being discharged. Actuaries take a long-term view in valuations and in any event, most pension scheme investments may consist of equities. The practical result is, however, that there is considerable potential for volatility since even small variations in settlement rates can have a material effect on pension cost.

FAS 88, the companion standard, requires immediate recognition of certain previously unrecognised amounts when certain transactions or events occur. It prescribes the method for determining the amount to be recognised in the profit and loss account when a pension obligation is settled or curtailed. There is no direct equivalent of these provisions in the UK. However, where a significant number of employees leave a scheme in the UK, this would effectively be a 'curtailment'. Under FAS 88 the effect of this would be recognised immediately whereas under SSAP 24 , unless regarded as an extraordinary event under SSAP 6, it would be dealt with in the periods when the reduction in contributions occurs but not over the working lives of those who remain as it arises in relation to those who left the scheme.

Comparison of FAS 87 and FAS 88 with SSAP 24

13.11 Comparative studies of FAS 87 and SSAP 24 have concluded that provided that the assumptions adopted for FAS 87 are not unreasonable, the expense can coincide with that of SSAP 24, but for how long this can be maintained is debatable. FAS 87 prescribes an actuarial valuation method, projected unit credit, (an accrued benefits method), to calculate regular cost. This method is acceptable in the UK provided that the flow of new entrants maintains the current membership profile. If this condition is not met, the regular cost may not remain the stable percentage of payroll required by SSAP 24. The use of a market-related discount rate rather than the expected long-term rate and the need to consider actuarial assumptions individually rather than as a whole can also provide areas of difference.

FAS 87 is almost legalistic in its approach to pension increases, allowing advance provision only where there is a 'substantive commitment' on the grounds that a present obligation does not exist for pension increases promised in future amendments and because of difficulties of quantification. SSAP 24 recommends that future increases to pensions in payment be allowed for in the actuarial assumptions, and while FAS 87 spreads forward the cost of increasing pensions in payment, SSAP 24 requires the capital cost to be charged to the profit and loss account when granted insofar as it cannot be charged against a surplus.

If there is a surplus, the cost is effectively spread forward as it is under FAS 87, since the reduction in surplus in this way reduces the favourable variation to be spread forward. In the absence of one, the cost is charged immediately.

FAS 87's approach to accounting for substantial reductions in the workforce, supplemented by FAS 88, is rather different from that of SSAP 24. For curtailments, settlements or terminations, any loss is to be recognised in the profit and loss account 'when it is probable that the curtailment will occur and the effects are reasonably estimable'. If there is a net gain, it is to be recognised when the employees terminate or the plan suspension or amendment is adopted. SSAP 24 allows departure from spreading material surpluses or deficiencies when contribution levels have changed as a result of a significant reduction in the number of employees but requires the effect to be spread over the period during which contributions are affected, unless the change is related to an 'extraordinary' event. In this instance, any surplus or deficiency is to be included as part of the extraordinary item and not spread at all. If a gain or loss is directly related to the disposal of a segment of business, FAS 88 requires the amount to be recognised as part of the transaction. This is in line with the treatment which would be adopted under UK statements.

Certain refunds of surpluses may under SSAP 24 be immediately credited to the profit and loss account. Under FAS 87 and FAS 88 withdrawal of excess assets is treated as a credit to accrued or prepaid pension cost and immediate credit to the profit and loss account is not permitted unless there is a curtailment. If a plan is terminated, and termination creates a gain or a loss, then an immediate credit or debit to the profit and loss account is permitted. The refund is treated as a gain from settlement.

Transitional provisions provide a further source of differences, as FAS 87 is more rigorous. It requires any surplus or deficit at the start of the year of implementation to be ascertained on a market value basis. The amount must be spread forward on a straight-line basis over the average remaining service lives of employees expected to receive benefits under the plan although if it is less than 15 years, the employer may elect to use 15 years. Restatement of prior years is not permitted. In the UK, a number of options are available in dealing with transitional surplus or deficit. In general terms, it may be treated as a prior year adjustment under SSAP 6 or spread forward from the date of implementation of SSAP 24 and in both cases as a variation from regular cost. Alternatively, it may be set up as a prepayment or provision, and amortised as cost and funding diverge over the estimated remaining service lives of employees until it is reduced to zero.

A detailed comparison of the main provisions of SSAP 24 and FAS 87 is shown in Appendix F. However, the main differences can be simply summarised as set out below.

(i) FAS 87 requires settlement rates to be used to discount the pension liability whereas under SSAP 24 a long-term interest rate, compatible with other assumptions made by the actuary in his valuation, would be used.

(ii) SSAP 24 has exceptions to the spreading rule for certain variations which would not be permitted under FAS 87, in particular accounting for refunds to be recognised in the profit and loss account when received.

(iii) FAS 87 treats increases in pensions which do not form part of a substantive commitment as a past service cost and amortises the effects over the working lives of members after the increase is awarded. SSAP 24, however, encourages expected increases to be provided for in advance by being built into the actuarial assumptions.

The Institute of Actuaries has issued a guidance note (GN 13),'Actuarial statements required in connection with the Statement of Financial Accounting Standard No 87 (FAS 87) in the USA' to its members in March 1988, effective from 1 April 1988. This was, of course, before SSAP 24 was published.

Practical implications for multinational employers

13.12 It is clear that, although the American and British standards have similar objectives, the differences between the bases of calculation of pension cost mean that often compliance with one of the standards will not mean compliance with the other. For UK holding companies with material American pensions obligations, it will be necessary to ask their actuaries to recalculate the US figures in line with SSAP 24 so that if there is a material difference, an appropriate adjustment can be made in the consolidated accounts to ensure compliance with UK GAAP. SSAP 24 states that an adjustment on consolidation will be necessary unless the commitment is very different, or because of the difficulties and costs of obtaining actuarial information. It is unlikely that these criteria could be said to apply in the case of US schemes.

For US companies with UK subsidiaries, and non-US companies with a US listing similar procedures will apply in relation to figures calculated under SSAP 24 to ensure compliance in the USA with FAS 87 and FAS 88. However, this will be a more demanding exercise, because while in the UK actuarial valuations undertaken on a triennial basis are adequate for the purposes of SSAP 24 (unless there are material changes affecting the pension scheme when a new valuation or interim review will be necessary), compliance with FAS 87 requires remeasurement every year.

Timing

13.13 As the time scale for preparation of final results is usually very tight, the complexity of FAS 87 and the recalculation requirements mean that this is not a matter to be left until the financial year end. It is clearly advisable to set a timetable for consultation with both the actuary and the auditor well in advance to anticipate the issues and problems and resolve any difficulties which may arise.

IAS (International Accounting Standard) 19

13.14 The International Accounting Standards Committee addressed the issue of pension cost in 1983 with the publication of IAS 19 'Accounting for retirement benefits in the financial statements of employers'. In many respects it is similar in approach to SSAP 24 but IAS 19 deals with actuarial methods in a little more detail and states that an accrued benefit valuation or a projected benefit valuation should be used. An appendix to IAS 19 gives examples of individual methods which fall under these classifications. The treatment of variations is rather different from that of SSAP 24 in that they can either be charged or credited to income as they arise or alternatively allocated systematically over a period not exceeding the expected remaining service lives of the participating employees.

The main provisions of IAS 19

13.15 IAS 19 is effective for accounting periods beginning on or after 1 January 1985. The main accounting rules set out in the standard are as follows.

(a) The cost of benefits should be determined by consistently using appropriate and compatible assumptions and an accrued benefit or a projected benefit valuation method. Pay-as-you-go and terminal funding methods should not be used.

(b) Current service costs should be charged to income systematically over the expected remaining service lives of the employees covered by the retirement plan. The cost is currently not required to be a level percentage of salary and hence assumptions on pay increases are not mandatory.

(c) Costs relating to past service, experience adjustments, and the effects of changes in actuarial assumptions should either be charged or credited to income as they arise or allocated systematically over a period not exceeding the expected remaining service lives of the participating employees. Amendments providing additional benefits for retired employees should be treated in the same way.

(d) The effect of changes in actuarial method should be accounted for and disclosed in accordance with IAS 8, 'Unusual and prior period items and changes in accounting policies'.

(e) When additional benefits which are a continuing commitment, e.g. permanent increases in pensions in payment, are granted to pensioners, the present value of the costs should be charged to the profit and loss account at the time the promise is made.

(f) When a plan is to be discontinued, the cost of any unfunded amounts should be charged to the profit and loss account immediately unless the remaining obligation is transferred to another scheme.

Disclosure requirements of IAS 19

13.16 There are numerous disclosures required such as:

(i) the accounting policy for pension costs;

(ii) the amount of any shortfall (if any) of the net realisable value of the fund assets compared with the value of the vested benefits;

(iii) a statement of the funding approach adopted;

(iv) the date of the latest actuarial valuation; and

(v) any difference between the amounts funded and the amounts charged to income, together with the amount of the resulting pension provision or prepayment and the funding approach adopted, if there is no systematic policy of funding.

IAS 19 has been drafted widely, such that although FAS 87 and FAS 88 are unlikely to produce the same pension cost as SSAP 24 from year to year, both US and UK statements have been accepted by their respective standards committees as complying with the international one.

There do, however, seem to be potential differences from the UK statement. For example, SSAP 24 requires that most variations from regular cost be spread forward over the expected or average remaining service lives of current employees. Under IAS 19, variations are charged or credited to income as they arise or allocated over a period not exceeding the expected remaining service lives of participating employees, effectively giving a choice which is usually only available in very limited circumstances under SSAP 24 in the case of a refund.

The International Accounting Standards Committee (IASC) has since issued an exposure draft, E32, 'Comparability of Financial Statements', which sets out proposals designed to eliminate most of the free choices of accounting treatment currently permitted under existing International Accounting Standards. These proposals affect IAS 19. The intentions are to require the incorporation of assumptions about projected salaries in assessing the liabilities of final pay plans. The proposals state that accrued benefit valuation methods are preferred, but that projected benefit valuation methods are to be permitted. Finally, past service costs, experience adjustments and the effects of changes in actuarial assumptions are to be recognised systematically over a period approximating the average of the expected remaining service lives of participating employees. It will no longer, if these proposals are carried through, be possible to recognise such variations in the income of the current period as they arise. It is anticipated that these proposals will be implemented substantially as originally intended, except that the IASC envisages immediate write off or the use of shorter amortisation periods for certain adjustments such as curtailments, settlements, some plan amendments and similar items. The timetable for the finalisation of these proposals is expected to be fairly lengthy, however.

Chapter 14

The audit of pension cost

Introduction

14.1 Auditors have long been familiar with the role of the actuary in relation to pension schemes. However, the issue in 1986 of ED 39 'Accounting for pension costs', Statement of Recommended Practice (SORP) 1 'Pension Scheme Accounts' and *The Occupational Pension Schemes (Disclosure of Information) Regulations* meant that auditors were required to develop a greater understanding of the work of an actuary. In 1987, the Auditing Practices Committee published an 'Audit Brief' entitled 'The work of a pension scheme actuary' which provides an insight into the rôle of the actuary and his work in relation to pension scheme valuation.

SSAP 24 and liaison between the actuary and the auditor

14.2 The issue of SSAP 24 and its requirement for the direct involvement of actuaries in the calculation of an accounting cost focussed renewed attention on the need for positive liaison between actuary and auditor. The Auditing Guideline 'Reliance on other specialists' was issued in May 1986 to provide guidance on the principles to be followed by an auditor when he wishes to place reliance on audit evidence provided by other specialists.

14.3 Following the 1986 Disclosure Regulations and *The Occupational Pension Schemes (Auditors) Regulations 1987 SI 1987 No 1102*, the Auditing Practices Committee issued an Auditing Guideline 'Pension Schemes in the United Kingdom' in May 1988. While this aims to give guidance on the special factors to be considered in the application of Auditing Standards to the audit of pension schemes, it does refer to the auditor's need to have an appreciation of the various matters considered by the actuary, and also provides some useful background reading on scheme arrangements and the social security and tax legislation.

14.4 This guidance was supplemented by an informal 'protocol' which dealt with liaison between the actuary and the auditor in relation to pension costs. This was widely circulated among firms of actuaries and auditors to provide a basis of interprofessional co-operation by setting out the responsibility of the auditors, their objectives in relation to pension cost and the procedures of liaison between the auditor and actuary. The document also included a list of questions which the auditor might ask of the actuary and *vice versa.*

The protocol was reviewed by the Auditing Practices Committee, and with some modifications, has now been adopted as 'Practice note 2'. It is reproduced as Appendix B to this book.

Auditors' responsibilities

14.5 The practice note, para 7, quoting from 'The auditor's operational standard', points out that

> 'the auditor should obtain relevant and reliable audit evidence sufficient to enable him to draw reasonable concusions therefrom'.

Auditors frequently have to place reliance on audit evidence from other specialists and, for pension costs of defined benefit schemes, this will be from a qualified actuary. The auditing guideline 'Reliance on other specialists' provides guidance on the principles to be followed, covering the areas of competence and objectivity, agreement on the scope of the work, evaluation of the findings and reporting.

Audit objectives in relation to pension cost

14.6 The auditors have a statutory responsibility to report to the members of a company as to whether in their opinion the company's balance sheet and profit and loss account have been properly prepared and whether the accounts give a true and fair view of the company's affairs. In relation to pension costs, the auditors' objectives will be to ensure that the company's pension costs and liabilities have been accounted for in accordance with SSAP 24.

The auditors will therefore need to be satisfied on the following points.

(a) whether the expected cost of providing pensions is recognised on a systematic and rational basis over the period during which the company derives benefit from the employees' services [*SSAP 24, para 77*];

(b) whether the effects of any significant changes of accounting policy or actuarial method and assumptions are correctly identified and incorporated and disclosed in the financial statements;

(c) whether events giving rise to exceptional or extraordinary items affecting pension costs have been identified and whether any consequential adjustment to pension cost has been properly made;

(d) whether the effect of changes in the pension benefits offered by the company have been taken into account;

(e) whether the expected remaining service lives of employees have been identified and whether the period for amortisation of variations has been properly determined;

(f) whether the accounting for and disclosure of any surplus or deficit identified by the latest actuarial valuation have been dealt with in accordance with SSAP 24.

Audit procedures

14.7 Audit procedures will depend on the materiality of pension costs and commitments in relation to the company's accounts. It is important to recognise firstly, that consultation with the actuary should ordinarily take place each year and that the mutual client should consent to such consultation at the outset and continue to be involved. Secondly, the judgment and calculations are complex. Initial discussions should take place well before the end of the relevant financial year so as to avoid delaying the timely production of the accounts.

As the practice note points out, the auditor is concerned with all pension costs including those for *ex gratia* and unfunded amounts as well as those provided through a funded scheme. The actuary's rôle in the assessment of pension cost may therefore extend beyond his normal rôle in relation to a prefunded occupational scheme, and the work he needs to perform should be agreed in advance with the auditor and the client.

14.8 The procedures set out in the practice note are as follows.

(i) Initial contact should be made with the actuary after client consent has been obtained.

The employer's own actuary should be approached first, but it is important to recognise that many actuaries whom the employer consults are in fact appointed by, and are the professional advisers of, the pension scheme, not the employing company. In such circumstances it may be necessary to obtain the consent of the pension scheme trustees to contact the actuary.

(ii) The auditor should obtain a copy of the most recent actuarial valuation for SSAP 24 purposes and background information relating to pension schemes and pension commitments. Such information would include correspondence between the client and scheme trustees, solicitors and actuary as well as the Occupational Pensions Board and Inland Revenue, and details of any changes in pension arrangements. Board minutes also need to be reviewed for indications of events with pension implications, such as redundancies or benefit improvements.

(iii) If necessary, the auditor and actuary should meet, normally with the mutual client, to discuss an agreed agenda.

(iv) Notes of the meeting should be exchanged and any further work agreed.

(v) Such further work should be agreed with the client.

(vi) As part of his post balance sheet review, the auditor should confirm whether or not there have been any changes of circumstance.

(vii) The auditor should obtain confirmation from management and trustees that the actuary has been advised of all the facts necessary for him to assess pension costs and liabilities.

(viii) The auditor should confirm whether or not the disclosure note in the accounts complies with SSAP 24 and *CA 1985*.

(ix) The auditor should recommend that the actuary's agreement with the notes on pension costs in the financial statements be obtained.

Questions for the auditor to ask the actuary

14.9 The practice note sets out, with the rationale, the questions the auditor might wish to pose to the actuary. In summary, these relate to:

(a) Whether the assumptions and valuation method used for funding are the same as those used to assess pension cost, and if not, why.

(b) What the effect would be of taking account of legislative changes (if any) which have occurred since the last valuation.

(c) Whether the actuarial method and assumptions used in the last valuation satisfy the basic accounting objectives of SSAP 24.

(d) Provision of the latest formal review of the scheme.

(e) What the actuary's recommendations are in respect of any material surplus or deficiency.

(f) Whether the actuary and auditor are using common data.

(g) Whether there have been any rule changes or events since the last valuation and whether these have been allowed for.

(h) Whether benefit improvements have been made and on what basis.

(i) Whether the basis for directors' pension contributions disclosure is appropriate.

(j) Whether there are any other matters of which the auditor should be aware.

The list is not comprehensive, nor would all these questions be relevant to every employer company, but they do point to areas for the auditor to examine.

The Practice note also includes as an appendix the latest version of Guidance Note (GN) 9, 'Retirement benefit schemes – actuarial reports' issued by the Institute of Actuaries. This note aims to ensure that reports contain sufficient information to enable the expected future course of a scheme's contribution rate and funding level to be appreciated.

Other audit matters

14.10 The level of detail of the audit work will depend on the materiality of pension costs and commitments, but it will be recognised that there is a considerable variety of pension arrangements and audit procedures will have to be tailored to the individual client. The practice note gives a number of pointers to appropriate steps to take in its procedures and questions. Additional matters might include:

(i) determination from the scheme rules whether it is defined contribution or defined benefit (see chapter 4);

(ii) if the pension scheme is defined contribution, determining whether the pension accrual includes amounts to be paid into the scheme in respect of services provided in the year.

If the scheme is a defined benefit scheme, the auditor should obtain a copy of the last actuarial valuation report, (which should be in accordance with GN 9), and financial statements of the pension scheme and seek responses to the questions set out in the practice note. In addition, he should undertake the following steps.

(i) Consider whether the actuarial assumptions in respect of the rate of return on investments and the rate of increase in salaries and pensions are reasonable and prudent and compatible with those in the financial statements and earlier years.. The practice note points out that it would not be usual to question the methods and assumptions of the actuary used to calculate a funding rate. However, the auditor should review the methods and assumptions used for calculating cost.

(ii) Determine whether any experience surplus or deficit revealed by the latest valuation report is spread over the expected remaining service lives of current employees. (Exceptions are where there has been a significant reduction in the number of employees in the scheme or where in limited circumstances prudence may require a material deficit to be recognised over a shorter period.)

This is an area where consultation with the actuary is desirable, to confirm the sources of the variation (see 6.3).

(iii) For a defined benefit scheme, verify that the pension accrual represents the pension cost less amounts paid into the scheme during the year.

(iv) Enquire of senior management whether ex *gratia payments* have been made or are agreed on a regular basis and if so, that they are accounted for in accordance with SSAP 24.

It is emphasised that the pension cost issues should be explored in advance of the financial year end and reviewed as part of the post balance sheet review. Reporting deadlines can be very tight and to allow inadequate time to discuss and review the issues can create unnecessary pressures on both actuary and auditor.

Timeliness of information

14.11 The effect of redundancies on a pension scheme can only be properly assessed by actuarial valuation and it may not be possible to complete the valuation before the accounts and the audit have to be completed. If the amount is potentially material, this may pose a problem for the auditor, particularly where there is a pension cost which is to be treated as part of an extraordinary or exceptional item.

Company does not comply with the disclosure requirements

14.12 Where a company does not comply with the disclosure requirements, the auditor should consider qualifying the accounts on the grounds of disagreement. This is discussed in para 9.18.

Company does not obtain an actuarial assessment of pension cost

14.13 Where the directors of a company with a defined benefit pension scheme fail to obtain an actuarially calculated best estimate of pension cost, it may be necessary to qualify the accounts both for failure to comply with SSAP 24 and uncertainty surrounding the pension cost charge in the accounts.

Appendix A

The text of SSAP 24

ACCOUNTING FOR PENSION COSTS

24

Accounting for pension costs

Contents

Appendix A

STATEMENT OF STANDARD ACCOUNTING PRACTICE

Accounting for pension costs

(Issued May 1988)

The provisions of this statement of standard accounting practice should be read in conjunction with the Explanatory Foreword to accounting standards *and need not be applied to immaterial items.*

Part 1 – Explanatory note

Importance of pension costs

1 The provision of a pension is part of the remuneration package of many employees. Pension costs form a significant proportion of total payroll costs and they give rise to special problems of estimation and of allocation between accounting periods. Accordingly, it is important that standard accounting practice exists concerning the recognition of such costs in the employers' financial statements. This statement deals with the accounting for, and the disclosure of, pension costs and commitments in the financial statements of enterprises that have pension arrangements for the provision of retirement benefits for their employees.

Types of pension schemes

2 Pension arrangements can take different forms. The employer may have a commitment arising from the contract of employment, the provision of pensions may have arisen from custom and practice or *ex gratia* arrangements may be made on a case by case basis. This Statement covers a scheme where an enterprise has entered into a commitment, whether legal, contractual or implicit in the employer's actions, to provide pensions for its employees. It also addresses situations where *ex gratia* or discretionary payments are made in the absence of such a commitment.

3 Pension schemes to which this Statement applies may basically be divided into defined contribution schemes and defined benefit schemes. In a defined contribution scheme, the employer will normally discharge his obligation by making agreed contributions to a pension scheme and the benefits paid will depend upon the funds available from these contributions and investment earnings thereon. The cost to the employer can, therefore, be measured with reasonable certainty. A number of pension schemes in the United Kingdom and Ireland, including many smaller ones, are defined contribution schemes.

4 In a defined benefit scheme, however, the benefits to be paid will usually depend upon either the average pay of the employee during his or her career or, more typically, the final pay of the employee. In these circumstances, it is impossible to be certain in advance that the contributions to the pension scheme, together with the investment return thereon, will equal the benefits to be paid. The employer may have a legal obligation to provide any unforeseen shortfall in funds or, if not, may find it necessary to meet the shortfall in the interests of maintaining good employee relations. Conversely, if a surplus arises the employer may be entitled to a refund of, or reduction in, contributions paid into the pension scheme. Thus, in this type of scheme the employer's commitment is generally more open than with defined contribution schemes and the final cost is subject to considerable uncertainty. The larger UK and Irish schemes are generally of the defined benefit kind and these cover the great majority of members of schemes.

ACCOUNTING FOR PENSION COSTS

Pension schemes may also be classified by the way in which they are financed, namely funded schemes or schemes where the benefits are paid directly by the employer. The same accounting principles apply to both types of scheme. 5

The trustees of a funded scheme may make use of the services of an insurance company – an approach that is particularly common amongst the smaller schemes. Insurance companies offer a wide variety of contracts, but, in the case of defined benefit schemes, these contracts are normally no more than investment management and administrative arrangements, possibly with life cover included, and do not relieve the employer of the responsibility to ensure that the scheme is adequately financed. 6

Actuarial considerations

In view of the very long-term nature of the pensions commitment, it is necessary to make use of actuarial calculations in determining the pension cost charge in respect of defined benefit schemes. In the case of defined contribution schemes there is no need for actuarial advice in order to establish the pension cost although such advice may be required for other purposes in connection with the operation of the scheme. 7

In defined benefit schemes, the choice of assumptions and the choice of valuation method can each have a major effect on the contribution rate calculated at each valuation. The choice of assumptions can be as significant as the choice of method. 8

The assumptions which the actuary must make in carrying out his valuation will be about matters such as future rates of inflation and pay increases, increases to pensions in payment, earnings on investments, the number of employees joining the scheme, the age profile of employees and the probability that employees will die or leave the company's employment before they reach retiring age. The actuary will view the assumptions as a whole; he will make assumptions which are mutually compatible, in the knowledge that, if experience departs from the assumptions made, the effects of such departures may well be offsetting, notably in the case of investment yields and increases in prices and earnings. 9

Most pension schemes undergo a formal actuarial valuation on a triennial basis. In such cases it is not intended that any special valuation exercise should be carried out by enterprises for the purpose of implementing this Statement for the first time. 10

The Councils of the Institute and Faculty of Actuaries published a paper in May 1986 entitled 'Pension Fund Terminology: specimen descriptions of commonly used valuation methods'. In addition, the Auditing Practices Committee has published an Audit Brief entitled 'The work of a pension scheme actuary'. This covers matters such as the valuation of defined benefit and defined contribution schemes, valuation assumptions and interprofessional co-operation. A glossary of pensions terminology for pension schemes has been published by The Pensions Management Institute and The Pensions Research Accountants Group. 11

The funding plan

The funding methods developed by actuaries are designed to build up assets in a prudent and controlled manner in advance of the retirement of the members of the scheme, in order 12

STATEMENT OF STANDARD ACCOUNTING PRACTICE

that the obligations of the scheme may be met without undue distortion of the employer's cash flow. The actuary's main concern is that the present and estimated future contribution levels should be at least sufficient to provide security for the payment of the promised benefits.

13 A range of actuarial methods is available for determining the level of contributions needed to meet the liabilities of the pension scheme. Some methods will tend to lead to higher levels of funding in the scheme than others.

14 In practice, it is common for actuaries to aim at a level contribution rate, as a proportion of pensionable pay in respect of current service. The contribution rate thus determined depends on the particular actuarial method used and the assumptions made regarding new entrants to the scheme. In broad terms, in projecting a stable contribution rate, accrued benefits methods rely on the assumption that the flow of new entrants will be such as to preserve the existing average age of the work-force; prospective benefits methods, on the other hand, normally look only to the existing work-force and seek a contribution rate that will remain stable for that group despite its increasing age profile until the last member retires or leaves. In a mature scheme both types of method may in practice achieve stable contribution rates but the size of the fund under a prospective benefits method will tend to be larger than under an accrued benefits method because it is intended to cover the ageing of the existing work-force.

15 From time to time it may be necessary to improve the level of funding because of deficiencies (where these are not expected to be offset by future surpluses). This may be done by an increase in the ordinary annual rate of contribution or by additional special payments over a limited period. On occasion the employer may make additional lump sum contributions which have the effect of reducing his future liabilities, if to do so is convenient in the context of the financial policy of the employer's business. Conversely, a previously high level of funding may be lowered by reducing or interrupting the contributions if there is a surplus in the fund or in times of financial stringency for the company. However, whilst the financial position of the sponsoring employer may influence the pattern of funding it will not provide a satisfactory basis for determining the pension charge for the period.

The accounting objective

16 From the point of view of the employee a pension may be regarded as deferred remuneration; from the point of view of the employer it is part of the cost incurred in obtaining the employee's services. The accounting objective therefore requires the employer to recognise the cost of providing pensions on a systematic and rational basis over the period during which he benefits from the employees' services. Many companies have, until now, simply charged the contributions payable to the pension scheme as the pension cost in each accounting period. In future, in order to comply with this Statement, it will be necessary to consider whether the funding plan provides a satisfactory basis for allocating the pension cost to particular accounting periods.

Defined contribution schemes

17 In the case of a defined contribution scheme the employer's obligation at any point in time is restricted to the amount of the contributions payable to date. The pension cost is, therefore, the amount of the contributions payable in respect of the particular accounting period.

ACCOUNTING FOR PENSION COSTS

Defined benefit schemes

The selection of the actuarial method and assumptions to be used in assessing the pension cost of a defined benefit scheme is a matter of judgement for the actuary in consultation with his client, taking account of the circumstances of the specific company and its workforce. This Statement requires that the actuarial valuation method and assumptions used for accounting purposes should satisfy the accounting objective. In order that full provision may be made over the employees' service lives for the expected costs of their pensions, the effect of expected future increases in earnings, including merit increases, up to the assumed retirement date or earlier date of withdrawal or death in service, should be recognised. Account will also need to be taken of expected future increases in deferred pensions and pensions in payment where the employer has an express or implied commitment to grant such increases. The calculation of benefit levels should be based on the situation most likely to be experienced and not on a contingent event not likely to occur. The actuarial method selected should be used consistently and should be disclosed. If there is a change of method this fact should be disclosed and the effect quantified. The actuarial assumptions and the actuarial method taken as a whole should be compatible and should lead to the actuary's best estimate of the cost of providing the pension benefits promised. 18

If the funding plan does not provide a satisfactory basis for determining the pension cost charge, separate actuarial calculations will be required. 19

Regular pension cost and variations in cost

The total cost of pensions in a year can notionally be divided into the regular cost, which is the consistent ongoing cost recognised under the actuarial method used, and variations from the regular cost. Where a stable contribution rate for regular contributions, expressed as a percentage of pensionable earnings, has been determined, that rate will provide an acceptable basis for calculating the regular cost under the stated accounting objective so long as it makes full provision for the expected benefits over the anticipated service lives of employees. 20

Variations from the regular cost may arise from: 21

(a) experience surpluses or deficiencies;

(b) the effects on the actuarial value of accrued benefits of changes in assumptions or method;

(c) retroactive changes in benefits or in conditions for membership;

(d) increases to pensions in payment or to deferred pensions for which provision has not previously been made.

Spreading variations from regular cost

Experience deficiencies or surpluses are part of the ongoing process of revising the estimate of the ultimate liabilities which will fall on the employer. Any effect on the cost should normally be taken into account by adjusting the current and future costs charged in the accounts and should not be treated as a prior year adjustment. 22

In accordance with the accounting objective, the normal period over which the effect of material deficiencies or surpluses should be spread for accounting purposes is the expected 23

STATEMENT OF STANDARD ACCOUNTING PRACTICE

remaining service lives of the current employees in the scheme after making suitable allowances for future withdrawals. A period representing the average remaining service lives of the current membership may be used if desired. This period, which will vary from scheme to scheme and from time to time, should be determined by the actuary. It would not be appropriate to credit or charge the entire surplus or deficiency against profits in one accounting period, except as provided in paragraphs 81 to 83.

24 The only circumstances in which there may be a departure from the normal principle of spreading material surpluses or deficiencies as set out in paragraph 23 are summarised in this paragraph and in paragraph 29 below. The full conditions which must be satisfied before there may be a departure from the normal spreading requirements are set out in paragraphs 81 to 83. The circumstances referred to below represent situations that properly lie outside the actuarial assumptions and normal running of the scheme and, accordingly, are expected to arise infrequently. They are:

(a) where there is a significant reduction in the number of employees covered by the company's and/or group's pension scheme arrangements;

(b) where, in the circumstances set out in paragraph 82, prudence requires a material deficiency to be recognised over a shorter period.

25 In many companies, there have been reorganisation programmes in recent years that have involved significant redundancies. These have often led to large non-reversing surpluses building up in related pension schemes. This Statement recognises that in such instances it would not be appropriate to spread the effect of the refund of such surpluses over the remaining service lives of the current employees in the scheme.

26 In the circumstances set out in paragraph 24(a) a refund of a surplus, contributions holiday or reduction in contributions should be accounted for as it becomes receivable and should not be anticipated, that is, if it is agreed that contributions will be reduced for a period of years the reduction should be recognised on a year by year basis and not accumulated and reflected in the financial statements in the period the first reduction becomes effective. Where a reduction in the number of employees is related to an extraordinary event, such as the closure of a business segment, it is accepted that it may not be possible to apply the rule set out in this paragraph. This is because SSAP 6 (Revised) 'Extraordinary items and prior year adjustments' requires the individual elements of income and expenditure which derive from a single extraordinary event to be aggregated and so it may not be appropriate to defer recognition of an associated pension cost or credit.

27 The exemption from the normal spreading principle relating to significant reductions in the total number of employees covered by a group's or company's pension arrangements does not cover situations where employees are transferred from one group scheme to another one.

28 As stated in paragraph 24(b), in strictly limited circumstances prudence may require that a material deficiency should be recognised over a period shorter than the expected remaining service lives of current employees in the scheme. A precondition of invoking this section is that significant additional contributions have had to be paid into the pension scheme. Furthermore, the additional payments should have been made as stated in paragraph 24 in respect of a major transaction or event outside the actuarial assumptions and normal

running of the scheme. A possible example of such a situation would be where there had been a major mismanagement of a pension scheme's assets. However, it is emphasised that each situation must be judged on its particular merits.

Where a refund that is subject to deduction of tax in accordance with the provisions of the UK Finance Act 1986, or equivalent legislation, is made to the employer, the enterprise may depart from the normal spreading principle and instead recognise the refund in the period in which it occurs. The accounting treatment adopted in respect of such refunds should be disclosed. 29

Changes in assumptions, valuation method and benefits

The effect of changes in the assumptions or valuation method on the cost of providing for past service is analogous to an experience deficiency or surplus and should be accounted for in a similar way. 30

Retroactive changes in benefits and membership are decided upon currently and it is thus not appropriate to charge any part of the costs arising from these decisions as a prior year adjustment. Past service costs should normally be written off over the remaining service lives of the current employees. 31

Where a surplus in a pension fund is utilised to provide benefits for which the company had previously established a provision in its financial statements, the provision, to the extent that it is no longer required, should be released over the estimated remaining service lives of the current employees. 32

Increases to pensions in payment and deferred pensions

Increases to pensions in payment up to a certain level may be specified in the rules of the pension scheme. Other increases may be granted in response to pensioners' needs and in the interests of continuing good industrial relations. In the United Kingdom, increases to deferred pensions, that is the prospective pensions of early leavers, are required by law to be made up to a specified level. 33

Increases specified in the pension scheme rules or required by law will be taken into account in the actuarial assumptions. The cost will, therefore, be charged over the service lives of the employees. Any divergence between the assumptions and experience will be accounted for as an element of any overall experience deficiency or surplus. 34

Other increases are, at least in form, discretionary at the time they are awarded, whether they are paid through the scheme or directly by the employer. Discretionary increases may be granted on the basis that the rules require there to be an annual review or because the employer has announced an intention to grant increases but no previous commitment has been made. The preferred treatment is for such increases, where they are likely to be granted on a regular basis, to be allowed for in the actuarial assumptions. They will then be recognised as part of the pension cost over the working lives of the beneficiaries. 35

Once an increase has been awarded it is very unlikely that it will be withdrawn and so it should be regarded thereafter as part of the employer's commitments. Accordingly, this 36

STATEMENT OF STANDARD ACCOUNTING PRACTICE

Statement provides that, if provision has not been made for the increase in the actuarial assumptions, the capitalised amount of the increase should be provided for in the period in which it is granted to the extent that it is not covered by a surplus.

37 Where a non-recurring ('one-off') increase is granted which applies to the current period but will not affect pensions paid in future periods, it should be treated as purely *ex gratia* and its cost should be charged in the period in which it is granted to the extent that it is not covered by a surplus.

38 Employers may occasionally grant *ex gratia* pensions to employees at the time of their retirement. An example would be a pension granted to a long-serving employee who for some reason had not been a member of the company's scheme and for whom the company decided to make provision. As with discretionary pension increases, the capital cost of any such *ex gratia* pensions should be charged in the period in which they are granted to the extent that they are not covered by a surplus.

Hybrid schemes

39 A few schemes are hybrid in nature combining features of defined contribution and defined benefit schemes. In such instances the rules or trust deed should be carefully studied and the operation of the scheme in practice, or its proposed method of operation, taken into account when determining the appropriate accounting treatment. The accounting treatment adopted should be in accordance with the underlying substance of the scheme.

Discounting

40 By their nature actuarial valuations make allowance for interest so that future cash flows are discounted to their present value. Financial statements, however, normally include items at their face value without discounting them. The question of whether items should be discounted in financial statements is a general one and this Statement does not attempt to establish standard practice. Interest effects arising from short-term timing differences between the payment of contributions and the recognition of cost are not likely to be material and can be ignored. If the difference is long-term, the situation becomes akin to that arising in respect of an unfunded scheme. If a scheme is unfunded the provision for pension costs is assessed and reviewed on a discounted basis and adjusted each year by an amount comprising two elements: a charge for the year (equivalent to a contribution in a funded scheme) and interest on the unfunded liability.

Foreign schemes

41 In principle, the pension costs charged in respect of all pension schemes included in group accounts should conform to the accounting objective and a consolidation adjustment should be made where the cost charged in the individual accounts of a group company does not do so.

42 No adjustment would normally be necessary in respect of UK and Irish schemes as the pension cost in the individual company accounts should already conform to the requirements of this Statement. On the other hand, in the case of foreign schemes, the commitment of the employer regarding the provision of pensions may be very different from that which

is customary in the United Kingdom and Ireland so that it would be inappropriate to adjust the pension cost charged. In some cases, for example, the employer's obligation may be discharged by prescribed payments under a nationwide or industry-wide scheme with characteristics similar to those of the State scheme in the United Kingdom. In such cases charging the contributions payable will satisfy the requirements of this Statement.

In other instances the nature of the employer's commitment may be similar to that in the UK and Ireland and the different determination of the pension cost charge may be caused solely by different accounting policies. An adjustment to the charge would then be appropriate although it is recognised that it may sometimes be impractical to make such an adjustment because of the difficulties and cost of obtaining compatible actuarial valuations in order to be able to recalculate the pension charge in accordance with the full provisions of this Statement. In such circumstances while an adjustment to the charge is not mandatory it is encouraged and suitable disclosure should be made. 43

Deferred taxation

For many enterprises the pension cost charge for the period has in the past been equal to the contributions payable. Under the requirements of this Statement the charge in the financial statements could be different from the contributions payable if, for example, a deficiency on valuation is being spread forward in the financial statements over the estimated remaining service lives of current employees although an additional lump-sum payment has been paid into the pension fund. Since taxation relief is generally granted in respect of payments made to the pension fund, accounting for pension costs in the manner prescribed by this Statement may have deferred tax implications. Where these occur they should be accounted for in accordance with SSAP 15 (Revised) 'Accounting for Deferred Tax'. 44

Disclosures

Sufficient information should be disclosed to give the user of the financial statements a proper understanding of the impact of the pension arrangements on the group's and/or the company's financial statements. 45

For a defined contribution scheme it will usually suffice to indicate the nature of the scheme and the amounts included in the profit and loss account and balance sheet. 46

For a defined benefit scheme more extensive disclosures are needed because of the greater and more uncertain obligations of the employer. Disclosures required include the accounting policy, the actuarial valuation method and major actuarial assumptions adopted, the cost charged, with explanations of it, and certain actuarial valuation information. In view of the significant long-term variable commitment of the employer, the disclosures should not only relate to the amounts in the financial statements for the periods presented but should also give an indication of significant changes in future costs that are expected under the actuarial assumptions and method used. Examples of how a small company and a large group may satisfy the disclosure requirements are given in Appendix 1. 47

As explained in paragraph 14, the effect of aiming for a level contribution rate varies according to the actuarial method used and the assumption made regarding new entrants. It is therefore necessary to disclose what assumption has been made in this regard unless it is immediately apparent from the disclosure of the actuarial method used. 48

STATEMENT OF STANDARD ACCOUNTING PRACTICE

49 This Statement requires the disclosure of an outline of the results of the most recent formal actuarial valuation or later review of the pension scheme on an ongoing basis. Specific disclosures to be made include the market value of scheme assets at the date of their valuation or review and the level of funding expressed in percentage terms. In certain instances it may be necessary to provide further information in order that details on the level of funding may be seen in their proper context. The level of funding and/or market values of scheme assets at the date of valuation or review may, for example, have subsequently changed markedly as a result of changes in general stock market values or in the level of contributions paid into the pension scheme. In particular, it should be considered whether the figures disclosed relating to the last valuation or review need to be amplified by a discussion of changes that have occurred since that date.

50 Disclosure is also required of changes in the group and/or company's pension scheme arrangements where these have had, or will have, a material effect on the future cost of providing pensions.

51 Where a company or group has more than one scheme it will often be necessary to give information on a combined basis in order to keep the volume of disclosures within reasonable limits. However, it is important that the combined figures should provide a proper understanding of the impact of the pension arrangements on the group's and/or company's financial position.

Group schemes

52 It is quite common for a number of companies within the same group to contribute to a single group scheme. With such schemes it is normally accepted that the same contribution rate, expressed as a percentage of payroll, should apply to the different member companies even though, if calculated on an individual company basis, the rate payable may vary between the employers within a group. This Statement permits the use of a common group rate for contributions payable by sponsoring employers. If a group scheme is in operation it may not be possible to estimate the pension obligations for which a particular group company is responsible and it would not be meaningful to provide information relating to the group as a whole in the subsidiary's financial statements. Provision is therefore made for reduced disclosure in the financial statements of subsidiary companies that are members of group schemes. The full details relating to the pension scheme should be disclosed in the financial statements of the holding company.

Transitional provisions

53 When, on implementing this Statement for the first time, a cumulative adjustment arises in respect of prior years, this may either be dealt with in accordance with the other provisions of this Statement or accounted for in accordance with the provisions of SSAP 6 (Revised) 'Extraordinary items and prior year adjustments'. That is, the cumulative adjustment may, except as discussed below, be spread over the expected remaining service lives of current employees in the scheme or accounted for as a prior year adjustment. To the extent that the adjustment relates to a variation from regular cost that, in accordance with the provisions of paragraphs 81 and 82, would not be eligible to be spread over the remaining service lives it should be accounted for as a prior year item. (An example of such an adjustment would be one arising from a significant reduction in the number of employees

covered by a company's pension scheme arrangements.) Similar considerations may also arise in respect of paragraphs 84 and 85 which deal with discretionary and *ex gratia* pension increases and *ex gratia* pensions. The cumulative adjustment should be calculated, as at the beginning of the accounting period in which this Statement is first applied, as the actuarial value of the surplus or deficiency on an ongoing basis as adjusted by any existing provision for unfunded pension costs or any existing pensions prepayment. In order that enterprises do not have to undertake a special valuation exercise for the purposes of implementing this Statement, they may base the calculation of the cumulative adjustment on the results of the last actuarial valuation so long as it was carried out on a basis broadly consistent with the requirements of this Statement. In arriving at the adjustment any surplus or deficiency at the last valuation date should be adjusted to take account of any additional payments or reduced contributions made since that date as a consequence of it. It may also be necessary to make allowance for major changes affecting the pension scheme since the last valuation.

The Republic of Ireland

The Republic of Ireland, unlike the United Kingdom, currently does not have any legislative requirement for defined benefit pension schemes to be actuarially assessed and the actuarial profession's involvement with pension schemes has tended to be less than in the United Kingdom. Legislation is to be introduced based on the recommendations contained in the First Report of the National Pensions Board but the first actuarial valuation for a number of schemes will not take place until the beginning of the next decade. Accordingly, the provisions of paragraphs 77, 79 to 85 and 88(g) and 88(h) will not be mandatory for non-quoted companies registered in the Republic of Ireland in respect of the financial statements of periods commencing before 1 January 1993. Such companies are, however, encouraged to comply with the full requirements of this Statement as soon as possible. 54

The full requirements of this Statement will apply to companies registered in the Republic of Ireland and quoted on the International Stock Exchange of the United Kingdom and the Republic of Ireland Limited from the same date as it applies to companies registered in the United Kingdom. 55

Part 2 – Definitions

Accrued benefits are the benefits for service up to a given point in time, whether the rights to the benefits are vested or not. They may be calculated in relation to current earnings or projected final earnings. 56

An *accrued benefits method* of actuarial valuation is a valuation method in which the actuarial value of liabilities relates at a given date to: 57

(a) the benefits, including future increases promised by the rules, for the current and deferred pensioners and their dependants; and

(b) the benefits which the members assumed to be in service on the given date will receive for service up to that date only.

STATEMENT OF STANDARD ACCOUNTING PRACTICE

Allowance may be made for expected increases in earnings after the given date, and/or for additional pension increases not promised by the rules. The given date may be a current or future date. The further into the future the adopted date lies, the closer the results will be to those of a prospective benefits valuation method.

58 The *average remaining service life* is a weighted average of the expected future service of the current members of the scheme up to their normal retirement dates or expected dates of earlier withdrawal or death in service. The weightings can have regard to periods of service, salary levels of scheme members and future anticipated salary growth in a manner which the actuary considers appropriate having regard to the actuarial method and assumptions used.

59 A *current funding level valuation* considers whether the assets would have been sufficient at the valuation date to cover liabilities arising in respect of pensions in payment, preserved benefits for members whose pensionable service has ceased and accrued benefits for members in pensionable service, based on pensionable service to and pensionable earnings at, the date of valuation including revaluation on the statutory basis or such higher basis as has been promised.

60 An *ex gratia pension* or *discretionary or ex gratia increase* in a pension is one which the employer has no legal, contractual or implied commitment to provide.

61 A *defined benefit scheme* is a pension scheme in which the rules specify the benefits to be paid and the scheme is financed accordingly.

62 A *defined contribution scheme* is a pension scheme in which the benefits are directly determined by the value of contributions paid in respect of each member. Normally the rate of contribution is specified in the rules of the scheme.

63 An *experience surplus or deficiency* is that part of the excess or deficiency of the actuarial value of assets over the actuarial value of liabilities, on the basis of the valuation method used, which arises because events have not coincided with the actuarial assumptions made for the last valuation.

64 A *funding plan* is the timing of payments in an orderly fashion to meet the future cost of a given set of benefits.

65 A *funded scheme* is a pension scheme where the future liabilities for benefits are provided for by the accumulation of assets held externally to the employing company's business.

66 The *level of funding* is the proportion at a given date of the actuarial value of liabilities for pensioners' and deferred pensioners' benefits and for members' accrued benefits that is covered by the actuarial value of assets. For this purpose the actuarial value of future contributions is excluded from the value of assets.

67 An *ongoing actuarial valuation* is a valuation in which it is assumed that the pension scheme will continue in existence and (where appropriate) that new members will be admitted. The liabilities allow for expected increases in earnings.

Past service is used in this Statement to denote service before a given date. It is often used, however, to denote service before entry into the pension scheme. 68

Pensionable payroll/earnings are the earnings on which benefits and/or contributions are calculated. One or more elements of earnings (eg overtime) may be excluded, and/or there may be a reduction to take account of all or part of the state scheme benefits which the member is deemed to receive. 69

A *pension scheme* is an arrangement (other than accident insurance) to provide pension and/or other benefits for members on leaving service or retiring and, after a member's death, for his/her dependants. 70

A *prospective benefits method* of valuation is a valuation method in which the actuarial value of liabilities relates to: 71

(a) the benefits for current and deferred pensioners and their dependants, allowing where appropriate for future pension increases; and

(b) the benefits that active members will receive in respect of both past and future service, allowing for future increases in earnings up to their assumed exit dates, and where appropriate for pension increases thereafter.

Regular cost is the consistent ongoing cost recognised under the actuarial method used. 72

Part 3 – Standard accounting practice

Scope

This Statement applies where the employer has a legal or contractual commitment under a pension scheme or one implicit in the employer's actions, to provide, or contribute to, pensions for his employees. It also addresses discretionary and *ex gratia* increases in pensions and *ex gratia* pensions. The same principles apply irrespective of whether the scheme is funded or unfunded. 73

This Statement applies to defined contribution schemes and defined benefit schemes. 74

Although this Statement primarily addresses pensions, its principles may be equally applicable to the cost of providing other post-retirement benefits. 75

This Statement does not apply to either state social security contributions or redundancy payments. 76

Pension cost

The accounting objective is that the employer should recognise the expected cost of providing pensions on a systematic and rational basis over the period during which he derives benefit from the employees' services. The ways in which this is to be achieved are detailed in paragraphs 78 to 92. 77

STATEMENT OF STANDARD ACCOUNTING PRACTICE

Defined contribution schemes

78 For defined contribution schemes the charge against profits should be the amount of contributions payable to the pension scheme in respect of the accounting period.

Defined benefit schemes

79 For defined benefit schemes the pension cost should be calulated using actuarial valuation methods which are consistent with the requirements of this Statement. The actuarial assumptions and method, taken as a whole, should be compatible and should lead to the actuary's best estimate of the cost of providing the pension benefits promised. The method of providing for expected pension costs over the service lives of employees in the scheme should be such that the regular pension cost is a substantially level percentage of the current and expected future pensionable payroll in the light of the current actuarial assumptions.

80 Subject to the provisions of paragraphs 81 to 83, variations from the regular cost should be allocated over the expected remaining service lives of current employees in the scheme. A period representing the average remaining service lives may be used if desired.

81 The provisions of paragraph 80 should not be applied where, and to the extent that, a significant change in the normal level of contributions occurs because contributions are adjusted to eliminate a surplus or deficiency resulting from a significant reduction in the number of employees covered by the enterprise's pension arrangements. Except where such treatment would be inconsistent with SSAP 6 in relation to an extraordinary item, any reduction in contributions arising in these circumstances should be recognised as it occurs. Amounts receivable may not be anticipated; for example, the full effect of a contribution holiday should not be recognised at the outset of the holiday, but rather spread over its duration.

82 In strictly limited circumstances prudence may require that a material deficit be recognised over a period shorter than the expected remaining service lives of current employees in the scheme. Such circumstances are limited to those where a major event or transaction has occurred which has not been allowed for in the actuarial assumptions, is outside the normal scope of those assumptions and has necessitated the payment of significant additional contributions to the pension scheme.

83 Where a refund that is subject to deduction of tax in accordance with the provisions of the UK Finance Act 1986, or equivalent legislation, is made to the employer, the enterprise may depart from the requirements of paragraph 80 and account for the surplus or deficiency in the period in which the refund occurs.

***Ex gratia* pensions and discretionary and *ex gratia* pension increases**

84 Where *ex gratia* pensions are granted the capital cost, to the extent not covered by a surplus, should be recognised in the profit and loss account in the accounting period in which they are granted.

85 Where allowance for discretionary or *ex gratia* increases in pensions is not made in the actuarial assumptions, the capital cost of such increases should, to the extent not covered by a surplus, be recognised in the profit and loss account in the accounting period in which they are initially granted.

ACCOUNTING FOR PENSION COSTS

Balance sheet

If the cumulative pension cost recognised in the profit and loss account has not been completely discharged by payment of contributions or directly paid pensions, the excess should be shown as a net pension provision. Similarly, any excess of contributions paid or directly paid pensions over the cumulative pension cost should be shown as a prepayment. 86

Disclosures

The following disclosures should be made in respect of a defined contribution scheme: 87

(a) the nature of the scheme (ie defined contribution);

(b) the accounting policy;

(c) the pension cost charge for the period;

(d) any outstanding or prepaid contributions at the balance sheet date.

The following disclosures should be made in respect of a defined benefit scheme: 88

(a) the nature of the scheme (ie defined benefit);

(b) whether it is funded or unfunded;

(c) the accounting policy and, if different, the funding policy;

(d) whether the pension cost and provision (or asset) are assessed in accordance with the advice of a professionally qualified actuary and, if so, the date of the most recent formal actuarial valuation or later formal review used for this purpose. If the actuary is an employee or officer of the reporting company, or of the group of which it is a member, this fact should be disclosed;

(e) the pension cost charge for the period together with explanations of significant changes in the charge compared to that in the previous accounting period;

(f) any provisions or prepayments in the balance sheet resulting from a difference between the amounts recognised as cost and the amounts funded or paid directly;

(g) the amount of any deficiency on a current funding level basis, indicating the action, if any, being taken to deal with it in the current and future accounting periods;

(h) an outline of the results of the most recent formal actuarial valuation or later formal review of the scheme on an ongoing basis.

This should include disclosure of:

(i) the actuarial method used and a brief description of the main actuarial assumptions;

(ii) the market value of scheme assets at the date of their valuation or review;

(iii) the level of funding expressed in percentage terms;

(iv) comments on any material actuarial surplus or deficiency indicated by (iii) above;

(i) any commitment to make additional payments over a limited number of years;

(j) the accounting treatment adopted in respect of a refund made in accordance with the provisions of paragraph 83 where a credit appears in the financial statements in relation to it;

(k) details of the expected effects on future costs of any material changes in the group's and/or company's pension arrangements.

STATEMENT OF STANDARD ACCOUNTING PRACTICE

89 Where a company or group has more than one pension scheme disclosure should be made on a combined basis, unless disclosure of information about individual schemes is necessary for a proper understanding of the accounts. For the purposes of paragraph 88(g) above, however, a current funding level basis deficiency in one scheme should not be set off against a surplus in another.

Group schemes

90 A subsidiary company which is a member of a group scheme should disclose this fact in its financial statements and disclose the nature of the group scheme indicating, where appropriate, that the contributions are based on pension costs across the group as a whole. Such a company is exempt from the disclosure requirements of paragraph 88(g) and (h) and should instead state the name of the holding company in whose financial statements particulars of the actuarial valuation of the group scheme are contained. This exemption only applies if the holding company is registered in the United Kingdom or the Republic of Ireland.

Foreign schemes

91 Where, in respect of foreign operations, the employer has an obligation to provide pensions, the pension charge should reflect that obligation and, therefore, be dealt with in accordance with the requirements of this Statement. An adjustment on consolidation will be necessary where the charge is not already calculated in accordance with the basis set out in this Statement, unless the nature of the employer's commitment is very different from that which is customary in the United Kingdom and Ireland. It is recognised, however, that in some cases it may be impractical to make the adjustment because of the difficulties and cost of obtaining the necessary actuarial information. In such cases, the amount charged to the profit and loss account and the basis of the charge should, as a minimum, be disclosed in the consolidated financial statements.

Transitional provisions

92 When, on implementing this Statement for the first time, a cumulative adjustment arises in respect of prior years this may either be dealt with in accordance with the other provisions of this Statement or accounted for in accordance with the provisions of SSAP 6 (Revised) 'Extraordinary items and prior year adjustments'. The way in which the transitional provisions have been applied should be disclosed in the financial statements for the period in which this Statement is first implemented.

Date from which effective

93 The accounting and disclosure requirements set out in this Statement should be adopted as soon as possible and, except in the case of certain companies registered in the Republic of Ireland as provided in paragraph 94, regarded as standard in respect of financial statements relating to accounting periods beginning on or after 1 July 1988.

94 In the case of companies that are registered in the Republic of Ireland and not quoted on the International Stock Exchange of the United Kingdom and Ireland paragraphs 77, 79 to 85 and 88(g) and 88(h) should be adopted as soon as possible and regarded as

standard in respect of financial statements relating to accounting periods beginning on or after 1 January 1993. The remainder of the required accounting practices and disclosures should be regarded as standard in respect of financial statements relating to accounting periods beginning on or after 1 July 1988. A cumulative adjustment that arises in respect of paragraph 84 on *ex gratia* pensions may either be dealt with in accordance with SSAP 6 (Revised) or allocated over the expected remaining service lives of current employees in the scheme.

Part 4 – Legal requirements in Great Britain and Northern Ireland

References are to the Companies Act 1985 and the Companies (Northern Ireland) Order 1986.

Paragraph 50(4) of Schedule 4 requires a company to give details of any pension commitments provided for in the company's balance sheet and also of any such commitments for which no provision has been made. Particulars of pension commitments to past directors of the company must be disclosed separately. 95

Paragraph 50(6) of Schedule 4 requires that disclosure under paragraph 50(4) should separately include details of commitments undertaken on behalf of, or for the benefit of, any holding company or fellow subsidiary of the company and any subsidiary of the company. 96

Paragraph 56(4) of Schedule 4 requires companies to disclose the total pension costs incurred in the year on behalf of all employees of the company, together with separate disclosure of social security costs incurred on their behalf. 97

By virtue of paragraphs 61 and 68 of Schedule 4, the above requirements also apply to group accounts. 98

Banking, insurance and shipping companies are exempt from the above requirements of Schedule 4. 99

Paragraph 28 of Schedule 5 requires companies to disclose the total amount of pension paid to directors or past directors, other than pensions funded substantially through a pension scheme. If they are so funded, the amount disclosed as emoluments has to include contributions to the scheme (paragraph 22). 100

Part 5 – Legal requirements in the Republic of Ireland

In this part references to companies legislation have been abbreviated as follows: 101

Companies Act 1963 — The 1963 Act

The Schedule to the Companies (Amendment) Act 1963 — The Schedule

STATEMENT OF STANDARD ACCOUNTING PRACTICE

102 Section 191 of the 1963 Act requires disclosure of the aggregate amount of directors' and past-directors' pensions, other than pensions under a scheme where contributions are substantially adequate for the maintenance of the scheme. The Section also requires disclosure of the aggregate amount of directors' emoluments; for the purpose of the Section emoluments include contributions paid in respect of directors to any pension scheme.

103 Paragraph 36(4) of the Schedule requires disclosure of any pension commitments included in the company's balance sheet and any such commitments for which no provision has been made. Where any such commitment relates wholly or partly to pensions payable to past directors of the company, separate particulars shall be given of that commitment so far as it relates to such pensions.

104 Information required to be disclosed under paragraph 36(5) of the Schedule is as follows:

(a) the nature of every pension scheme operated by or on behalf of the company including information as to whether or not each scheme is a defined benefit scheme or a defined contribution scheme;

(b) whether each such scheme is externally funded or internally financed;

(c) whether any pension costs and liabilities are assessed in accordance with the advice of a professionally qualified actuary and, if so, the date of the most recent relevant actuarial valuation;

(d) whether, and if so where, any such actuarial valuation is available for public inspection.

Part 6 – Compliance with International Accounting Standard No 19 'Accounting for Retirement Benefits in the Financial Statements of Employers'

105 Compliance with the requirements of this Statement will automatically ensure compliance with International Accounting Standard No 19 'Accounting for Retirement Benefits in the Financial Statements of Employers'.

ACCOUNTING FOR PENSION COSTS

Appendix 1

This appendix is for general guidance and does not form part of the statement of standard accounting practice.

Examples of disclosures

(a) *Defined contribution scheme*

The company operates a defined contribution pension scheme. The assets of the scheme are held separately from those of the company in an independently administered fund. The pension cost charge represents contributions payable by the company to the fund and amounted to £500,000 (1986 £450,000). Contributions totalling £25,000 (1986 £15,000) were payable to the fund at the year-end and are included in creditors.

(b) *Defined benefit scheme*

(i) Small company

The company operates a pension scheme providing benefits based on final pensionable pay. The assets of the scheme are held separately from those of the company, being invested with insurance companies. Contributions to the scheme are charged to the profit and loss account so as to spread the cost of pensions over employees' working lives with the company. The contributions are determined by a qualified actuary on the basis of triennial valuations using the projected unit method*. The most recent valuation was as at 31 December 1987. The assumptions which have the most significant effect on the results of the valuation are those relating to the rate of return on investments and the rates of increase in salaries and pensions. It was assumed that the investment returns would be 9% per annum, that salary increases would average 7% per annum and that present and future pensions would increase at the rate of 4% per annum.

The pension charge for the period was £50,000 (1986 £48,000). This included £5,200 (1986 £5,000) in respect of the amortisation of experience surpluses that are being recognised over 10 years, the average remaining service lives of employees.

The most recent actuarial valuation showed that the market value of the scheme's assets was £1,200,000 and that the actuarial value of those assets represented 104% of the benefits that had accrued to members, after allowing for expected future increases in earnings. The contributions of the company and employees will remain at 11% and 5% of earnings respectively.

(ii) Large group

The group operates a number of pension schemes throughout the world. The major schemes, which cover 85% of scheme members, are of the defined benefit type. With the exception of the main scheme in Germany, the assets of the schemes are held in separate trustee administered funds.

The total pension cost for the group was £2,050,000 (1986 £1,585,000) of which £300,000 (1986 £285,000) relates to the overseas schemes. The pension cost relating to the UK schemes is assessed in accordance with the advice of a qualified actuary

STATEMENT OF STANDARD ACCOUNTING PRACTICE

using the attained age method*. The latest actuarial assessment of those schemes was as at 31 December 1985. The assumptions which have the most significant effect on the results of the valuation are those relating to the rate of return on investments and the rates of increase in salaries and pensions. It was assumed that the investment return would be 9% per annum, that salary increases would average 7% per annum and that present and future pensions would increase at the rate of 4% per annum. The cost has risen significantly as a result of the acquisition of ABC Limited at the beginning of the period and the resultant increase in group scheme members. Of the total cost, £350,000 (1986 £300,000) is attributable to amortisation of past service liabilities that are being written off over a ten-year period ending in 1988.

At the date of the latest actuarial valuation, the market value of the assets of the UK scheme was £32.1m and the actuarial value of the assets was sufficient to cover 85% of the benefits that had accrued to members, after allowing for expected future increases in earnings. This deficiency should be eliminated by 1991 at the current employer's contribution rate of 12% of pensionable earnings.

The element of the total pension cost relating to foreign schemes includes £280,000 (1986 £250,000) where the charge has been determined in accordance with local best practice and regulations in the Federal Republic of Germany.

A provision of £5,500,000 (1984, £5,000,000) is included in creditors, this being the excess of the accumulated pension cost over the amount funded. The major part of this provision relates to the unfunded German scheme.

*** These and other actuarial funding methods are described in 'Pension Fund Terminology: specimen descriptions of commonly used valuation methods' issued by the Institute and Faculty of Actuaries.**

Appendix B

APC practice note

PRACTICE NOTE 2

ACCOUNTING FOR PENSION COSTS UNDER SSAP 24
LIAISON BETWEEN THE ACTUARY AND THE AUDITOR

Guidance note issued in June 1990 in respect of communications between actuaries and auditors in response to SSAP 24.

CONTENTS

This Practice Note is issued by the Auditing Practices Committee of CCAB Limited, whose members are:

The Institute of Chartered Accountants in England and Wales
The Institute of Chartered Accountants of Scotland
The Institute of Chartered Accountants in Ireland
The Chartered Association of Certified Accountants
The Chartered Institute of Management Accountants
The Chartered Institute of Public Finance and Accountancy

Practice Notes are intended to provide guidance and information to assist auditors. They do not require the approval of the Councils of the members of CCAB Limited, and they do not have the same authority as either Auditing Standards or Auditing Guidelines.

ACCOUNTING FOR PENSION COSTS UNDER SSAP 24
LIAISON BETWEEN THE ACTUARY AND THE AUDITOR

This Practice Note has been prepared after full consultation with the Councils of the Institute of Actuaries and the Faculty of Actuaries in Scotland.

Introduction

1 SSAP 24, Accounting for Pension Costs, issued in May 1988 deals with the accounting treatment of pension costs* in companies' financial statements. For many companies with defined benefit schemes this will have the effect of companies changing their accounting policy from accounting simply on the basis of charging the contributions payable by the company in each accounting period to that of recognising the cost of providing a pension for an employee over the period that the employer benefits from an employee's services, in accordance with the accruals concept.

2. The purpose of this Practice Note is to explain the responsibilities of the auditor of a company in respect of the pension costs in the financial statements of the company and consequently his relationship with the actuary to the company's pension scheme. It is only applicable in respect of companies with defined benefit pension schemes. It is not intended to explain the responsibilities of the auditor of a pension scheme. The Auditing Guideline, 'Pension schemes', should be consulted for guidance on this. Many of the principles described in this Practice Note, however, will also apply to the relationship between the pension scheme auditor and actuary.

3 SSAP 24 gives guidance on the basis for determining the costs of pension arrangements and appropriate disclosures in a company's financial statements. The ASC has stated, however, in TR 756, that paragraph 75 of that standard is intended to suggest to companies how they might account for post-retirement benefits other than pensions, in the absence of an accounting standard. If companies do follow paragraph 75 of SSAP 24 and they do use actuaries to help them implement that paragraph, it would be appropriate for auditors to follow procedures analogous to those set out in this Practice Note when liaising with those actuaries.

4 This Practice Note outlines the procedures an auditor should normally follow and the questions auditors should consider asking actuaries in order to audit pension costs. It supplements the general guidance given in the Auditing Guideline, 'Reliance on other specialists'. Whether it will be necessary to carry out all the procedures mentioned in this Practice Note will depend on the materiality of pension costs in the company's financial statements.

---

* In this Practice Note, 'pension costs' is used to refer to pension costs, liabilities, assets, commitments and relevant disclosures in the financial statements.

Directors' Responsibilities

5 Under the Companies Act 1985, the responsibility for preparing the financial statements, including the implementation of an appropriate accounting policy for pension costs, is that of the directors of the company.

6 For defined contribution schemes, the pension cost is the amount of contributions payable in respect of the accounting period. For defined benefit schemes, SSAP 24 paragraphs 18 and 19 require that:

> 'the actuarial valuation method and assumptions used for accounting purposes should satisfy the accounting objective. In order that full provision may be made over the employees' service lives for the expected costs of their pensions, the effect of expected future increases in earnings, including merit increases, up to the assumed retirement date or earlier date of withdrawal or death in service, should be recognised. Account will also need to be taken of expected future increases in deferred pensions and pensions in payment where the employer has an express or implied commitment to grant such increases. The calculation of benefit levels should be based on the situation most likely to be experienced and not on a contingent event not likely to occur. The actuarial method selected should be used consistently and should be disclosed. If there is a change of method this fact should be disclosed and the effect quantified. The actuarial assumptions and the actuarial method taken as a whole should be compatible and should lead to the actuary's best estimate of the cost of providing the pension benefits promised.
>
> If the funding plan does not provide a satisfactory basis for determining the pension cost charge, separate actuarial calculations will be required.'

Auditor's Responsibilities

7 The auditor's operational standard states that:

> 'The auditor should obtain relevant and reliable audit evidence sufficient to enable him to draw reasonable conclusions therefrom'.

The Auditing Guideline, 'Reliance on other specialists', provides guidance on the principles to be followed by the auditor when he wishes to place reliance on audit evidence provided by other specialists. In the case of pension costs stated in a company's financial statements this involves an auditor relying on the opinion of the actuary to the company's pension scheme. This reliance will be achieved by the auditor evaluating audit evidence provided by the specialist to determine whether it is sufficient, relevant and reliable enough for him to draw reasonable conclusions from it.

8 For defined contribution schemes, the pension cost can be verified without involving an actuary.

Objectives

Actuaries

9 An actuary can value defined benefit pension schemes for a number of reasons such as:

a) estimating the extent to which benefits are covered by existing assets;

b) estimating the future cost of the scheme and contributions to the scheme (i.e. determining the future contribution rate); or

c) distributing the fund's assets on a break-up of the trust.

10 The methods used by an actuary will vary according to the reasons for which the valuation is carried out, the professional judgement of the actuary and the client's instructions e.g. regarding the level of funding acceptable within actuarial parameters. When carrying out a valuation for SSAP 24 purposes, however, SSAP 24 requires that the actuarial assumptions and methods taken as a whole should be compatible and should lead to the actuary's best estimate of the cost of providing the pension benefits promised. The actuary may be able to assure the auditor that a valuation carried out for some other purpose is also suitable for SSAP 24.

Auditors

11 The auditor has to be satisfied that the company's pension costs have been dealt with in accordance with SSAP 24. The starting point for the auditor's work will often be to obtain, in conjunction with the actuary, an understanding of the actuarial valuation of the scheme and the annual contributions paid to to it, and to establish whether they are suitable for the purposes of SSAP 24.

12 To meet this objective the auditor will wish to establish whether:

a) The expected cost of providing pensions is recognised on a systematic and rational basis over the period during which the company derives benefit from the employees' services;

b) The effects of any material changes of accounting policy and in the basis of the actuarial valuation i.e. the actuary's methods and assumptions have been disclosed and incorporated in the financial statements;

c) Events giving rise to exceptional or extraordinary items affecting pension costs have been identified and their effects incorporated in the financial statements as appropriate. These might include acquisitions and disposals of business segments, redundancy or early retirement programmes and branch closures;

d) The effect of changes in the pension benefits promised by the company have been identified by management and incorporated in the financial statements as appropriate;

e) The expected average remaining service lives of employees have been identified, so that the period of amortisation of variations can be determined; and

f) The accounting for and disclosure of any surplus or deficit identified by the latest actuarial valuation has been dealt with in a manner which meets the requirements of SSAP 24.

13 To fulfil the above objectives an auditor will often need to liaise with the pension scheme's actuary to ensure that he obtains the requisite information from him.

Procedures

14 The degree of detail of the auditor's work will depend on the materiality of pension costs to the financial statements of the company. The following points should be considered when the auditor plans his work.

a) The auditor should encourage the company to include liaison with the actuary in its financial statements preparation timetable and to obtain the actuary's agreement to this. In the past actuarial work may not have needed to be completed at the same time as the preparation and audit of a company's annual financial statements.

b) Any contact between the auditor and the actuary to the pension scheme should be made with the knowledge and consent of their mutual client(s).

c) Actuarial valuations of pension schemes will probably not take place every year. An auditor, however, is required to give an opinion on the financial statements prepared by management every year, and so should consider contacting the actuary annually, especially if the circumstances warrant this, for example when there has been a substantial increase or decrease in the number of employees.

d) The judgements and the actuary's calculations required to calculate pension costs are complex and time consuming. It will usually be appropriate, therefore, with management's consent, for initial discussions between the auditor and the actuary to take place well in advance of the year end, as the financial statements may be subject to a tight deadline. The responsibility for initiating discussions lies with the auditor but the actuary may initiate these discussions. It also may be appropriate for discussions to take place at any time before signing the audit report, if circumstances indicate that such discussions would be useful.

e) The auditor should consider the overall pension commitments of the company, not only those which are provided through a pension scheme. For example, there may be *ex gratia* payments to former employees or their dependants which are made direct from company funds. He may, therefore, ask questions which go beyond the normal scope of the actuary's work for his client. The approach to asking and answering these questions and the arrangements for meeting associated professional fees, if any, should be agreed between the client, the auditor and the actuary in advance of the work being carried out.

f) The principles and objectives of pension cost accounting (i.e. to show a true and fair view in financial statements) might be different from the principles and objectives of calculating a contribution rate for funding purposes. (e.g. to comply with legal requirements, in statute or contract, for a particular level of funding or to achieve a pattern of funding consistent with the employer's cash flow requirements). Management will normally have liaised with the actuary during the preparation of the financial statements. To ensure, however, he has sufficient background information to enable him to form a view on these matters, the auditor also will need to ask questions to establish whether or not the actuary's methods and assumptions are appropriate to the calculation of pension costs for the annual financial statements. He should also establish whether the data supplied to the actuary by management is consistent with that used in preparing the financial statements and, if it is not, what the effects are. It would not be usual to question the methods and assumptions used by the actuary to calculate a contribution rate for funding *per se*.

g) Sometimes one actuary will be employed to advise the trustees of the pension fund and another actuary will be employed to advise the management of the employing company. In these circumstances, the auditor should approach the actuary advising the management, in the first instance.

15 The sequence of events in the audit of pension costs could be as follows:

a) Initial contact should be made with the actuary after having obtained the consent of the client.

b) The auditor should obtain from the client a copy of the most recent actuarial valuation, for SSAP 24 purposes, and review relevant correspondence which concerns the client's pension costs, between the client and the actuary, the solicitors and the trustees of any pension fund, the OPB and the Inland Revenue and details of any changes to the company's pension arrangements. He should also, by discussion with management and review of minutes of the board and any relevant committees, establish whether any events with major pension implications have happened or are expected to happen. Such events might include acquisitions and disposals of business segments, redundancy or early retirement programmes, branch closures and revision of pension benefits.

c) If necessary, the auditor and the actuary should arrange a meeting which client personnel would normally attend. An agenda for this meeting should be agreed in advance to enable any necessary preparatory work to be carried out. The points covered should normally include those set out in paragraph 16 below.

d) Notes of the meeting should be prepared and exchanged and arrangements for any further work should be agreed.

e) Any additional work requested or required should be agreed with the client.

f) Before completing the audit the auditor should contact the actuary to establish whether there have been any changes in circumstances. This would form part of his post balance sheet events review.

g) The auditor should obtain formal confirmation from management and trustees that to the best of their knowledge and belief all matters necessary to enable the actuary to assess pension costs have been disclosed to him.

h) The auditor should establish whether the company's proposed disclosure concerning pension costs complies with SSAP 24 and the relevant legislation.

i) As a matter of professional courtesy, the auditor should recommend to management that he obtains the actuary's agreement to the note concerning pension costs in the company's financial statements prior to publication.

16 **Examples of questions which the auditor may wish to ask the actuary**

The reason for asking the question is given in square brackets beneath it.

Notes: (1) *These examples are drawn up on the basis that the auditor has a copy of the actuary's latest valuation report prepared in accordance with Guidance Note 9 (GN9) 'Retirement Benefit Schemes - Actuarial Reports' published by the Institute and Faculty Actuaries. A copy of GN9 is attached for reference (see Appendix 1). An explanation of actuarial reports and how they are drawn up is given in the Audit Brief, 'The Work of a Pension Scheme Actuary'.*

(2) *References to 'the valuation report' should be read to include any written statement made by the actuary to the client company relevant to accounting for pension costs by that company.*

(3) *Management should have considered the matters referred to below when preparing the financial statements.*

(4) *Where the answers to the questions are unsatisfactory or indicate that the valuation does not recognise all costs required by SSAP 24, the auditor should discuss with the client whether to ask the actuary to conduct further work.*

(5) *It is only necessary to ask questions if they have not been dealt with satisfactorily in the actuary's written report(s).*

a) Where, in order to assess pension costs for accounting purposes, you have issued statements additional to your formal valuation of the pension fund prepared in accordance with GN9:

i) have these statements been prepared using valuation bases, methods and assumptions consistent with that formal valuation? If not, please explain the reasons for the differences.

ii) what was the reason for the statements being issued?

[Reason - to enable the auditor to establish whether all pension costs have been calculated on a common basis and, if not, whether there are valid reasons for the difference.]

b) What would be the effect on the valuation of taking account of legislative changes (if any) which have occurred since the date of the valuation?

[Reason - the financial statements should be prepared on the basis of a current estimate of pension costs.]

c) Can you confirm that the actuarial method and assumptions adopted for the most recent formal valuation satisfy the basic accounting objectives of SSAP 24 and provide within the parameters of SSAP 24 your best estimate of the cost of providing the pension benefits promised? In particular;

i) To what extent does the valuation method allow for the effect of expected future increases in earnings, including merit increases?

ii) What provisions (either explicit or implicit) have been made for future increases to deferred pensions or pensions in payment?

iii) How does the valuation method allow for new entrants?

[Reason - valuations prepared for funding purposes are often prepared on a prudent rather than a best estimate basis and the method and assumptions may be chosen to achieve a funding plan which meets the cash plans of a company rather than to achieve a true and fair view for accounting purposes. This question is designed to test whether the valuation prepared for funding purposes is also suitable for accounting purposes].

d) Please provide an outline of the latest formal review of the scheme covering in particular the following points from SSAP 24 paragraph 88(h):

i) the actuarial method used and a brief description of the main actuarial assumptions;

ii) the market value of the scheme assets at the date of their valuation or review;

iii) the level of funding expressed in percentage terms; and

iv) comments on any material actuarial surplus or deficiency indicated by (iii) above.

[Reason - to ensure sufficient information is available to meet the requirements of paragraph 88(h) of SSAP 24 and to enable the auditor to understand the background to those disclosures].

e) What are your recommendations for dealing with any material surplus or deficiency?

[Reason - to assist the auditor to establish whether paragraphs 80 - 85 and 88(h) of SSAP 24 have been complied with].

f) Can we ascertain the commonality of the data which you used for your latest formal valuation or review with the data used in the financial statements? Examples of such data are:

i) The investment holdings of the pension fund, their value and who holds them;

ii) The membership data at the time of the formal actuarial valuation;
[Note that the actuary may obtain the membership data for his valuation from a different source from that of the auditor.] and

iii) Contributions paid to the scheme over the relevant period on the basis recommended or agreed by you.

Note that it may be necessary for the auditor to contact the trustees and to liaise also with the auditor of the pension scheme to confirm the completeness and accuracy of relevant data. Some of such data may be found in the financial statements of the pension scheme.

[Reason - to enable the auditor to establish whether the data provided to the actuary is the same as that used to prepare the financial statements.]

g) Can you list any rule changes or major events (in pension terms),including changes in pension increase policy, that have occurred since the last valuation where the financial effects were allowed for in the valuation report? Are there any changes which were not allowed for and, if so, please quantify the financial effects?

[Reason - the financial statements should be prepared on the basis of a current estimate of pension costs.]

h) What is the cost of any past service benefit awards (including increases to pensions in payment and deferred pensions) made since the effective date of the last formal valuation for which no explicit allowance was made in the funding plan and how was this determined?

[Reason - the financial statements should be prepared on the basis of a current estimate of pension costs dealt with in accordance with SSAP 24.]

i) Is the basis proposed by the directors for providing for the pension contributions to be included in the disclosure of directors' emoluments appropriate?

[Reason - to assist the auditor to establish whether Schedule 5 of the Companies Act 1985 has been complied with].

j) Are there any other matters regarding the actuarial valuations of the company's pension arrangements in general of which the auditor should be aware?

[Reason - the auditor should form his opinion on the basis of all relevant available information].

APPENDIX 1

GUIDANCE NOTE GN9

RETIREMENT BENEFIT SCHEMES - ACTUARIAL REPORTS

[GN9 may be revised. This version was revised with effect from 1 April 1988. Members should ensure that they have an up to date version.]

1. INTRODUCTION

1.1 When a retirement benefit scheme is to be set up, and at intervals thereafter, an actuarial report should be prepared.

1.2 These guidelines apply to such reports, including those on valuations which are required under the Occupational Pension Schemes (Disclosure of Information) Regulations 1986 (SI 1986 No.1046) - as amended by the Occupational Pension Schemes (Disclosure of Information) (Amendment) Regulations 1986 (SI 1986 No.1717) - to which reference is made in this note.

1.3 These guidelines relate primarily to defined benefit schemes where the ultimate costs are initially unknown but the guidelines should also be followed as far as possible for other types of schemes.

1.4 The guidelines have been prepared with United Kingdom requirements and conditions in mind. Where a member is practising outside the United Kingdom and the Council of the Institute or the Faculty (as the case may be) has agreed, the guidelines may be replaced by guidance given by an actuarial body of the country in which the actuary practises.

2. PURPOSE OF THE GUIDELINES

2.1 The purpose of the guidelines is to ensure that reports contain sufficient information to enable the expected future course of a scheme's contribution rate and funding level to be appreciated.(See Regulation 8(1)(a).) It is not intended to restrict the actuary's freedom of judgment in choosing the method of valuation and the underlying assumptions.

2.2 Although any report will be addressed to the actuary's client, normally the employer or the trustees, the actuary needs to bear in mind that his advice may be made available to third parties who can reasonably be expected to rely on it. In connection with the actuarial reports required under the Regulations, these specify in paragraphs 8(10)-(12) the third parties to whom trustees must make reports available.

3. THE REPORT

3.1 The items in the following list are normally to be regarded as essential components of any report. Other information may often be desirable and suitable explanations of some features may be very important, for example, the effect on the funding level of an improvement in benefits with retroactive effect.

Basic Information

3.1.1 An opening statement showing to whom the report is addressed, the purpose for which the valuation is made and the dates as at which the current valuation and, if applicable, the immediately preceding valuation were conducted.

3.1.2 A statement of benefits which have been valued (for example, by a summary of the terms of the scheme or by reference to appropriate documents). Reference should be made to the extent to which allowance has been made for discretionary increases in benefit especially where there has been a recent practice of granting such increases.

3.1.3 A brief summary of the data on which the investigation is based including a description of the assets. If the actuary has any reservations as to the reliability of the data, such explanation or qualification as is appropriate should be given.

Inter-valuation Period

3.1.4 A statement of the rates of contribution payable during the inter-valuation period; and a commentary on any material developments during such period and on any significant variations in experience from the assumptions made at the previous valuation.

Funding Objectives

3.1.5 An explanation of the funding objectives and of the method being employed to achieve those objectives. The implications in terms of stability of contribution rates and of future funding levels should also be explained.

Valuation Assumptions and Method

3.1.6 A statement of the assumptions made in valuing both the liabilities and the assets and of the method employed in deriving the contribution rate in 3.1.8 below. Attention should be directed particularly to those assumptions to which the contribution is sensitive.

3.1.7 Comments on the compatibility of the basis of valuing the assets with that of valuing the liabilities. The actuary should also comment if it is considered that the investment policy is inappropriate to the form and incidence of the liabilities.

Contribution Rate

3.1.8 The contribution rate recommended to achieve the funding objectives. If such objectives imply a changing contribution rate (as a percentage of the relevant earnings), an indication as to the extent and timing of such change should be given.

Current Funding Levels

3.1.9 A statement as to whether or not, in the actuary's opinion, the assets would have been sufficient at the valuation date to cover liabilities arising (including any dependents' contingent benefits) in respect of pensions in payment, preserved benefits for members whose pensionable service has ceased and accrued benefits for members in pensionable service which will normally be related to pensionable service to, and pensionable earnings at, the date of valuation including revaluation on the statutory basis (or on such higher basis which has been promised). If there is any shortfall in the coverage, an indication of the degree of shortfall should be given having regard to the priorities attaching to various categories of benefits on winding-up.

3.1.10 A statement as to the on-going funding position if this is not otherwise conveyed by the comments on the funding objectives and the contribution rate.

General

3.1.11 A statement as to whether the valuation has been prepared in accordance with GN9 current at the date of signature of the valuation report (Regulation 8(1)(b)). Regulation 8(1)(c) states that any material departures from GN9 should be indicated. The actuary is however expected to comply with GN9 unless in exceptional circumstances he is convinced that full compliance would be inappropriate in which case he should give a complete explanation.

4. THE ACTUARIAL STATEMENT

4.1 This section relates to the Actuarial Statement required under Regulation 8(7) and Schedule 4 to the Regulations.

4.1.1. For the purpose of Section 1 of the Statement it should be assumed that the scheme is not discontinuing. Regulation 8(8)(b) describes how accrued rights and liabilities are to be calculated and valued for this purpose and these are stated to be the benefits to which the member would be entitled on leaving pensionable service. This statement may thus be less rigorous than the requirement in 3.1.9. If the actuary feels that there is likely to be misinterpretation of the expression 'liabilities' by members, he should feel free to include an explanation under Section 3 bearing in mind that the word 'liabilities' also appears in Section 2 in a rather different sense.

4.1.2. Section 2 of the Statement requires an opinion from the actuary on the adequacy of the resources of the scheme 'in the normal course of events', In interpreting this expression at the date of each statement the actuary should take a prudent view of the future without taking into account every conceivable unfavourable development.

The actuary should regard this as excluding the possibilities of events - including those external to the scheme - which he cannot reasonably be expected to have allowed for in a conservative approach to the matter. The certificate cannot say more than can be inferred from the actuarial valuation to which the statement relates. The actuary will not generally need to give a negative or qualified opinion provided that the contribution rate specified reflects that referred to in 3.1.8. above and provided that any statement under 3.1.10. does not indicate cause for concern. If a negative or qualified opinion is given, attention should be drawn to the relevant sections of the latest valuation report.

4.1.3. For the purpose of Section 3, use may be made of the specimen descriptions of commonly-used valuation methods in a note entitled Pension Fund Terminology and issued by the Institute and Faculty in May 1986. The actuary should endeavour to express the summary in language which is likely to be understood by the members. It is sufficient to describe the key funding assumptions; these are not necessarily limited to the financial assumptions. Members may be referred to the latest valuation report for fuller details, although such reference of itself does not satisfy the Regulations.

4.2. Regulation 8(7) refers to the inter-valuation period. This is not designed to require the actuary to monitor the situation continuously; however, if he is made aware or becomes aware of developments which materially affect the continuing validity of the latest Statement, then a revised Statement should be prepared and issued under Regulation 8(7).

Appendix C

Summary of Inland Revenue Limits on Occupational Pension Scheme Benefits

Defined benefits scheme – members joining before 17 March 1987

Member's pension	normally ⅔ x final remuneration including pension exchanged for lump sum.
Death after retirement pension	⅔ x the maximum pension which could have been provided to the member at retirement.
Normal pension age	a specified age within the range of 60 (males) or 55 (females) and 70. Lower ages may be possible subject to Inland Revenue approval
Lump sum at retirement	1½ x final remuneration at normal pension age, ie 3/80 final remuneration per year of service.

Accelerated accrual rate based on 'uplifted sixtieths' table

Member's pension	⅔ x final remuneration as a maximum pension available after 10 years service.

Accelerated accrual of lump sums based on 'uplifted eightieths' table

Death in service lump sum	4 x remuneration at date of death, plus employee's contributions (with interest).
Death in service pension	⅔ x the maximum potential pension which could have been provided for the member.
Early retirement pension	a proportion of the maximum permissible pension at normal pension age, based on the ratio of completed to potential service.
Lump sum at retirement	maximum lump sum available after 20 years' service.

Employee contributions (including any additional voluntary contributions) must not exceed 15% of remuneration.

The calculation of remuneration and final remuneration must meet certain requirements.

No commutation of new additional voluntary contribution arrangements within the scheme, if the employee had not entered into arrangements to pay additional voluntary contributions within the scheme before 8th April 1987.

Generally, limits must take account of retained benefits, other approved schemes of the employer and free-standing additional voluntary contributions.

Schemes may provide that these members be given the option to be treated for Inland Revenue limits purposes as if they had joined the scheme on or after 1st June 1989.

Differences applicable to members joining schemes existing before 14th March 1987 between 17th March 1989 and 31st May 1989 (inclusive)

Maximum pension available after 20 years' service.

Accelerated accrual rate is 1/30th of final remuneration up to 20 years' service

Accelerated accrual of lump sums above 3/80 ths must be in proportion to the pension enhancement above n/60 ths.

Lump sum at retirement	1 ½ x final remuneration, up to a maximum final remuneration of £100,000.

Maximum lump sum available after 20 years provided a ⅔ rds pension can be provided for the same period of service.

These members have the right to opt to be treated as if they joined the scheme on or after 1st June 1989.

Differences applicable to members joining a scheme established on or after 14th March 1989 or joining a scheme existing before that date on or after 1st June 1989

Earnings which may be pensionable are limited to £64,800 for the tax year 1990/91. This limit is increased each year in line with the Retail Prices Index, rounded up to the nearest £600. As a result of this cap, the following cash limits apply for 1990/91:

maximum pension of £43,200 pa;

maximum retirement lump sum of £97,200;

maximum death in service lump sum of £259,200 (plus a return of contributions with interest);

maximum employee contributions, including additional voluntary contributions, of £9,720 pa.

In addition to the cash limits above, the maximum retirement lump sum will be the higher of:

3/80ths of final remuneration for each year of service up to a maximum of 40;

and

2¼ x the initial annual rate of actual pension (including pension secured by AVCs and FSAVCs paid during the period of membership of the scheme) before commutation or any allocation to dependants' pensions, both up to a maximum of £97,200.

Full ⅔rds pension is permitted after 20 years' service on retirement at any age between 50 and 75, irrespective of normal pension age.

Appendix D

The terms in this appendix have been reproduced from the booklet *Pensions terminology* (third edition 1988) with the kind permission of the Pensions Management Institute.

Definitions

Accelerated accrual

Provision by a scheme of an accrual rate greater than one sixtieth of pensionable earnings for each year of pensionable service. Also often used as an alternative term for uplifted 60ths.

Accounting bases

The methods adopted concerning particular items in preparing annual accounts to determine the income and expenditure of the accounting period and the amounts of assets and liabilities shown in the balance sheet or net assets statement, having regard to the application of fundamental accounting concepts.

Accounting policies

The **accounting bases** adopted with the object of presenting fairly the financial position of a pension scheme and changes therein.

For a typical larger scheme these might embrace decisions about amortisation, conversion of foreign currency, valuation of investments, and the extent if any to which the cash basis is used.

Accounting Standards Board

A committee appointed by the Financial Reporting Council to set standards and through the Review Panel, to monitor and where necessary enforce accounting standards.

This definition is not included in the PMI terminology book but has been included to alert readers to current developments.

Accounting Standards Committee

The body charged in the UK with narrowing the areas of difference and reducing the variety in accounting policies. It issued mandatory Statements of Standard Accounting Practice (SSAPs), non-mandatory Statements of Recommended Practice (SORPs) and, as an interim procedure, Statements of Intent (SOIs) and Exposure Drafts (EDs). Its successor body from 1st August 1990 is the Accounting Standards Board.

Accrual rate

The rate at which pension benefit increases as pensionable service is completed in a defined benefit scheme.

Accruals concept

The accounting practice whereby revenues and costs are recognised as they are earned or incurred, rather than when money is received or paid.

See also matching.
In some circumstances the accruals concept may be overridden by the **prudence concept.**

Accrued benefits

The benefits for service up to a given point in time, whether **vested rights** or not. They may be calculated in relation to current earnings or projected earnings.

Allowance may also be made for revaluation and/or pension increases required by the scheme rules or legislation.

Accrued benefits valuation method

A **valuation method** in which the **actuarial liability** at the valuation date relates to:

(a) the benefits for current and deferred pensioners and their dependants, allowing where appropriate for future increases, and

(b) the **accrued benefits** for members in service on the valuation date.

A recommended contribution rate may allow for earnings and service projected to the end of a specified period (the control period). In that case allowance may be made for replacing members assumed to leave during that period.

Accrued rights

A term sometimes used to describe accrued benefits.

The term is given specific definitions for the purposes of preservation (SSA 73), contracting out and the Disclosure Regulations (SSPA 75).

Accrued rights premium

A type of state scheme premium which may be paid for a member below state pensionable age when a defined benefit scheme ceases to be contracted out, in return for which the state scheme will take over the obligation to provide his/her **guaranteed minimum pension.**

Active member

A member of a pension scheme who is at present accruing benefits under that scheme in respect of current service.

Actuarial assumptions

The set of assumptions as to rates of return, inflation, increase in earnings, mortality etc, used by the actuary in an actuarial valuation or other actuarial calculations.

Actuarial basis

A term commonly used to mean valuation method and/or actuarial assumptions.

Actuarial certificate

A certificate given by an actuary, and arising out of actuarial work.

Particular examples are:

(a) the certificate in respect of the OPB solvency test which is required for some contracted out schemes;

(b) the certificate given to the SFO in connection with the rules for dealing with pension scheme surpluses under ICTA 88.

Actuarial deficiency

The excess of the **actuarial liability** over the **actuarial value of assets**, on the basis of the **valuation method** used.

If an actuarial report refers to a surplus or deficiency, it must be studied to ascertain precisely what assets and liabilities have been taken into account. In a stricter sense, the terms surplus and deficiency might be used in relation to the results of a **discontinuance valuation**.

Actuarial liability

The value placed on the liability of a pension fund for outgoings due after the **valuation date**.

See prospective benefits valuation method and accrued benefits valuation method.

Actuarial report

A report on an actuarial valuation, or actuarial advice on the financial effects of changes in a pension scheme.

A report on an actuarial valuation must conform to actuarial guidance issued by the Institute and the Faculty of Actuaries.

Actuarial statement

The statement required by the Disclosure Regulations to be included in the **annual report**. It must show in the prescribed form the security of the accrued and prospective rights of members and be signed by an actuary.

Actuarial surplus

The excess of the **actuarial value of assets** over the **actuarial liability** on the basis of the valuation method used.

See notes under actuarial deficiency.

Actuarial valuation

An investigation by an actuary into the ability of a pension scheme to meet its liabilities. This is usually to assess the **funding level** and a **recommended contribution rate** based on comparing the **actuarial value of assets** and the **actuarial liability.**

Actuarial value of assets

The value placed on the assets by the actuary. This may be market value, **present value** of estimated income and proceeds of sales or redemptions, or some other value.

Actuarial value of liabilities

See actuarial liability.

Actuarial value of future contributions

The **present value** of assumed future contributions and income therefrom.

Actuary

An adviser on financial questions involving probabilities relating to mortality and other contingencies.

For statutory purposes in the UK, the term automatically includes Fellows of the Institute of Actuaries and of the Faculty of Actuaries. Persons with other actuarial qualifications can be approved by the Secretary of State for a specific purpose of the legislation.

Added years

The provision of extra pension benefit by reference to an additional period of pensionable service in a defined benefit scheme, arising from the receipt of a transfer payment, the paying of additional voluntary contributions or by way of **augmentation.**

Additional component

The earnings related element of the state pension, over and above the **basic component**.

Additional Voluntary Contributions

Contributions over and above a member's normal contributions, if any, which a member elects to pay to the scheme in order to secure additional benefits.

See also free standing additional voluntary contributions.

Administrator

The person or persons regarded by the SFO and where relevant the OPB as responsible for the management of a pension scheme.

In a less formal sense, the person who manages the day to day administration of the scheme.

Aggregate method

A valuation method in which the recommended contribution rate is obtained directly as that which, if paid on behalf of existing members over their future periods of active membership, would provide for the excess of the present value of all their benefits over the actuarial value of assets.

Allocation

The facility for a member to give up (or allocate) part of his/her pension in exchange for a pension payable to the member's spouse or dependant.

Amortisation

A term used by accountants to mean the amount by which the carrying value of a wasting asset, such as leasehold property, is reduced when presented in financial statements to recognise reduction in value caused by the passage of time.

Sometimes used to mean the discharge of a liability by instalments.

Annual report

The means by which the trustees of a pension scheme communicate general, financial and other information about the scheme to members, employers and other interested parties.

The term is used in particular to describe the information which is required to be made available by trustees in relation to each scheme year under the disclosure of information requirements of SSPA 75. This must include a copy of the audited accounts and of the latest actuarial statement and other information as specified in the Disclosure Regulations, including a financial review by the trustees and an investment report. It may contain additional information not required by the Regulations.

Pension schemes often publish a simplified annual report for members containing the above material suitably summarised and, perhaps, illustrated.

Annuity

A series of payments, which may be subject to increases, made at stated intervals until a particular event occurs. This event is most commonly the end of a specified period or the death of the person receiving the annuity.

Appropriate personal pension scheme

A personal pension scheme or free standing AVC scheme granted an appropriate scheme certificate by the OPB, enabling its members to use it for the purpose of contracting out.

Appropriate scheme certificate

The certificate issued by the OPB to a personal pension scheme or to a free standing AVC scheme confirming that the scheme satisfies the conditions required for contracting out.

Approved scheme

A retirement benefits scheme which is approved by the Inland Revenue under Chapter I of Part XIV of ICTA 88, including a free standing AVC scheme. The term may also be used to describe a personal pension scheme approved under Chapter IV of that Part.

See also exempt approved scheme.

Attained age method

A prospective benefits valuation method in which the contribution rate, which, if paid on behalf of existing members over their future working lifetime, would provide for the benefits that will accrue to them after the valuation date, is taken as the **standard contribution rate**.

Auditing guidelines

Guidelines issued by the Auditing Practices Committee which give guidance to auditors on particular commercial or legal circumstances.

Augmentation

The provision of additional benefits in respect of particular members, normally where the cost is borne by the pension scheme and/or the employer.

Average earnings scheme

A scheme where the benefit for each year of membership is related to the pensionable earnings for that year.

Basic component

The single person's flat rate state pension paid to all who have met the minimum contribution requirements.

Benefit statement

A statement or estimate of benefits payable in respect of an individual on the occurrence of specified events.

Book reserve scheme

A pension scheme under which the employer is responsible for the payment of the benefits, which are financed by a **provision** in the employer's accounts.

Bulk transfer

The transfer of a group of members from one pension scheme to another, usually with a transfer payment in respect of their accrued benefits under the first scheme.

The SFO should be consulted about any such transfer payments.

Buy back

A term used to describe the payment of a type of **state scheme premium** by means of which a member's rights are fully reinstated under SERPS.

Buy out

The purchase by pension scheme trustees of an insurance policy or bond in the name of the beneficiary, in lieu of entitlement to benefit from the scheme.

Capitalised value

An alternative term for present value.

Career average scheme

An alternative term for average earnings scheme.

Cash accumulation policy

An insurance policy under which contributions, net of expense charges, are accumulated in a pool to which interest and usually bonuses are added. The proceeds are applied to provide pensions and other benefits as they become due.

Cash equivalent

The amount which a member of a pension scheme may under Schedule 1A of SSPA 75, require to be applied as a transfer payment to another permitted pension scheme or to a buy out policy.

Cash option

An alternative term for commutation.

Centralised scheme

A pension scheme operated on behalf of several employers.

Certificate of existence

A document confirming that a person entitled to a pension is still alive.

At the same time, confirmation may be sought about other conditions affecting entitlement.

Certified amount

That part of a **contributions equivalent premium** which may be recovered out of any refund of scheme contributions to the member.

Closed scheme

A pension scheme which does not admit new members.

Contributions may or may not continue and benefits may or may not be provided for future service.

Commingled fund

A term sometimes used to describe a common investment fund.

Common investment fund

An arrangement whereby the assets of two or more pension schemes, usually operated by a single employer, are pooled for investment.

Commutation

The giving up of a part or all of the pension payable from retirement for an immediate cash sum.

Concentration of investment

Placing a significant proportion of the assets of a pension scheme in any single investment.

The amounts requiring compulsory disclosure and reporting are laid down by the OPB and Disclosure Regulations.

Consistency concept

The accounting practice whereby there is identical accounting treatment of like items from year to year.

Where a change in accounting treatment is made the effect would be disclosed in the first year after the change, probably as a 'prior year adjustment'.

Consulting actuary

An actuary whose sole or main business is consultancy.

Contracted out money purchase scheme

An alternative term for a money purchase contracted out scheme.

Contracted out rebate

The amount by which National Insurance contributions in respect of **upper band earnings** are reduced in respect of employees who are contracted out by virtue of their membership of an occupational pension scheme.

The term is also commonly used to describe the equivalent payment made by the DSS as **minimum contributions** *to a personal pension scheme.*

Contract out

To use a statutory arrangement under which members of a pension scheme which meets certain conditions obtain rights under it in place of part of their earnings related state scheme benefits. Contributions to the state scheme are reduced in respect of such employees or, in the case of a personal pension scheme or free standing AVC scheme, partly repaid to the scheme.

Contracting out certificate

The certificate issued by the OPB, in respect of an occupational pension scheme which satisfies the conditions for contracting out, confirming that employees in the employments named in the certificate are to be treated as being in contracted out employment.

Contributions equivalent premium

A type of state scheme premium which may be paid when a member leaves after a relatively short period of contracted out employment, in return for which the state scheme will take over the obligation to provide his/her **guaranteed minimum pension.**

Contribution holiday

A period during which employers' and/or members' contributions are temporarily suspended, normally when the fund is in surplus. The term is sometimes used loosely when contributions continue to be paid but at a reduced rate.

Contributory scheme

A scheme which requires contributions from active members unless they are temporarily suspended during a **contribution holiday**.

Controlled funding

A **funding plan** which has regard to the pension scheme's liabilities as a whole rather than those for individual members.

This term is most commonly used in connectic with insured final earnings schemes.

Corporate trustee

A company which acts as a trustee.

Current funding level

The **funding level**, at the present time, where the **actuarial liability** in respect of active members is taken as the present value of accrued benefits calculated in relation to current earnings, revalued as for preserved pensions on the statutory basis (or such higher basis as has been promised).

Current unit method

An accrued benefits valuation method in which the **actuarial liability** is based on earnings at the **valuation date.** The standard contribution rate is that necessary to cover the cost of benefits which will accrue in the year following the valuation date by reference to earnings projected to the end of that year.

Deed of adherence

A legal document admitting a new employer to a scheme and containing an undertaking by the new employer to comply with the provisions of the scheme.

Deed of appointment

A legal document by which a new trustee is appointed.

Deferred annuity

An annuity which commences from a future date.

Deferred pensioner

A person entitled to **preserved benefits.** Sometimes referred to as a deferred member.

The term is also sometimes used to describe a member on postponed retirement.

Deferred retirement

An alternative term for postponed retirement.

Deficiency

See actuarial deficiency.

Defined benefit scheme

A pension scheme in which the rules specify the benefits to be paid, and the scheme is financed accordingly.

Defined contribution scheme

An alternative term for a money purchase scheme, normally one where the rate of contribution is specified in the rules.

Definitive trust deed

The detailed trust deed which follows an interim trust deed.

Dependant

A person who is financially dependent on a member or pensioner or was so at the time of death or retirement of the member or pensioner.

For SFO purposes a spouse qualifies automatically as a dependant and a child of the member or pensioner may always be regarded as a dependant until attaining the age of 18 or ceasing to receive full time educational or vocational training, if later.

Deposit administration

An alternative term for a cash accumulation policy, normally one for a group of employees.

Determination

Exercise of a statutory power, usually by the OPB or the Secretary of State, either to take action in specified circumstances or to decide whether in certain situations the requirements of the law are met. The term is also sometimes used as an alternative term for winding up.

Disability benefit

A benefit paid to an employee who is unable to work for medical reasons, for example an ill health early retirement benefit, a **prolonged disability insurance** benefit or a benefit consequent on an injury at work.

Disclosure regulations

Regulations issued under SSPA 75 requiring disclosure of information about pension schemes and benefits to interested parties.

Discontinuance

The cessation of contributions to a pension scheme leading either to **winding up** or to the scheme becoming a **frozen scheme**.

Discontinuance funding valuation method

An out of date term for current unit method.

Discontinuance valuation

An **actuarial valuation** carried out to assess the position if the scheme were to be discontinued and the trustees were to wind it up in accordance with the requirements of the trust instrument. The valuation may take into account the possible exercise of any discretion to augment benefits.

Discretionary increase

An increase in a pension in payment or in a preserved benefit arising other than from a system of **escalation** or **indexation.** Such an increase may be of a regular or an ad hoc nature.

Discretionary scheme

A scheme in which the employees to be included are selected by the employer. Often the benefits, or the contributions from which they are to be provided, are also decided individually for each member.

Dynamisation/Dynamism

A term sometimes used to describe escalation or indexation. It is also used to describe index linking of earnings, either for calculating scheme benefits, or for determining **final remuneration** for the purpose of SFO limitations.

Early leaver

A person who ceases to be an active member of a pension scheme, other than on death, without being granted an immediate retirement benefit.

Early retirement

The retirement of a member with immediate retirement benefit, before normal pension date.

The benefit may be reduced because of early payment.

Earmarked policy

A term used in the Practice Notes to denote a policy held by a pension scheme, where each annuity or sum assured is earmarked to provide benefits for or in respect of an individual member.

Employer

The person or body with whom the member of a pension scheme has a contract of employment relevant to that scheme.

This term is to be preferred to 'company' as having more general application in the context of pension schemes.

Entry age method

A prospective benefits valuation method in which the new entrant contribution rate is taken as the **standard contribution rate**.

Escalation

A system whereby pensions in payment and/or preserved benefits are automatically increased at regular intervals and at a fixed percentage rate. The percentage may be restricted to the increase in a specified index.

Ex gratia benefit

A benefit provided by the employer which he is neither legally nor contractually required to provide.

Executive scheme

A scheme for selected directors or employees.

Exempt approved scheme

An approved scheme other than a personal pension scheme which is established under irrevocable trusts (or exceptionally, subject to a formal direction under S.592(1)(b) of ICTA 88) thus giving rise to the tax reliefs specified in ICTA 88.

Experience deficiency/surplus

An actuarial deficiency or surplus which arises because events have not coincided with the actuarial assumptions made for the last valuation.

External investment manager

An investment manager not solely employed by the trustees or by the employer.

Final average earnings

Final pensionable earnings which are based on the average of earnings in a number of consecutive years.

Final earnings scheme

A pension scheme where the benefit is calculated by reference to the member's pensionable earnings for a period ending at or before normal pension date or leaving service.

Final pensionable earnings

The pensionable earnings, at or near retirement or leaving service, on which the pension is calculated in a final earnings scheme.

Final remuneration

The term used by the SFO for the maximum amount of earnings which it will permit to be used for the purpose of calculating maximum approvable benefits.

The permissible alternatives are set out fully in the Practice Notes.

Final salary scheme

An alternative term for final earnings scheme.

Fixed benefit scheme

A pension scheme where the benefit is not related to earnings, contributions or service.

Flat rate scheme

A pension scheme which provides benefits for each year of pensionable service not related to earnings.

Franking

A practice at one time followed by some schemes, whereby the statutory increases in **guaranteed minimum pension** between termination of contracted out employment and state pensionable age were offset against other scheme benefits rather than being added to a member's total preserved benefits. This procedure is now forbidden in respect of members whose contracted out employment ended on or after 1 January 1985.

Free standing additional voluntary contributions

A pension contract separate from a company pension scheme effected by an active member of that scheme. Benefits are secured with a pension provider by contributions from the member only.

Free standing AVC scheme

A scheme established by a pension provider to accept free standing additional voluntary contributions.

Frozen benefit

A **preserved benefit**, strictly one not subject to **revaluation**.

Frozen scheme

A **closed scheme** where no further contributions are payable and members are entitled to **preserved benefits**.

Fully insured scheme

A scheme where the trustees have effected an insurance contract in respect of each member which guarantees benefits corresponding at all times to those promised under the rules.

Sometimes used to mean insured scheme.

Funding

The provision in advance for future liabilities by the accumulation of assets, normally external to the employer's business.

Funding level

The relationship at a specified date between the **actuarial value of assets** and the **actuarial liability.**

The funding level may be calculated separately in respect of different categories of liability e.g. pensions in payment and AVCs.

Funding objective

See funding plan.

Funding plan

The arrangement of the incidence over time of payments with the aim of meeting the future cost of a given set of benefits.

Possible objectives of a funding plan might be that, if the **actuarial assumptions** are borne out by events:

(a) A specific **funding level** should be reached by a given date.

(b) The level of contributions should remain constant, or should after a planned period be the **standard contribution** rate required by the **valuation method** used in the actuarial valuation.

Funding rate

A term sometimes used to describe the recommended contribution rate.

Group personal pension scheme

An arrangement made for the employees of a particular employer to participate in a personal pension scheme on a grouped basis.

Guaranteed minimum pension

The minimum pension which an occupational pension scheme (other than a money purchase contracted out scheme) must provide as one of the conditions of **contracting out**.

For an employee contracted out under any occupational or personal pension scheme, an amount equal to this amount is deducted from his/her benefit under the state scheme.

Guaranteed pension

A term which may be used to describe the minimum benefit available from an insurance policy.

Also sometimes used to denote minimum pension or pension guarantee.

Guidance Notes

1. Notes published by the SFO describing the requirements for tax approval in respect of specified types of schemes, in particular those relating to personal pension schemes. See also Practice Notes.
2. Notes published by professional bodies such as the Institute of Actuaries, advising their members on the appropriate course of action in specified circumstances.

Hancock annuity

A term describing a certain kind of annuity purchased by the employer at the time of an employee's retirement, the capital cost of which is normally allowed for tax relief in the year of purchase.

Hybrid scheme

A pension scheme in which the benefit is calculated usually as the better of two alternatives, for example of a final earnings and a money purchase basis.

Index linking

A term describing adjustment in line with an index (usually of prices or earnings). In relation to pensions, an alternative term for indexation.

Indexation

A system whereby pensions in payment and/or preserved benefits are automatically increased at regular intervals and by reference to a specified index of prices or earnings.

The term is also occasionally used in relation to index linking of final pensionable earnings or final remuneration: see explanation under dynamisation.

Individual arrangement

An occupational pension scheme with only one member where the documentation, often a letter of exchange, relates only to that member.

An employer may have several individual arrangements for different employees.

Industry-wide scheme

A centralised scheme for non-associated employers in a particular industry.

Inflation proofing

A term commonly used to describe indexation.

Insured scheme

A pension scheme where the sole long term investment medium is an insurance policy (other than a **managed fund** policy).

Integration

The design of pension scheme benefits to take into account all or part of the state scheme benefits which the member is deemed to received.

One form of integration involves a state pension disregard.

Interim trust deed

A form of trust deed commonly used to establish a pension scheme on broadly stated terms leaving the detailed provisions and the rules to be provided later by a definitive trust deed.

A scheme may be established by other methods, for example by a board resolution, declaration of trust or letter of exchange.

Investment performance measurement

The comparison of the rate of return of a given pension fund with one or more of:

(a) the notional return of a model fund;

(b) the actual rates of return of other funds; and

(c) stock market indices over the same period.

Joint office

The Joint Office of the OPB and the SFO.

Joint office memoranda

Explanatory memoranda issued by the Joint Office of the OPB and the SFO.

Late retirement

The retirement of a member, with immediate retirement benefit, after normal pension date.

The benefit may be increased because of late payment.

Level of funding

An alternative term for funding level.

Liabilities

Amounts which a pension scheme has an obligation to pay now or in the future. The amounts may not be immediately ascertainable and some liabilities may be dependent on the occurrence of future events.

Life assurance scheme

A scheme which provides a benefit only on the death of a member.

Lower earnings limit

The minimum amount, approximately equivalent to the **basic component,** which must be earned in any pay period before contributions become payable to the state scheme.

Once the limit is exceeded, contributions are payable in respect of earnings both above and below this limit.

Managed fund

An investment contract by means of which an insurance company offers participation in one or more pooled funds. Sometimes also used to denote an arrangement where the scheme assets are invested on similar lines to unit trusts by an external investment manager.

Matching

The policy of selecting investments of a nature, term or currency similar to that of the expected outgoings.

Also as an accounting term, an element of the accruals concept whereby revenue and costs are matched with one another so far as their relationship can be established or justifiably assumed.

Maximum approvable benefit

The maximum benefit for an individual which is allowable under an approved scheme (other than a personal pension scheme or a simplified defined contribution scheme).

Member

A person who has been admitted to membership of a pension scheme and is entitled to benefit under the scheme. Sometimes used to refer only to an **active member**.

For some statutory purposes the term 'members' may include employees who are prospective members.

Member's normal contributions

The regular contributions required from an active member by the scheme rules.

Minimum benefit

An amount of benefit which a scheme promises if the normal benefit for a particular member is smaller.

Minimum contributions

Contributions payable to a personal pension scheme or to a free standing AVC scheme by the DSS in respect of a member who has elected to contract out. The contributions consist of a partial rebate of National Insurance contributions, together with a 2% incentive where applicable.

The term could also be used in respect of any minimum amount which a member is required to contribute in order to be a member of an occupational or personal pension scheme, or in order to make additional voluntary contributions.

Minimum payments

The minimum amount which an employer must pay into a money purchase contracted out scheme. This amount corresponds to the reduction in national insurance contributions which applies in respect of employees who are contracted out.

Minimum pension

See minimum benefit.

Model rules

Specimen rules produced by the OPB and/or the SFO for certain categories of pension schemes to facilitate approval and/or the issue of a contracting out or appropriate scheme certificate.

Modified premium value

A **premium value** which excludes the loadings made by the insurer in premium rating for initial expenses, such as issue expenses, brokerage and stamp duty.

Money purchase

The determination of an individual member's benefits by reference to contributions paid into the scheme in respect of that member, usually increased by an amount based on the investment return on those contributions.

Money purchase contracted out scheme

The term used in SSPA 75 (as amended by SSA 86) to describe an occupational pension scheme which is contracted out by reference to the payment of a minimum level of contributions in respect of each member rather than by reference to provision of a **guaranteed minimum pension**.

Money purchase scheme

A scheme where the benefits are determined on a **money purchase** basis.

Money purchase underpin

A minimum benefit provided in a final earnings scheme, calculated on a **money purchase** basis.

Net relevant earnings

Earnings from self employment or non pensionable employment after deducting losses and certain business charges on income, used in determining the maximum contributions to a retirement annuity or **personal pension scheme** which qualify for tax relief. The maximum is currently 17.5% of net relevant earnings with higher contribution limits for persons aged over fifty.

New entrant contribution rate

A rate of contribution estimated as being sufficient to provide benefits for future entrants, including any contribution required from the members.

New money

The flow into a fund of contributions and transfer payments less outgoings. Normally not considered to include income from existing assets.

Non-contributory scheme

A pension scheme which does not require contributions from its active members.

Not to be confused with a contributory scheme where contributions are suspended during a **contribution holiday**.

Normal pension age

The age by reference to which the **normal pension date** is determined.

SSPA 75 uses the term in a sense similar to that of normal pension date.

Normal pension date

The date at which a member of a pension scheme normally becomes entitled to received his/her retirement benefits.

Normal retirement age

The age by reference to which the **normal retirement date** is determined.

Normal retirement date

Commonly used with the same meaning as normal pension date.

Normal pension date is probably preferable in this context. The date of normal retirement is strictly a matter for the contract of employment, and can in some cases be different from the normal pension date because of legislative requirements.

Occupational pension scheme

An arrangement organised by an employer or on behalf of a group of employers to provide pensions and/or other benefits for or in respect of one or more employees on leaving service or on death or retirement.

A more detailed definition is to be found in S.51(3)(a) of SSA 73.

Occupational Pensions Board

A statutory body set up under SSA 73, with functions derived from that Act and SSPA 75. The Board is responsible for issuing **contracting out** or **appropriate scheme certificates** for pension schemes which meet the statutory requirements, for supervising those schemes to ensure that guaranteed minimum pensions and protected rights are secure and for ensuring that equal access and preservation requirements are satisfied. The Board is required to report to the Secretary of State when he/she seeks their advice and to comment on draft regulations affecting occupational pension schemes.

Ordinary annual contributions

A term used in the Practice Notes to denote the contributions payable to an occupational pension scheme by the employer on a regular basis in accordance with the trust instrument.

Partially approved scheme

A pension scheme only partially approved by the SFO because it provides some benefits which are not approvable, for example for overseas employees.

Not to be confused with partial loss of tax exemptions which occurs under Schedule 22 of ICTA 88 if a pension scheme which is excessively overfunded fails to take action to reduce the surplus.

Past service

Service before a given date. Often used to denote service before entry into the pension scheme.

Past service benefit

A benefit granted for **past service** and/or **pre-scheme service**.

Pay as you go

An arrangement under which benefits are paid out of revenue and no provision is made for future liabilities.

The state scheme is pay as you go.

Pension costs

The cost of retirement benefits charged to the profit and loss account of an employer over one or more years. This will not necessarily match on a year by year basis the payments made to any relevant pension scheme.

Pension fraction

The fraction of pensionable earnings for each year of pensionable service which forms the basis of the pension in a final earnings scheme or an average earnings scheme.

Pension fund

Strictly speaking the assets of a pension scheme but very often used to denote the pension scheme itself.

Pension increase

An increase in a pension in payment. In practice the term may also embrace revaluation of preserved benefits.

Such an increase may arise as a result of **escalation** *or* **indexation**, *or may be a* **discretionary increase**.

Pension scheme

An occupational pension scheme, a personal pension scheme or a free standing AVC scheme.

Pension tax relief at source

The right of an employed contributor to a free standing AVC scheme or to a personal pension scheme to deduct basic rate tax relief from contributions which he/she pays to the scheme.

Pensionable earnings

The earnings on which benefits and/or contributions are calculated.

One or more elements of earnings (e.g. overtime) may be excluded, and/or there may be a **state pension disregard**.

Pensionable employment

An alternative term for pensionable service.

Pensionable service

The period of service which is taken into account in calculating pension benefit.

SSA 73 gives the term a statutory definition for the purposes of preservation, which also applies for the purposes of the revaluation and transfer payment requirements of SSPA 75.

Pensioner

A person who is currently entitled to a pension from a pension scheme.

Permanent health insurance

An alternative term for prolonged disability insurance.

Personal pension

An alternative term for a personal pension arrangement.

The term is also frequently used to describe a retirement annuity effected under the tax legislation in force before July 1988.

Personal pension arrangement

An individual contract made under a **personal pension scheme**.

Personal pension scheme

Usually used to mean a scheme approved under Chapter IV of Part XIV of ICTA 88, under which individuals who are self employed or in non pensionable employment make pension provision by means of insurance, unit trust or deposit account contracts.

SSA 86 uses a slightly different definition which excludes a scheme open only to the self employed but also includes a free standing AVC scheme.

Practice Notes

Notes on the approval of retirement benefits schemes by the SFO published as Joint Office Publication IR12 (1979). Notes on the approval of free standing AVCs have been issued as a supplement to the Practice Notes.

See also Guidance Notes.

Pre-scheme service

Service before the start of the relevant pension scheme.

Prepayment (pension)

A balance sheet item on the assets side of the employer's accounts representing that part of a funding payment to a pension scheme which under SSAP 24 falls to be set against the revenue of the business in future years.

Present value

The total of the amounts of a series of future payments or receipts discounted at interest to a current date, usually the **valuation date,** and allowing for the probabilities of payment or receipt.

The concept of the present values of income and outgoings is essentially the same as discounted cash flow.

Preserved benefits

Benefits arising on an individual ceasing to be an active member of a pension scheme, payable at a later date.

Principal employer

The term commonly used in the trust instrument for the particular participating employer in which is vested special powers or duties in relation to such matters as the appointment of trustees, amendments and winding up. Usually this will be the employer which established the scheme or its successor in business.

Priority liabilities

Benefits and other liabilities which are given precedence in accordance with the **priority rule** when a scheme is wound up.

Under S.40(3) of SSPA 75 a contracted out scheme other than a money purchase scheme must contain a rule which gives priority, in the event of the scheme winding up, to guaranteed minimum pensions and certain other liabilities.

Priority rule

The provisions contained in the trust deed or rules of a pension scheme setting out the order of precedence to be followed if the scheme is wound up with insufficient assets to meet all liabilities.

Projected unit method

An accrued benefits valuation method in which the **actuarial liability** makes allowance for projected earnings. The **standard contribution rate** is that necessary to cover the cost of all benefits which will accrue in the year following the **valuation date** by reference to earnings projected to the dates on which benefits become payable.

Prolonged disability insurance

Insurance effected outside a pension scheme against long-term sickness or disability, providing a regular income during such periods of absence before retirement.

Normally, the income becomes payable only after a minimum period. Not to be confused with ill-health early retirement benefit.

Prospective benefits valuation method

A **valuation method** in which the **actuarial liability** is the **present value** of:

(a) the benefits for current and deferred pensioners and their dependants, allowing where appropriate for future pension increases, and

(b) the benefits which active members will receive in respect of both past and future service, allowing for projected earnings up to their assumed exit dates and, where appropriate, for pension increases thereafter, less the **present value** of future contributions payable in respect of current members at the **standard contribution rate**.

Protected rights

The benefits under an appropriate personal pension scheme or a money purchase contracted out scheme, deriving respectively from at least the **minimum contributions** or **minimum payments**, which are provided in a specified form as a necessary condition for contracting out.

The term may also be used in a general sense to describe rights given to certain members on change of rules or change of pension scheme which are superior to those of a new entrant. It also has a special meaning in relation to the termination of former old code approval, as set out in the Practice Notes.

Provision

An amount written off to provide for depreciation or diminution in value of assets. Also an amount retained as reasonably necessary to provide for any liability or loss which is likely to be incurred but the amount or date of which is uncertain. (See Companies Act 1985, Schedule 4 para 88).

See also reserve. Pension costs in employers' accounts should be actuarially assessed. If, as a result, there is a sum set aside on the liabilities side of the balance sheet, it will be a provision rather than a reserve.

Prudence concept

The accounting practice whereby revenue and profits are not included in financial statements until cash is received or their ultimate realisation in cash form can be assessed with reasonable certainty. Provision is none the less made for all known liabilities, expenses and losses, even though quantifiable only as a best estimate.

See accruals concept with which the prudence concept may conflict.

Rate of return

The change in value of an investment over a period, taking into account both the income from it and the change in its market value. Normally expressed as an equivalent annual rate.

Real rate of return

The difference between the **rate of return** of an investment and a selected measure of inflation over the same period.

The measure of inflation used should be specified, but will often be the index of retail prices.

Recommended contribution rate

The contribution rate recommended by the actuary. It is usually obtained by adjusting the standard contribution rate for differences between the **actuarial liability** and the **actuarial value of assets** taking into account the objectives of the funding plan.

The pension scheme's auditor is required to report if the employers have not been paying the contributions recommended by the actuary.

Regular pension cost

An accounting term denoting the part of the **pension cost** which results from spreading over the average remaining service lifetime the **liabilities** of the pension scheme that, under the actuarial method in use, are attributed to future service.

Reserve

An amount appropriated from the profits of a business and set aside on the balance sheet as part of the capital employed.

Any amount which ought properly to be regarded as a **provision** *should not be included in a reserve.*

Retirement benefits scheme

An arrangement for the provision of benefits consisting of or including relevant benefits.

The full definition is set out in S.611 of ICTA 88.

Revaluation

The application, particularly to preserved benefits, of **indexation, escalation** or the awarding of **discretionary increases.** SSPA 75 imposes revaluation in the calculation of **guaranteed minimum pension** and of preserved benefits other than **guaranteed minimum pension**.

Revaluation is also an accounting term for the revision of the carrying value of an asset, usually having regard to its market value.

Rules

The detailed provisions of a pension scheme, brought into operation by a definitive trust deed or in some other formal way, for example by a trustees' resolution.

Salary related scheme

A **defined benefit scheme** in which benefits are related to earnings, i.e. a final earnings scheme or an average earnings scheme.

Salary sacrifice

An agreement between the employer and employee whereby the employee forgoes part of his earnings in return for a corresponding contribution by the employer to a pension scheme.

This is not the same as an **additional voluntary contribution**.

Section 21 orders

The Orders issued each year in accordance with S.21 of SSPA 75 specifying the rates of increase to be applied to the earnings factors on which the additional component and guaranteed minimum pensions are based. This revaluation is based on the increase in national average earnings.

Section 32 policy

A term widely used to describe an insurance policy used for **buy out** purposes.

The term came into use as a result of S.32 of FA 81, which gave prominence to the possibility of effecting such policies (now ICTA 88).

Segregated fund

An arrangement whereby the investments of a particular pension scheme are managed by an external investment manager independently of other funds under its control. Often used to indicate such an arrangement with an insurance company.

Self administered scheme

A pension scheme where the assets are invested, other than wholly by payment of insurance premiums, by the trustees, an in-house manager or an external investment manager.

Although on the face of it the term self administered should refer to the method of administering contributions and benefits, in practice the term has become solely related to the way in which the investments are managed.

Self investment

The investment of a scheme's assets in the business of the employer or that of an associated company, including loans made to the employer or associated company.

The amounts of self investment requiring compulsory disclosure and reporting are laid down by the OPB and Disclosure Regulations. The SFO imposes restrictions on self investment by small self administered schemes.

Simplified defined contribution scheme

A money purchase scheme subject to the simplified approval procedure described in Joint Office Memorandum No. 94.

Small self administered scheme

A self administered scheme with few members (generally less than 12) which is subject on this account to certain special conditions for approval under ICTA 88.

Special contributions

Contributions payable by the employer or by the members for a limited period or as a single payment, often to provide new benefits or to meet deficiencies.

Standard contribution rate

The contribution rate required by a particular valuation method before taking into account any differences between the **actuarial liability** and the **actuarial value of assets**.

State earnings related pension scheme

A term widely used to describe the additional component of the state pension scheme.

State scheme premium

A payment made to the state scheme in certain circumstances.

The categories of state scheme premiums are: accrued rights premium, contracted out protected rights premium, contributions equivalent premium, limited revaluation premium, pensioner's rights premium, personal pension protected rights premium, transfer premium.

State pension disregard

A reduction in pension or pensionable earnings to achieve **integration**.

Superannuation Funds Office

The branch of the Inland Revenue which deals with the approval of pension schemes under the relevant tax legislation.

Surplus

See actuarial surplus.

Rather confusingly, the term may also be used to describe an excess of income over expenditure in a scheme's annual accounts.

Terminal funding

An arrangement whereby a payment to meet the present value of a benefit is made only at or about the time when the benefit is due to commence.

Not common in the UK except in respect of discretionary pension increases.

Total earnings scheme

A type of average earnings scheme where the pension is a specified fraction of the member's aggregate earnings throughout his/her period of membership.

Transfer payment

A payment made from a pension scheme to another pension scheme, or to an insurance company to purchase a **buy out** policy, in lieu of benefits which have accrued to the member or members concerned, to enable the receiving arrangement to provide alternative benefits.

The transfer payment may be made in accordance with the scheme rules or in exercise of a member's statutory rights under SSPA 75.

Transfer value

A term commonly used to mean transfer payment.

True and fair view

An approach adopted by accountants when keeping financial records and drawing up accounts whereby the fairness of the presentation of the information presented is given as much emphasis as the factual correctness.

According to the Disclosure Regulations and SORP 1, the accounts of a UK pension scheme should present a true and fair view of the scheme's income and expenditure, the net assets and a reconciliation of the net assets movements.

Trustee

A person or company appointed to carry out the purposes of a trust in accordance with the provisions of the trust instrument and general principles of trust law.

2% Incentive

Payments which SSA 1986 requires the DSS to make in certain cases to an appropriate personal pension scheme or to a newly contracted out occupational pension scheme.

Unfunded scheme

A pension scheme for which the employer does not set aside and accumulate assets in advance of the benefits commencing to be paid. The basis may be **pay as you go** or **terminal funding**.

Uplifted 60ths

Benefits in excess of one sixtieth of final remuneration for each year of service to the extent permitted by the SFO in an approved occupational pension scheme (other than a simplified scheme).

Upper band earnings

Earnings between the **lower earnings limit** and the **upper earnings limit** on which the **additional component** is calculated.

Also used in the calculation of a guaranteed minimum pension.

Upper earnings limit

The maximum amount of earnings (equal to approximately seven times the **lower earnings limit**) on which contributions are payable to the state scheme by employees.

Valuation balance sheet

A comparison of the **actuarial value of assets** with the **actuarial liability** showing the elements of these amounts in the form of a balance sheet, with an amount for surplus or deficiency as a balancing item.

The results of an actuarial valuation may be presented in other ways.

Valuation basis

A term commonly used by actuaries to mean **valuation method** and/or **actuarial assumptions**.

Valuation date

The date by reference to which an **actuarial valuation** is carried out.

Valuation method

An approach used by the actuary in an **actuarial valuation**. The main categories of approach are described under **accrued benefits valuation method** and **prospective benefits valuation method**. A variety of methods can be used but the method or methods used in a particular case should be adequately described in the actuarial report.

Valuation report

See actuarial report.

Vested rights

(a) For active members, benefits to which they would unconditionally be entitled on leaving service;

(b) for deferred pensioners, their preserved benefits;

(c) for pensioners, pensions to which they are entitled;

including where appropriate the related benefits for spouses or other dependants.

Winding up

The process of terminating a pension scheme, usually by applying the assets to the purchase of immediate and deferred annuities for the beneficiaries, in accordance with the trust instrument.

See also priority rule.

With profits policy

An insurance policy under which a share of the surpluses disclosed by actuarial valuations of the insurance company's life and pensions business is payable as an addition to the guaranteed benefits or in reduction of future premiums.

Appendix E

These definitions are those included in *Pension fund terminology* published by the Institute and Faculty of Actuaries.

Descriptions of main actuarial valuation methods

Name	**Standard contribution rate**	**Target fund**
Projected unit method	The present value of all benefits which will accrue in the year following the valuation date (by reference to service in that year and projected final earnings) divided by the present value of current members' earnings in that year.	The present value of all benefits accrued at the valuation date (based on projected final earnings for members in service).
Current unit method	The sum of (i) the present value of benefits which will accrue in the year following the valuation date (by reference to service in that year and projected earnings at the end of that year), and (ii) the present value of all benefits accrued at the valuation date multiplied by the expected percentage increase in earnings over the next year divided by the present value of current members' earnings in that year.	The present value of all benefits accrued at the valuation date (based on earnings at the valuation date for members in service).

Name	Standard contribution rate	Target fund
Entry age method	The present value of all future benefits based on projected final earnings for a member entering at the normal entry age divided by the present value of total projected earnings throughout his expected future membership.	The present value of total benefits (based on projected final earnings for members in service) less the value of the standard contribution rate multiplied by the present value of total projected earnings for all members throughout their expected future membership.
Attained age method	The present value of all benefits which will accrue to present members after the valuation date (by reference to service after the valuation date and projected final earnings) divided by the present value of total projected earnings for all current members throughout their expected future membership.	The present value of all benefits accrued at the valuation date (based on projected final earnings for members in service)
Aggregate method	The 'Aggregate Method' does not define a standard contribution rate of a target fund. The method simply derives a single, overall contribution rate. This rate is obtained by dividing the excess of the present value of all benefits which have accrued and will accrue over the value placed on the scheme assets for valuation purposes by the present value of total projected earnings for all members throughout their expected future membership. The method is a special case of the attained age method with the standard contribution rate compounded with any additional contribution required to cover a shortfall in assets from the target fund	

Appendix F

SSAP 24 and FAS 87 Comparison

	SSAP 24	FAS 87
1. Actuarial method	One which results in regular cost being a substantially level percentage of current and future pensionable payroll	Projected unit credit (in UK termed projected unit).
2. Actuarial assumptions	Long-term overall best estimates.	Where appropriate market related individual best estimates.
3. Discretionary pension increases	Preferably allowance for likely increases in advance. Otherwise recognised in period when granted unless covered by surplus.	Only allowed for in advance if substantive commitment. Otherwise cost spread forward when granted.
4. Amortisation	Over working life as level percentage of pensionable payroll or on some other acceptable basis.	Usually over working life on straight-line basis.
5. Asset valuation	Any reasonable method.	Market or market-related value based on a maximum period of 5 years.
6. Extraordinary events	Surplus or deficiency aggregated with other financial effects in accordance with SSAP 6.	Immediate recognition of parts of unrecognised transitional surplus, experience gain or losses, or unrecognised costs of benefit improvements.

	SSAP 24	FAS 87
7. Reduction in work force	Surplus or deficiency recognised over the period during which the relevant adjustment to contribution occurs.	Immediate recognition of parts of unrecognised transitional surplus, experience gain or losses, or unrecognised costs of benefit improvements.
8. Refund on surplus	Either credit for net refund in period received or spread forward as a variation from regular cost.	Gross refund treated as accrued pension cost in balance sheet; excise tax treated as expense.
9. Disclosures	Requires statement as to whether the costs are assessed in accordance with the advice of an actuary.	N/A
	Requires level of funding expressed in percentage terms.	Requires reconciliation of funded status with the amounts which appear in the employer's balance sheet.

Appendix G

Summary of treatment of variations from regular cost

Source of surplus or deficit	Recognition spread over expected remaining service life	Shorter term treatment
Events allowed for in the actuarial assumptions (including pension increases) differ in magnitude from those assumed	Yes	No
Changes in actuarial assumptions or method	Yes	No
Retrospective benefit improvements (other than pension increases)	Yes	No
Pension increases and *ex-gratia* pensions for which no allowance has been made in the actuarial assumptions	Yes if there is a surplus No if there is no surplus	Immediate recognition of capital cost to the extent that it is not covered by surplus
An 'extraordinary event' for accounting purpose	No	Immediate recognition aggregating with other financial effects of that event
Significant reduction in workforce which is not an 'extraordinary event' for accounting purposes	Yes, if a change to the actual contributions is effective over the expected remaining service lives	If reflected in a change to the actual contributions, should be recognised over the period of that change

Source of surplus or deficit	Recognition spread over expected remining service life	Shorter term treatment
A major event, outside the normal scope of actuarial assumptions, giving rise to a deficit	Yes, if no significant extra contributions to the scheme are paid, or prudence does not dictate a shorter period	May recognise over a short period but only if prudence dictates and significant extra contributions to the scheme are actually paid
Refund of surplus under ICTA 1988 ss601-603, 22 Sch	Yes, if desired	Recognition in period received if desired

SSAP 24: Amortisation of a variation – a worked example

Amortisation of variation as a percentage of payroll, straight line and mortgage method

Assumptions	
Interest:	10.00%
Pay Increase:	8.00%
Surplus:	£5,000,000
Payroll:	£10,000,000
Regular Pension cost (%):	10.00%
Amortisation period:	10 years
Contributions paid in line with:	
% of pay	(H(i))
straight line method	(H(ii))
mortgage method	(H(iii))
contribution holiday	(H(iv))
Payment Timing:	Start of year

Appendix H (i)

				Comparisons:		% of Pay Amortisation			"Straight Line" Amortisation (level capital content)			"Mortgage" Amortisation (level [capital + interest])		
Year	Payroll £	Contributions Paid £	%	Regular Pension Cost £	%	Pension Cost £	%	Balance Sheet Item @ 31.12	Pension Cost £	%	Balance Sheet Item @ 31.12	Pension Cost £	%	Balance Sheet Item @ 31.12
Totals:	£189,771,265	£11,121,288		£18,977,126		£11,121,288			£11,121,288			£11,121,288		
0								£0			£0			£0
1	£10,000,000	£457,716	4.58%	£1,000,000	10.00%	£457,716	4.58%	£0	£54,228	0.54%	£403,487	£240,501	2.41%	£217,214
2	£10,800,000	£494,333	4.58%	£1,080,000	10.00%	£494,333	4.58%	£0	£148,218	1.37%	£749,602	£303,118	2.81%	£408,428
3	£11,664,000	£533,879	4.58%	£1,166,400	10.00%	£533,879	4.58%	£0	£254,692	2.18%	£1,028,789	£375,082	3.22%	£567,226
4	£12,597,120	£576,590	4.58%	£1,259,712	10.00%	£576,590	4.58%	£0	£375,145	2.98%	£1,230,234	£457,575	3.63%	£686,241
5	£13,604,890	£622,717	4.58%	£1,360,489	10.00%	£622,717	4.58%	£0	£511,243	3.76%	£1,341,708	£551,915	4.06%	£757,042
6	£14,693,281	£672,534	4.58%	£1,469,328	10.00%	£672,534	4.58%	£0	£664,837	4.52%	£1,349,405	£659,576	4.49%	£770,000
7	£15,868,743	£726,337	4.58%	£1,586,874	10.00%	£726,337	4.58%	£0	£837,988	5.28%	£1,237,755	£782,201	4.93%	£714,136
8	£17,138,243	£784,444	4.58%	£1,713,824	10.00%	£784,444	4.58%	£0	£1,032,987	6.03%	£909,212	£921,622	5.38%	£576,958
9	£18,509,302	£847,199	4.58%	£1,850,930	10.00%	£847,199	4.58%	£0	£1,252,382	6.77%	£584,029	£1,079,880	5.83%	£344,277
10	£19,990,046	£914,975	4.58%	£1,999,005	10.00%	£914,975	4.58%	£0	£1,499,005	7.50%	£0	£1,259,253	6.30%	£0
11	£21,389,250	£2,158,925	10.00%	£2,158,925	10.00%	£2,158,925	10.00%	£0	£2,158,925	10.00%	£0	£2,158,925	10.00%	£0
12	£23.316,390	£2,331,639	10.00%	£2,331,639	10.00%	£2,331,639	10.00%	£0	£2,331,639	10.00%	£0	£2,331,639	10.00%	£0

The graphs on H(v) illustrate the effects on the amortisation of a variation on the basis of different funding approaches.

				Comparisons:		% of Pay Amortisation			"Straight Line" Amortisation (level capital content)			"Mortgage" Amortisation (level [capital + interest])		
Year	Payroll £	Contributions Paid £	%	Regular Pension Cost £	%	Pension Cost £	%	Balance Sheet Item @ 31.12 £	Pension Cost £	%	Balance Sheet Item @ 31.12	Pension Cost £	%	Balance Sheet Item @ 31.12
Totals:	£189,771,265	£11,931,672		£18,977,126		£11,931,672			£11,931,672			£11,931,672		
0								£0			£0			£0
1	£10,000,000	£90,909	0.91%	£1,000,000	10.00%	£494,396	4.94%	(£403,487)	£90,909	0.91%	£0	£277,182	2.77%	(£186,273)
2	£10,800,000	£216,364	2.00%	£1,080,000	10.00%	£562,478	5.21%	(£749,602)	£216,364	2.00%	£0	£371,264	3.44%	(£341,173)
3	£11,664,000	£348,218	2.99%	£1,166,400	10.00%	£627,406	5.38%	(£1,028,789)	£348,218	2.99%	£0	£468,609	4.02%	(£461,564)
4	£12,597,120	£486,985	3.87%	£1,259,712	10.00%	£688,429	5.46%	(£1,230,234)	£486,985	3.87%	£0	£569,414	4.52%	(£543,993)
5	£13,604,890	£633,216	4.65%	£1,360,489	10.00%	£744,690	5.47%	(£1,341,708)	£633,216	4.65%	£0	£673,889	4.95%	(£584,665)
6	£14,693,281	£787,510	5.36%	£1,469,328	10.00%	£795,207	5.41%	(£1,349,405)	£787,510	5.36%	£0	£782,249	5.32%	(£579,405)
7	£15,868,743	£950,511	5.99%	£1,586,874	10.00%	£838,860	5.29%	(£1,237,755)	£950,511	5.99%	£0	£894,724	5.64%	(£523,619)
8	£17,138,243	£1,122,915	6.55%	£1,713,824	10.00%	£874,372	5.10%	(£989,212)	£1,122,915	6.55%	£0	£1,011,550	5.90%	(£412,253)
9	£18,509,302	£1,305,476	7.05%	£1,850,930	10.00%	£900,293	4.86%	(£584,029)	£1,305,476	7.05%	£0	£1,132,974	6.12%	(£239,752)
10	£19,990,046	£1,499,005	7.50%	£1,999,005	10.00%	£914,975	4.58%	(£0)	£1,499,005	7.50%	£0	£1,259,253	6.30%	£0
11	£21,589,250	£2,158,925	10.00%	£2,158,925	10.00%	£2,158,925	10.00%	(£0)	£2,158,925	10.00%	£0	£2,158,925	10.00%	£0
12	£23,316,390	£2,331,639	10.00%	£2,331,639	10.00%	£2,331,639	10.00%	(£0)	£2,331,639	10.00%	£0	£2,331,639	10.00%	£0

				Comparisons:		% of Pay Amortisation			"Straight Line" Amortisation (level capital content)			"Mortgage" Amortisation (level [capital + interest])		
Year	Payroll £	Contributions Paid £	%	Regular Pension Cost £	%	Pension Cost £	%	Balance Sheet Item @ 31.12	Pension Cost £	%	Balance Sheet Item @ 31.12	Pension Cost £	%	Balance Sheet Item @ 31.12
Totals:	£189,771,265	£11,579,609		£18,977,126		£11,579,609			£11,579,609			£11,579,609		
0								£0			£0			£0
1	£10,000,000	£260,248	2.60%	£1,000,000	10.00%	£477,462	4.77%	(£217,214)	£73,975	0.74%	£186,273	£260,248	2.60%	£0
2	£10,800,000	£340,248	3.15%	£1,080,000	10.00%	£531,463	4.92%	(£408,428)	£185,348	1.72%	£341,173	£340,248	3.15%	£0
3	£11,664,000	£426,648	3.66%	£1,166,400	10.00%	£585,445	5.02%	(£567,226)	£306,258	2.63%	£461,564	£426,648	3.66%	£0
4	£12,597,120	£519,960	4.13%	£1,259,712	10.00%	£638,975	5.07%	(£686,241)	£437,531	3.47%	£543,993	£519,960	4.13%	£0
5	£13,604,890	£620,737	4.56%	£1,360,489	10.00%	£691,539	5.08%	(£757,042)	£580,065	4.26%	£584,665	£620,737	4.56%	£0
6	£14,693,281	£729,576	4.97%	£1,469,328	10.00%	£742,534	5.05%	(£770,000)	£734,837	5.00%	£579,405	£729,576	4.97%	£0
7	£15,868,743	£847,123	5.34%	£1,586,874	10.00%	£791,258	4.99%	(£714,136)	£902,909	5.69%	£523,619	£847,123	5.34%	£0
8	£17,138,243	£974,072	5.68%	£1,713,824	10.00%	£836,895	4.88%	(£576,958)	£1,085,438	6.33%	£412,253	£974,072	5.68%	£0
9	£18,509,302	£1,111,178	6.00%	£1,850,930	10.00%	£878,497	4.75%	(£344,277)	£1,283,680	6.94%	£239,752	£1,111,178	6.00%	£0
10	£19,990,046	£1,259,253	6.30%	£1,999,005	10.00%	£914,975	4.58%	(£0)	£1,499,005	7.50%	(£0)	£1,259,253	6.30%	£0
11	£21,589,250	£2,158,925	10.00%	£2,158,925	10.00%	£2,158,925	10.00%	(£0)	£2,158,925	10.00%	(£0)	£2,158,925	10.00%	£0
12	£23,316,390	£2,331,639	10.00%	£2,331,639	10.00%	£2,331,639	10.00%	(£0)	£2,331,639	10.00%	(£0)	£2,331,639	10.00%	£0

				Comparisons:		% of Pay Amortisation			"Straight Line" Amortisation (level capital content)			"Mortgage" Amortisation (level [capital + interest])		
Year	Payroll £	Contributions Paid £	%	Regular Pension Cost £	%	Pension Cost £	%	Balance Sheet Item @ 31.12	Pension Cost £	%	Balance Sheet Item @ 31.12	Pension Cost £	%	Balance Sheet Item @ 31.12
Totals:	£189,771,265	£12,822,981		£18,977,126		£12,822,981			£12,822,981			£11,822,981		
0								£0			£0			£0
1	£10,000,000	£0	0.00%	£1,000,000	10.00%	£503,487	5.03%	(£503,487)	£100,000	1.00%	(£100,000)	£286,273	2.86%	(£286,273)
2	£10,800,000	£0	0.00%	£1,080,000	10.00%	£594,115	5.50%	(£1,097,602)	£248,000	2.30%	(£348,000)	£402,900	3.73%	(£689,173)
3	£11,664,000	£0	0.00%	£1,166,400	10.00%	£697,027	5.98%	(£1,794,629)	£417,840	3.58%	(£765,840)	£538,230	4.61%	(£1,227,404)
4	£12,597,120	£0	0.00%	£1,259,712	10.00%	£813,712	6.46%	(£2,608,341)	£612,267	4.86%	(£1,378,107)	£694,697	5.51%	(£1,922,100)
5	£13,604,890	£0	0.00%	£1,360,489	10.00%	£945,823	6.95%	(£3,554,164)	£834,349	6.13%	(£2,212,456)	£875,021	6.43%	(£2,797,121)
6	£14,693,281	£1,181,784	8.04%	£1,469,328	10.00%	£977,026	6.65%	(£3,349,405)	£969,328	6.60%	(£2,000,000)	£964,068	6.56%	(£2,579,405)
7	£15,868,743	£1,586,874	10.00%	£1,586,874	10.00%	£975,224	6.15%	(£2,737,755)	£1,086,874	6.85%	(£1,500,000)	£1,031,088	6.50%	(£2,023,619)
8	£17,138,243	£1,713,824	10.00%	£1,713,824	10.00%	£965,281	5.63%	(£1,989,212)	£1,213,824	7.08%	(£1,000,000)	£1,102,459	6.43%	(£1,412,253)
9	£18,509,302	£1,850,930	10.00%	£1,850,930	10.00%	£945,748	5.11%	(£1,084,029)	£1,350,930	7.30%	(£500,000)	£1,178,429	6.37%	(£739,752)
10	£19,990,046	£1,999,005	10.00%	£1,999,005	10.00%	£914,975	4.58%	£0	£1,499,005	7.50%	£0	£1,259,253	6.30%	£0
11	£21,589,250	£2,158,925	10.00%	£2,158,925	10.00%	£2,158,925	10.00%	£0	£2,158,925	10.00%	£0	£2,158,925	10.00%	£0
12	£23,316,390	£2,331,639	10.00%	£2,331,639	10.00%	£2,331,639	10.00%	£0	£2,331,639	10.00%	£0	£2,331,639	10.00%	£0

SSAP 24 Amortisation Methods

Pension Cost – the effect of different funding approaches

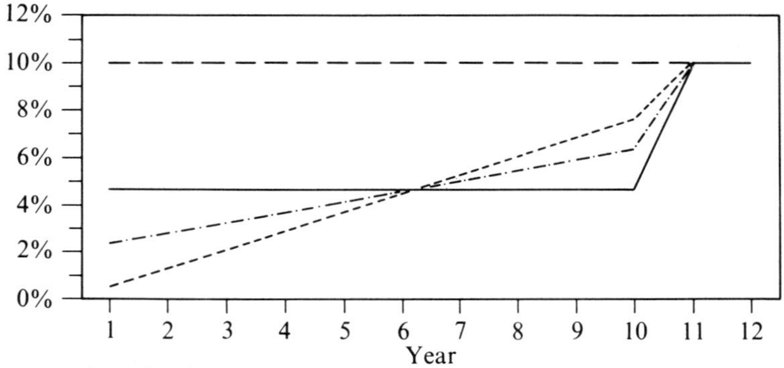

Contributions in line with % of pay method

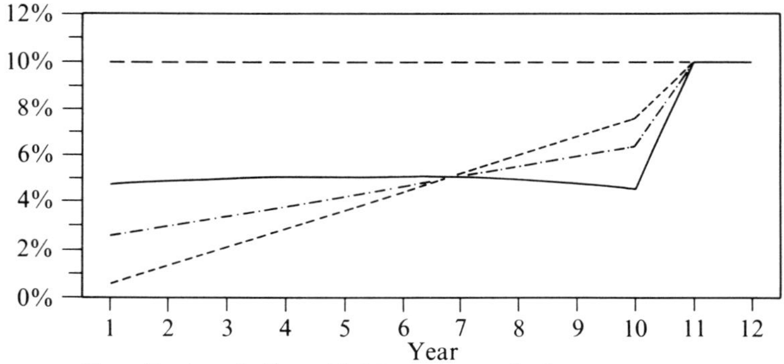

Contributions in line with Mortgage method

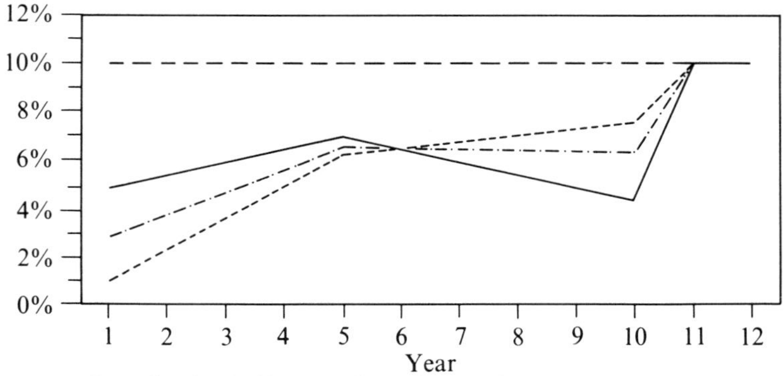

Contribution holiday until surplus used

% of Pay —— Straight Line ----- Mortgage —·—·— Regular — — —

Appendix H (vi)

Detailed analysis of pension cost and amortisation calculations

% of pay amortisation
Funding basis, % of pay

Appendix H (vi) cont.

Year	Payroll £	Contributions Paid £	Contributions Paid %	Regular Pension Cost £	Regular Pension Cost %	Regular Pension Cost (net of amortisation) £	Regular Pension Cost (net of amortisation) %	Pension Cost £	Pension Cost %
Totals:	£189,771,265	£11,121,288		£18,977,126		£11,121,288		£11,121,288	
0									
1	£10,000,000	£457,716	4.58%	£1,000,000	10.00%	£457,716	4.58%	£457,716	4.58%
2	£10,800,000	£494,333	4.58%	£1,080,000	10.00%	£494,333	4.58%	£494,333	4.58%
3	£11,664,000	£533,879	4.58%	£1,166,400	10.00%	£533,879	4.58%	£533,879	4.58%
4	£12,597,120	£576,590	4.58%	£1,259,712	10.00%	£576,590	4.58%	£576,590	4.58%
5	£13,604,890	£622,717	4.58%	£1,360,489	10.00%	£622,717	4.58%	£622,717	4.58%
5	£14,693,281	£672,534	4.58%	£1,469,328	10.00%	£672,534	4.58%	£672,534	4.58%
7	£15,868,743	£726,337	4.58%	£1,586,874	10.00%	£726,337	4.58%	£726,337	4.58%
8	£17,138,243	£784,444	4.58%	£1,713,824	10.00%	£784,444	4.58%	£784,444	4.58%
9	£18,509,302	£847,199	4.58%	£1,850,930	10.00%	£847,199	4.58%	£847,199	4.58%
10	£19,990,046	£914,975	4.58%	£1,999,005	10.00%	£914,975	4.58%	£914,975	4.58%
11	£21,589,250	£2,158,925	10.00%	£2,158,925	10.00%	£2,158,925	10.00%	£2,158,925	10.00%
12	£23,316,390	£2,331,639	10.00%	£2,331,639	10.00%	£2,331,639	10.00%	£2,331,639	10.00%

Calculation of Pension Cost

Year	Regular Pension Cost	Amortisation Amount	Interest on B/Sheet Item	Pension Cost
Totals:	£18,977,126	(£7,855,838)	£0	£11,121,288
0				
1	£1,000,000	(£542,284)	£0	£457,716
2	£1,080,000	(£585,667)	£0	£494,333
3	£1,166,400	(£632,521)	£0	£533,879
4	£1,259,712	(£683,122)	£0	£576,590
5	£1,360,489	(£737,772)	£0	£622,717
5	£1,469,328	(£796,794)	£0	£672,534
7	£1,586,874	(£860,537)	£0	£726,337
8	£1,713,824	(£929,380)	£0	£784,444
9	£1,850,930	(£1,003,731)	£0	£847,199
10	£1,999,005	(£1,084,029)	£0	£914,975
11	£2,158,925	£0	£0	£2,158,925
12	£2,331,639	£0	£0	£2,331,639

	Calculations of Balance Sheet Items				Analysis of Amortisation Amount				
Year	Amount at 1.1	Conts. Paid – (reg. pens. cost – amort'n)	Amount at 2.1	Amount at 31.12	Amortisation Amount	Capital Content	Unamortised Balance	Interest	Discounted Value
Totals:		£0			£7,855,838	£5,000,000		£2,855,838	£5,000,000
0				£0			£5,000,000		
1	£0	£0	£0	£0	£542,284	£96,513	£4,903,487	£445,772	£542,284
2	£0	£0	£0	£0	£585,667	£153,885	£4,749,602	£431,782	£532,425
3	£0	£0	£0	£0	£632,521	£220,813	£4,528,789	£411,708	£522,744
4	£0	£0	£0	£0	£683,122	£298,556	£4,230,234	£384,567	£513,240
5	£0	£0	£0	£0	£737,772	£388,526	£3,841,708	£349,246	£503,908
6	£0	£0	£0	£0	£796,794	£492,302	£3,349,405	£304,491	£494,746
7	£0	£0	£0	£0	£860,537	£611,651	£2,737,755	£248,887	£485,751
8	£0	£0	£0	£0	£929,380	£748,543	£1,989,212	£180,837	£476,919
9	£0	£0	£0	£0	£1,003,731	£905,183	£1,084,029	£98,548	£468,248
10	£0	£0	£0	£0	£1,084,029	£1,084,029	£0	£0	£459,734
11	£0	£0	£0	£0	£0	£0	£0	£0	£0
12	£0	£0	£0	£0	£0	£0	£0	£0	£0

Appendix H (vii)

Detailed analysis of pension cost and amortisation calculations

Straight line amortisation (level capital content)
Funding basis, % of pay

										Calculation of Pension Cost			
								Pension Cost Amounts					
Year	Payroll £	Contributions Paid £	%	Regular Pension Cost £	%	Regular Pension Cost (net of amortisation) £	%	Pension Cost £	%	Regular Pension Cost	Amortisation Amount	Interest on B/Sheet Item	Pension Cost
Totals:	£189,771,265	£11,121,288		£18,977,126		£11,931,672		£11,121,288		£18,977,126	(£7,045,455)	(£810,384)	£11,121,288
0													
1	£10,000,000	£457,716	4.58%	£1,000,000	10.00%	£90,909	0.91%	£54,228	0.54%	£1,000,000	(£909,091)	(£36,681)	£54,228
2	£10,800,000	£494,333	4.58%	£1,080,000	10.00%	£216,364	2.00%	£148,218	1.37%	£1,080,000	(£863,636)	(£68,146)	£148,218
3	£11,664,000	£533,879	4.58%	£1,166,400	10.00%	£348,218	2.99%	£254,692	2.18%	£1,166,400	(£818,182)	(£93,526)	£254,692
4	£12,597,120	£576,590	4.58%	£1,259,712	10.00%	£486,985	3.87%	£375,145	2.98%	£1,259,712	(£772,727)	(£111,839)	£375,145
5	£13,604,890	£622,717	4.58%	£1,360,489	10.00%	£633,216	4.65%	£511,243	3.76%	£1,360,489	(£727,273)	(£121,973)	£511,243
5	£14,693,281	£672,534	4.58%	£1,469,328	10.00%	£787,510	5.36%	£664,837	4.52%	£1,469,328	(£681,818)	(£122,673)	£664,837
7	£15,868,743	£726,337	4.58%	£1,586,874	10.00%	£950,511	5.99%	£837,988	5.28%	£1,586,874	(£636,364)	(£112,523)	£837,988
8	£17,138,243	£784,444	4.58%	£1,713,824	10.00%	£1,122,915	6.55%	£1,032,987	6.03%	£1,713,824	(£590,909)	(£89,928)	£1,032,987
9	£18,509,302	£847,199	4.58%	£1,850,930	10.00%	£1,305,476	7.05%	£1,252,382	6.77%	£1,850,930	(£545,455)	(£53,094)	£1,252,382
10	£19,990,046	£914,975	4.58%	£1,999,005	10.00%	£1,499,005	7.50%	£1,499,005	7.50%	£1,999,005	(£500,000)	£0	£1,499,005
11	£21,589,250	£2,158,925	10.00%	£2,158,925	10.00%	£2,158,925	10.00%	£2,158,925	10.00%	£2,158,925	£0	£0	£2,158,925
12	£23,316,390	£2,331,639	10.00%	£2,331,639	10.00%	£2,331,639	10.00%	£2,331,639	10.00%	£2,331,639	£0	£0	£2,331,639

Appendix H (vii) cont.

	Calculation of Balance Sheet Items				Analysis of Amortisation Amount				
Year	Amount at 1.1	Conts. Paid – (reg. pens. cost – amort'n)	Amount at 2.1	Amount at 31.12	Amortisation Amount	Capital Content	Unamortised Balance	Interest	Discounted Value
Totals:		(£810,384)			£7,045,455	£5,000,000		£2,045,455	£5,000,000
0				£0			£5,000,000		
1	£0	£366,806	£366,806	£403,487	£909,091	£500,000	£4,500,000	£409,091	£909,091
2	£403,487	£277,969	£681,456	£749,602	£863,636	£500,000	£4,000,000	£363,636	£785,124
3	£749,602	£185,661	£935,263	£1,028,789	£818,182	£500,000	£3,500,000	£318,182	£676,183
4	£1,028,789	£89,605	£1,118,394	£1,230,234	£772,727	£500,000	£3,000,000	£272,727	£580,561
5	£1,230,234	(£10,499)	£1,219,734	£1,341,708	£727,273	£500,000	£2,500,000	£227,273	£496,737
6	£1,341,708	(£114,976)	£1,226,732	£1,349,405	£681,818	£500,000	£2,000,000	£181,818	£423,355
7	£1,349,405	(£224,174)	£1,125,232	£1,237,755	£636,364	£500,000	£1,500,000	£136,364	£359,211
8	£1,237,755	(£338,471)	£899,284	£989,212	£590,909	£500,000	£1,000,000	£90,909	£303,230
9	£989,212	(£458,276)	£530,936	£584,029	£545,455	£500,000	£500,000	£45,455	£254,459
10	£584,029	(£584,029)	£0	£0	£500,000	£500,000	£0	£0	£212,049
11	£0	£0	£0	£0	£0	£0	£0	£0	£0
12	£0	£0	£0	£0	£0	£0	£0	£0	£0

Appendix H *(viii)*

Detailed analysis of pension cost and amortisation calculations

Mortgage method (level capital + interest)
Funding basis % of pay

Appendix H (viii) cont.

				Pension cost Amounts						Calculation of Pension Cost			
Year	Payroll £	Contributions Paid £	%	Regular Pension Cost £	%	Regular Pension Cost (net of amortisation) £	%	Pension Cost £	%	Regular Pension Cost	Amortisation Amount	Interest on B/Sheet Item	Pension Cost
Totals	£189,771,265	£11,121,288		£18,977,126		£11,579,609		£11,121,288		£18,977,126	(£7,045,455)	(£458,320)	£11,121,288
0													
1	£10,000,000	£457,716	4.58%	£1,000,000	10.00%	£260,248	2.60%	£240,501	2.41%	£1,000,000	(£739,752)	(£19,747)	£240,501
2	£10,800,000	£494,333	4.58%	£1,080,000	10.00%	£340,248	3.15%	£303,118	2.81%	£1,080,000	(£739,752)	(£37,130)	£303,118
3	£11,664,000	£533,879	4.58%	£1,166,400	10.00%	£426,648	3.66%	£375,082	3.22%	£1,166,400	(£739,752)	(£51.566)	£375,082
4	£12,597,120	£576,590	4.58%	£1,259,712	10.00%	£519,960	4.13%	£457,575	3.63%	£1,259,712	(£739,752)	(£62,386)	£457,575
5	£13,604,890	£622,717	4.58%	£1,360,489	10.00%	£620,737	4.56%	£551,915	4.06%	£1,360,489	(£739,752)	(£68,822)	£551,915
5	£14,693,281	£672,534	4.58%	£1,469,328	10.00%	£729,576	4.97%	£659,576	4.49%	£1,469,328	(£739,752)	(£70,000)	£659,576
7	£15,868,743	£726,337	4.58%	£1,586,874	10.00%	£847,123	5.34%	£782,201	4.93%	£1,586,874	(£739,752)	(£64,921)	£782,201
8	£17,138,243	£784,444	4.58%	£1,713,824	10.00%	£974,072	5.68%	£921,622	5.38%	£1,713,824	(£739,752)	(£52,451)	£921,622
9	£18,509,302	£847,199	4.58%	£1,850,930	10.00%	£1,111,178	6.00%	£1,079,880	5.83%	£1,850,930	(£739,752)	(£31,298)	£1,079,880
10	£19,990,046	£914,975	4.58%	£1,999,005	10.00%	£1,259,253	6.30%	£1,259,253	6.30%	£1,999,005	(£739,752)	£0	£1,259,253
11	£21,589,250	£2,158,925	10.00%	£2,158,925	10.00%	£2,158,925	10.00%	£2,158,925	10.00%	£2,158,925	£0	£0	£2,158,925
12	£23,316,390	£2,331,639	10.00%	£2,331,639	10.00%	£2,331,639	10.00%	£2,331,639	10.00%	£2,331,639	£0	£0	£2,331,639

	Calculations of Balance Sheet Items				Analysis of Amortisation Amount				
Year	1.1	Conts. Paid – (reg. pens. cost – amort'n)	Amount at 2.1	Amount at 31.12	Amortisation Amount	Capital Content	Unamortised Balance	Interest	Discounted Value
Totals:		(£458,320)			£7,397,518	£5,000,000		£2,397,518	£5,000,000
0				£0			£5,000,000		
1	£0	£197,467	£197,467	£217,214	£739,752	£313,727	£4,686,273	£426,025	£739,752
2	£217,214	£154,085	£371,299	£408,428	£739,752	£345,100	£4,341,173	£394,652	£672,502
3	£408,428	£107,231	£515,660	£567,226	£739,752	£379,610	£3,961,564	£360,142	£611,365
4	£567,226	£56,630	£623,855	£686,241	£739,752	£417,571	£3,543,993	£322,181	£555,786
5	£686,241	£1,980	£688,220	£757,042	£739,752	£459,328	£3,084,665	£280,424	£505,260
6	£757,042	(£57,042)	£700,000	£770,000	£739,752	£505,260	£2,579,405	£234,491	£459,328
7	£770,000	(£120,786)	£649,215	£714,136	£739,752	£555,786	£2,023,619	£183,965	£417,571
8	£714,136	(£189,629)	£524,508	£576,958	£739,752	£611,365	£1,412,253	£128,387	£379,610
9	£576,958	(£263,979)	£312,979	£344,277	£739,752	£672,502	£739,752	£67,250	£345,100
10	£344,277	(£344,277)	£0	£0	£739,752	£739,752	£0	£0	£313,727
11	£0	£0	£0	£0	£0	£0	£0	£0	£0
12	£0	£0	£0	£0	£0	£0	£0	£0	£0

Appendix I

Extracts from published accounts illustrating examples of disclosure of pension costs under SSAP 24

This appendix is designed to show how listed companies have dealt with disclosure of pension cost and the examples are included for illustrative purposes only. The first example compares pre-SSAP 24 disclosure with that in the first year of compliance. Subsequent examples are designed to illustrate the ways in which particular aspects of disclosure have been tackled.

Comparison of disclosure of pension cost before and after the introduction of SSAP 24

I.1 This comparison is demonstrated by the following extracts from ICI's accounts for 1988 and 1989.

Accounting policy and accounts disclosures 1988

Pensions funding

The Company and most of its subsidiaries operate pension schemes which cover the majority of employees (including directors) in the Group. The amounts charged against profit are calculated with actuarial advice in accordance with local practice, and represent a proper charge to cover the accruing liabilities on a continuing basis. With minor exceptions these schemes are financed through separate trustee-administered funds.

Extract from the note on emoluments of directors and employees

The average number of people employed by the Group in 1988 was 130,400 (1987 127,800) and the staff costs incurred during the year in respect of those employees were:

	1988 £m	1987 £m
Salaries	1,844	1,737
Social security costs	179	163
Pension fund contributions, pensions and gratuities (including severance costs £69m (1987 £48m))	244	256
Other employment costs	40	32
Employees' profit-sharing bonus	63	54
	2,370	2,242
Less: amounts allocated to capital expenditure, etc.	(33)	(43)
Charged to profit and loss account	2,337	2,199

Accounting policy and accounts disclosures 1989

Pension costs

Pension costs have been accounted for this year for the first time in accordance with the UK Accounting Standard No. 24 "Accounting for Pension Costs" issued in May 1988.

The pension costs relating to UK retirement plans are assessed in accordance with the advice of independent qualified consulting actuaries. The amounts so determined include the regular cost of providing the benefits under the plans which it is intended should remain a level percentage of current and expected future earnings of the employees covered under the plans. Variations from the regular pension cost are spread on a systematic basis over the estimated average remaining service lives of current employees in the plans.

Retirement plans of non-UK subsidiaries are accounted for in accordance with local conditions and practice. With minor exceptions, these subsidiaries recognize the expected cost of providing pensions on a systematic basis over the average remaining service lives of employees in accordance with the advice of qualified actuaries.

Extract from the note on emoluments of directors and employees

The average number of people employed by the Group in 1989 was 133,800 (1988 130,400) and the staff costs incurred during the year in respect of those employees were:

	1989 £m	1988 £m
Salaries	2,094	1,844
Social security costs	189	179
Pension costs	143	166
Severance costs	46	69
Other employment costs	68	49
Employees' profit-sharing bonus	62	63
	2,602	2,370
Less: amounts allocated to capital expenditure etc	(44)	(33)
Charged to profit and loss account	2,558	2,337

Pension costs

The Company and most of its subsidiaries operate retirement plans which cover the majority of employees (including directors) in the Group. These plans are generally of the defined benefit type under which benefits are based on employees' years of service and average final remuneration and are funded through separate trustee-administered funds.

Prior to 1989 the pension cost charged in the Group profit and loss account in respect of funded retirement plans equalled the annual contributions to these plans by companies in the Group. In the case of a small number of plans which are unfunded, the pension cost was the amount of pensions paid net of the movement on the provisions for pension costs which were actuarially valued. From 1989, the method of accounting for pension costs for the year is as set out under accounting policies on page 43. The effect of this change in accounting policy on the 1989 results was not material.

The total pension cost for the Group for 1989 was £143m (1988 £166m). Formal actuarial valuations of the Group's main plans are undertaken triennially. Actuarial valuations of these funds have been undertaken on varying dates. The actuarial assumptions used to calculate the projected benefit obligation of the Group's pension plans vary according to the economic conditions of the country in which they are situated. The weighted average discount rate used in determining the actuarial present values of the benefit obligations was 9.2 per cent. The weighted average expected long-term rate of return on investments was 9.3 per cent. The weighted average rate of increase of future earnings was 6.8 per cent. The actuarial value of the fund assets of these plans was sufficient to cover 105 per cent of the benefits that had accrued to members after allowing for expected future increases in earnings.

The market value of the assets of the major plans in the Group at the date of the latest valuations was £5,582m. Accrued pension costs amounted to £52m and are included in other creditors (note 9); provisions for the benefit obligation of the small number of unfunded plans mentioned above amounted to £81m (1988 £73m) and are included in provisions for employee benefits (note 20). Prepaid pension costs amounting to £33m are included in other debtors (note 16).

Extract from the Directors' Report

Pensions UK pensions were increased by 7.5 per cent from 1st November 1989 and a guarantee was given that pensions being paid would in future rise by 4.5 per cent or, if lower, the increase in the retail Price Index. These improvements were financed by resources already provided within the Funds. The 1989 valuations of the UK Pension Funds showed they were satisfactorily solvent.

Accounting policy where schemes are both final salary and defined contribution

I.2 British Vita, which operates both types of scheme, has the following accounting policy note for pension costs in its 1989 accounts.

Pension costs recorded in the year represent contributions payable under money purchase schemes and, in the case of final salary schemes, the estimated regular cost of the benefits accruing during the year, adjusted to spread any variations from regular cost over the expected remaining working lives of employees. Differences between pension costs and contributions paid are recorded as assets or liabilities in the balance sheet.

Disclosure of defined contribution scheme costs

I.3 Tesco PLC includes in its pension cost note (1989 accounts) the details of its defined contribution scheme.

The group also operates a defined contribution pension scheme for part-time employees which was introduced on 6th April 1988. The assets of the scheme are held separately from those of the group, being invested with an insurance company. The pension cost represents contributions payable by the group to the insurance company and amounted to £1.6m (1988 – £Nil). There were no material amounts outstanding to the insurance company at the year end.

Reason for change in pension cost

I.4 Godfrey Davis (Holdings) Plc disclosed in its 1989 accounts these reasons for increased pension cost.

> The increased pension cost in 1989 arises as the result of harmonisation of the benefits of the two major schemes, a high level of new entrants in certain subsidiaries as employees attained eligibility and the inclusion of a full year's costs in respect of the Elliott group of companies acquired with Falcon Industries in September 1988.

Vaux Group plc gives the following reason in its 1988 accounts.

> From 6th April 1988 the group decided to contract out of the state earnings related pension scheme and to provide improved benefits from the group's own schemes. As a result, the costs of the group's schemes increased and there was a reduction in the rate of contributions to the state scheme. This is the principal reason for the increase in the pension scheme costs shown in note 2c.

Pension provisions and prepayments

I.5 Ibstock Johnson PLC discloses in its 1989 accounts the pension prepayment and provision in the pension schemes note thus.

> The 1989 UK pension cost charged in the profit and loss account totalled £1.4 million. This is less than the total Company contributions payable of £1.7 million, resulting in a prepayment in the balance sheet at 31 December 1989 of £0.3 million.
>
> Provisions have been made by certain overseas subsidiaries for the actuarial assessment of future pension liabilities. There are other overseas schemes which have continued to charge contributions paid.

The pension prepayment is clearly disclosed as 'prepaid pension costs' under the heading of debtors recoverable after more than one year. The pension provision under the heading liabilities and charges is set out as follows.

Pension provision	£000 1989	£'000 1988
At 31 December 1988	3,030	1,361
Currency adjustment	312	(87)
Transfer from profit and loss account	691	156
Provision in companies acquired	–	1,600
At 31 December 1989	4,033	3,030

Berisford International plc disclosed both a prepayment and provision in its 1989 accounts.

> The total pension cost for the year was £5.8m (1988 £7.7m) and at 30 September 1988 included in prepayments and other long term creditors are amounts of £1.4m and £1.9m, being the deficiency and excess of contributions paid to the schemes respectively.

Measures being taken to eliminate a deficiency

I.6 The Midland Group plc's 1988 accounts disclosures on this point are as follows.

> The latest valuation was made as at 31 December 1987 at which date the market value of the scheme assets was £1,784m. This valuation was prepared on the attained age method and showed that the level of funding at that date was 95%, significantly higher than at 31 December 1984, the date of the last actuarial valuation. The actuaries recommended future contributions of 20% of pensionable salary (1984 27%) of which 1.4% (1984 7.7%) represents the amount expected to be necessary to achieve a funding level of 100% by 31 December 2006. Participating companies have agreed to make these contributions from 1 January 1988.

The note includes additional comment.

> The actuaries also confirmed that, on the basis of the actuarial assumptions and methods used, the scheme's assets at 31 December 1987 fully covered its liabilities based on then current salary levels and service to valuation date.

Bowthorpe Holdings' 1989 accounts reveals a deficiency in one scheme and the measures being taken to eliminate it.

At the date of the last valuation the market value of the assets for these two UK schemes was £13,036,000. The actuarial value of the assets provided cover of 104% of the accrued liabilities for the Staff Plan and 85% of the accrued liabilities for the Cash Plan based on members' projected salaries and allowing for the benefit improvements introduced then. The current company contribution rates of 9.8% and 2.8% respectively are considered appropriate and the latter rate is expected to redress the deficiency position over the long term.

Comments on and measures being taken to eliminate a surplus

I.7 BAA plc's 1989 accounts contain the following paragraph.

> At the date of the latest actuarial valuation, the actuarial value of the assets of the scheme was £296.0m with a market value of £299.3m. The actuarial value of the assets of the scheme was sufficient to cover 113% of the benefits that had accrued to members, after allowing for expected future increases in earnings. This surplus should be eliminated by 2003 at the current employer's contribution rate of 14% of pensionable earnings.

Fisons plc reveals the following in its pensions note to its 1989 accounts.

> The surpluses, arising primarily through good investment performance, have been amortised over the average remaining service lives of current scheme employees.

Disclosure of assumptions

I.8 Marley plc discloses in its 1989 accounts the actuarial assumptions for pension cost and the different assumptions for funding as follows.

> The principal actuarial assumptions adopted in calculating the pension cost charged in the accounts were:

Investment return	10.5% per annum
General salary inflation	8.0% per annum
Pension increases	5.0% per annum
Dividend growth	5.5% per annum

> For the funding of the schemes, the investment return and dividend growth assumptions have been taken at 0.5% less than those shown above.

For Marley, the SSAP 24 assumptions are less prudent than the funding assumptions. TI Group plc's 1989 accounts implied that the SSAP 24 assumptions were more prudent than those used at the last actuarial valuation.

> The main UK schemes are the TI Group Staff and General Pension Schemes. The assets of these schemes are held in separate trustee administered funds. The latest actuarial valuation of these schemes was carried out by independent actuaries as at 5th April 1989 using the attained age method which assumes no new entrants to the schemes. The principal actuarial assumptions adopted in that valuation were that the long term annual rate of return on investments would be 9%, annual dividend increases would be 4%,the average annual increases in pensionable salaries (inclusive of promotion and merit increases) and pensions in payment would be 7½% and 1½-3% respectively. Actuarial surpluses amounted to £91.65m. Under the constitution of the schemes no refund of the surplus to the Company is possible; the Company and the schemes' actuary are considering actions to be taken to utilise the surplus. The market value of the assets of the scheme at the date of the actuarial valuation was £472.4m
>
> In accordance with SSAP24, the actuary to the TI Group Staff and General Pension Schemes has calculated the pension cost on the method and assumptions stated above but with a higher allowance for pension increases and allowing an additional ½% for dividend growth. The combined actuarial value of the assets of the schemes on this prudent basis was sufficient to cover 115% of the benefits that had accrued to members after allowing for expected future increases in pensionable pay.

Some companies have not disclosed the absolute percentages but differentials. Barclays Bank PLC did this in its 1988 accounts.

> The principal actuarial assumptions adopted at that valuation [March 1987] were that, over the long term, the annual rate of return on new investments would be 2% higher than the annual increase in total pensionable remuneration, 4½% higher than the annual increase in present and future pensions in payment, and 4½% higher than the annual increase in dividends receivable

Period of amortisation of a surplus or deficit

I.9 Trust House Forte indicated a period of 12 years in its 1989 accounts.

> This surplus, less the cost of funding benefit improvements, has been allocated over the future service lives of the members of the scheme, which is estimated to be twelve years.

Smiths Industries plc used a period of 10 years. using the average basis.

> The variation from regular cost, which recognises the excess of assets over liabilities in the pension schemes existing at the time of initially adopting the present accounting policy, has been spread over 10 years, being the average remaining working life.

Comparative figures in the year of implementation

Method 1 Cumulative adjustment spread forward

I.10 SmithKline Beecham's accounting policy in its 1989 accounts states:

> As permitted by the Standard, [SSAP 24], surpluses or deficits arising in respect of prior years are being spread over the expected remaining service lives of employees rather than accounted for as a prior year adjustment; consequently, comparative figures have not been restated.

Method 3 Surplus at implementation date taken on to the balance sheet.

Costain's accounts show the transitional surplus net of deferred tax being added to the profit and loss account balance brought forward at 1 January 1989 to give a restated balance at that date, leaving the balance sheet as at 31 December 1988 unchanged.

	Profit and loss account £m
At 1 January 1989	205.0
Pension surplus (less taxation)	41.8
At 1 January 1989 as restated	246.8

Transitional provisions

I.11 As illustrated in I.10 above, Costain Group PLC took the surplus at implementation of SSAP 24 on to the balance sheet, describing the approach in its 1989 accounts in the following way.

> Under a change of accounting policy to comply with the provisions of Statement of Standard Accounting Practice 24 "Accounting for pension costs", the surplus has been recognised as a prepayment in the consolidated balance sheet. The pension cost charge for these schemes of **£0.4m** is net of interest accrued on the surplus (1988 £0.7m).

The notes to the accounts on debtors disclose a pension prepayment in the group of £64.3 million. Although it is not cross-referenced in the pensions cost note, the provisions for liabilities and charges for the group reveals the following.

	At beginning of year £m	**Pension surplus £m**	**Movement in year £m**	**At end of year £m**
Deferred taxation	11.8	22.5	4.3	38.6
Other provision	4.6	–	(1.8)	2.8
	16.4	22.5	2.5	41.4

	1989 £m	**1988 £m**
Accelerated capital allowances	16.2	22.9
Pension prepayment	22.5	–
Other timing differences	5.5	(6.8)
Advance corporation tax recoverable	(5.6)	(4.3)
	38.6	11.8

Johnson Matthey, in its 1989 accounts, has the following paragraph in its accounting policy note.

> The cumulative adjustment arising on implementation of SSAP 24 on the main UK scheme is being spread over the average remaining service lives of current employees in accordance with the terms of the Standard....That part of the cumulative adjustment relating to past extraordinary events has been accounted for within extraordinary items.

The pensions note discloses the resulting prepayment.

> The prepaid pension cost recognised in the group and company balance sheets at 31st March 1989 amounted to £6.2 million (1988 nil).

The same wording appears in the accounting policy note in the 1990 accounts and the note on extraordinary items contains the following.

	1990 £ million	1989 £ million
Pension fund surplus from rationalisations	2.6	3.5

Post-retirement benefits other than pensions

I.12 SmithKline Beecham plc, which does not accrue such costs but accounts for them on a pay-as-you-go basis, included this paragraph in its 1989 accounts.

> In addition to pension benefits, substantially all employees in the United States become eligible for certain healthcare and life assurance benefits upon retirement. The cost of providing these benefits is recognised as an expense in the year in which payments are made. The amounts charged to profit and loss account were £3.8 million (1988 – £3.8 million). the present value of the unfunded amounts relating to such benefits was approximately £200 million (1988 – £150 million).

Grand Metropolitan provides for the unfunded liability, as its accounts demonstrate.

> The group also operates a number of plans which provide employees with other post-retirement benefits principally in respect of US medical costs. The unfunded liability is assessed by professionally qualified actuaries and is included in provisions in the balance sheet.

Negative pension cost

I.13 BOC plc, in its accounts for 1989, showed how the regular cost was exceeded by the amortisation of the variation.

	£ million
Regular pension cost based on a constant percentage of earnings over the employees' service lives with the group	(22.8)
Variations from regular cost based on a constant percentage of current and estimated future earnings over the average remaining service lives of current employees	24.1
Net pension credit to operating profit	1.3

Treatment of pension scheme surplus or deficit as an asset or liability on acquisition

I.14 The notes to the accounts of the Granada group have this sentence included as part of the notes to the details of group reserves.

> Included in the net movement on goodwill is a credit of £57.1 million relating to the acquisition in 1988 of the Electronic Rentals Group plc (comprising the surplus on the ERG pension scheme net of reorganisation provisions)....stated net of associated taxation.

The pensions note provides further information.

> A prepayment of £88.9 million is included in debtors representing the surplus on the assessment of the Electronic Rentals Group pension scheme at 31 December 1988 and the excess of the pension credit to profit over the amounts funded during the year.

This amount is not separately disclosed in debtors nor is it included in debtors due after more than one year.

More than one major pension scheme

I.15 Where a company operates more than one significant scheme, it may be advisable to include details of each scheme, as Godfrey Davis (Holdings) Plc did in its 1989 accounts.

> Details of the most recent valuations of the two major schemes, which together account for 90% of the pension cost, are as follows:

	Godfrey Davis	**Sunlight**
Effective date	**31st March 1988**	**1st January 1989**
Valuation method	**Aggregate**	**Projected unit**
Main assumptions:		
Investment returns	9% pa	9% pa
Pensionable salary	8% pa	8% pa
Employer's contribution level as a percentage of pensionable salary	18.5%	9% – 21.3% (dependent upon category of employee)
Market value of scheme assets	£5,590,000	£6,479,000

Disclosure in a subsidiary's accounts

I.16 Lombard North Central PLC indicated in the pensions note to its 1989 accounts that it has its own schemes but that most employees are covered by the parent company's scheme. It does however include full disclosure of of its own pension scheme.

> Lombard North Central PLC and its subsidiaries operate nine pension schemes. The major schemes, which are defined benefit schemes, cover approximately 98% of staff and are the National Westminster Bank Pension Scheme and the Lombard Banking Pension and Assurance Scheme.
>
> The total pension cost for the group was £11.3 million (1988 £9.3 million). The pension cost relating to the main schemes, which are funded, is assessed in accordance with the advice of qualified actuaries using a projected benefit method known as attained age funding.
>
> The details of the National Westminster Bank Pension Scheme will be given in the 1989 Accounts of the National Westminster Bank PLC; the latest available actuarial valuation was at 31 March 1989.
>
> The Lombard Banking Pension and Assurance Scheme which covers approximately 14% of staff was valued on 31 March 1989. The assumptions which have the most significant effects on the results of the valuation are those relating to the rate of return on investments, the rates of increase in salaries and pensions and the increase in equity dividends. It was assumed that the investment return would be 9% per annum, that salary inflation would average 7% per annum, that present and future pensions would increase at an average rate of 5% per annum and that equity dividends would increase by 4% per annum.
>
> At the date of the latest valuation, the calculated value of the assets of the Lombard Banking Pension and Assurance Scheme was £22.9 million. The actuarial value of the assets was sufficient to cover 115% of the benefits that had accrued to members, after allowing for expected future increase in earnings.

Disclosure of the variation from regular cost

I.17 TI Group plc's 1989 pensions note include this statement.

> Net pension costs, after allowing for a credit of £6.7m in respect of the spreading of an actuarial surplus on the main UK schemes (which

takes into account proposed benefit improvements), were £5.5m (1988 £10.8m). Costs of overseas schemes were £7.0m (1988 £4.4m).

Disclosure of overseas costs

I.18 British Vita PLC in its accounts for 1989 explains its overseas pension costs in some detail.

> Money-purchase schemes are operated in France, Holland, Belgium and Australia and employer contributions to these schemes are charged to the profit and loss accounts in the year in which they are payable.
>
> A number of unfunded, final salary related schemes are operated in Germany in accordance with the recommendations of the consultant actuary, International Pension Consultants GmbH. Actuarial valuations are undertaken every two years on the 'Attained age' method based on the major assumptions of a 7% per annum interest rate, remuneration increases of 4% per annum and increases to pensions in payment of 2.5% per annum. The last valuation, undertaken as of 31 December 1988, disclosed a deficit which has now been fully accrued by reclassification of amounts provided for in the previous year.

Johnson Matthey PLC in its 1990 accounts justifies the local best practice approach on grounds of cost.

> Pension costs relating to foreign schemes where the charge has been determined in accordance with local best practice using a different accounting policy are not material. The cost of obtaining compatible actuarial valuations for the purposes of making adjustments to the pension charge is considered to be out of proportion to the benefits obtained.

Non-compliance with SSAP 24

I.19 Tozer Kemsley and Millbourn had this paragraph in the SSAP 24 note in the 1989 accounts.

> Pension costs are charged to the profit and loss account when employers' contribution payments are made to the scheme, as in the opinion of the directors this policy is most appropriate to the business and best reflects the Group's current and anticipated future funding position with the scheme. However, the pension cost has also been

assessed in accordance with the UK Statement of Standard Accounting Practice Number 24 using the assumptions described above. [*The results of the actuarial valuation as at 6 April 1989 are included in the note*]. The Standard requires that surpluses and deficits be amortised over the expected working lifetime of current members of the scheme. Following SSAP 24 the amortisation of the surplus would fully offset the regular cost and the net cost of the scheme would thereby be reduced to nil. Compliance with the Standard would have no effect on the Group's profit before taxation for the year ended 31 December 1989. There were no outstanding or prepaid contributions at the balance sheet date.

Table of Statutes and Statutory Instruments

Statutes

Statutory Instruments

Table of References to SSAP 24

SSAP paragraph	References in text
2	3.8
7	9.4
16	1.2
17	10.1
18	5.3, 9.4
20	6.1, 6.2
22	6.23
23	6.23
24	6.23
25	6.23
26	6.23
27	6.23
28	6.23
29	6.19, 6.23, 9.3
30	6.23
31	6.23
32	6.23
35	3.9, 6.12
39	4.4
40	6.26
41	6.29, 11.4
42	6.29, 11.4
43	6.29, 11.4
44	8.10
45	9.1
47	9.4, 9.18
48	9.4
49	9.4, 9.9
50	9.7
51	9.12
52	9.13, 11.2
53	7.1, 7.7, 7.14, 7.15
56	9.9, 9.10
59	9.10, 11.3
62	4.6
63	5.3
66	5.3, 9.9
67	9.9

SSAP paragraph	References in text
75	3.15
78	6.37
79	6.2, 6.23, 7.14
80	6.3, 6.23, 6.31
81	6.14, 6.17, 6.23, 7.15
82	6.18, 6.23, 7.15
83	6.19, 6.21, 6.22, 6.23, 11.18
84	6.13, 12.4
85	6.13
86	8.1, 8.2, 9.19
87	10.4
88	9.1, 9.2, 9.4, 9.5, 9.6, 9.8, 9.9, 9.10, 9.11, 9.16, 9.17, 9.18, 11.2
89	9.12, 10.5, 11.3
90	9.13, 11.2, 11.11
92	7.4, 9.1, 9.3
93	1.1
99	9.14
Appendix 1	5.3

Index

T

Further reading

'The new UK accounting standard for pension costs – SSAP 24 compared with FAS 87 and FAS 88' Peter Morgan and Robin Arnold *Benefits and Compensation International* August 1988 pp5-12

'A problem of compatability' Richard Davis and Tony Bingham *Accountancy* June 1989 pp84-86

'Time to sort out the balance sheet' Ron Paterson *Accountancy* November 1990 pp 27-28

Pensions Pocket Book 1991 Bacon & Woodrow 1991

Auditing Guideline 306: Pension Schemes in the United Kingdom Auditing Practices Committee 1988

Auditing Guideline 413: Reliance on Other Specialists Auditing Practices Committee 1986

Pensions Terminology Pensions Management Institute and the Pension Research Accountants Group 3rd edition 1988

International Accounting Standard No 19, 'Accounting for Retirement Benefits in the Financial Statements of Employers', International Accounting Standards Committee 1983

Statement of Financial Accounting Standards No.87 Employers' Accounting for Pensions Financial Accounting Standards Board Stamford Connecticut 1985

A Guide to Implementation of Statement 87 on Employers' Accounting for Pensions Questions and Answers Joan Lordi Amble and Jules M Cassel, Financial Accounting Standards Board Special Report 1986

Statement of Financial Accounting Standards No.88, Employers' accounting for Settlements and Curtailments of Defined Benefit Pension Plans and for Termination Benefits Financial Accounting Standards Board Stamford Connecticut 1985

Further reading

A Guide to Implementation of Statement 88 on Employers' Accounting for Settlements and Curtailments of Defined Benefit Pension Plans and for Termination Benefits Questions and Answers Joan Lordi Amble and Jules M Cassel, Financial Accounting Standards Board Special Report 1988

Proposed Statement of Financial Accounting Standards Employers' Accounting for Postretirement Benefits Other Than Pensions Financial Accounting Standards Board Stamford Connecticut 1989

Pension schemes and best estimates D J Parsons FIA, paper presented to the Staple Inn Actuarial Society on 8th May 1990

Papers produced by the Pensions Research Accountants' Group SSAP 24 working party. These cover a number of topics in detail and are obtainable from PRAG.

Order form

To: Tolley Publishing Company Ltd., Tolley House, 2 Addiscombe Road, Croydon, Surrey CR9 5AF England. Telephone: 081-686 9141

Please send me the following book(s), as shown below. I understand that if, for any reason, I am not satisfied with my order and return the book(s) in saleable condition within 21 days, Tolley will refund my money in full.

If you wish to place a standing order for any book(s) and obtain the benefits of the Tolley Subscriber Service, please tick the relevant standing order box(es) All books placed on standing order are sent post-free within the U.K. Please add 5% towards postage and packing if not placed on standing order.

Title	Price per copy	No. of copies	Standing order	Amount £
			☐	
			☐	
			☐	
			☐	
			☐	
			☐	

Plus VAT (if applicable) ______

Plus 5% postage and packing (if applicable) ______

Total £ ______

Cheque is enclosed for total amount of order £ ______

Please debit Access/Visa* account number

[ ] Access VISA Signature ______

*Please delete as necessary

Please send me a copy of the full Tolley catalogue ☐

Name† ______

Firm ______

Position ______

Address† ______

______

______ Post Code ______

Telephone No ______ Date ______

†If paying by credit card, please enter name and address of cardholder

Registered No. 729731 England VAT No. 243 3583 67

Code 262

Tolley